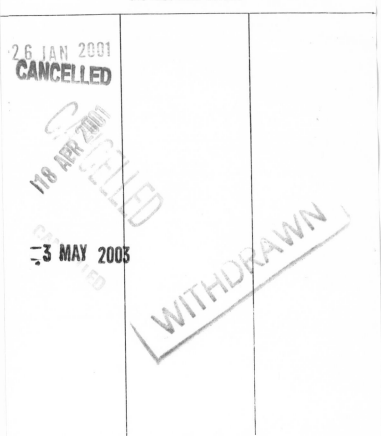

STRATEGY AND INTELLIGENCE

STRATEGY
AND INTELLIGENCE

———

BRITISH POLICY DURING THE
FIRST WORLD WAR

EDITED BY
MICHAEL DOCKRILL AND DAVID FRENCH

THE HAMBLEDON PRESS
LONDON   AND   RIO GRANDE

Published by the Hambledon Press 1996
102 Gloucester Avenue, London NW1 8HX (UK)
P.O. Box 162, Rio Grande, Ohio 45674 (USA)

ISBN 1 85285 099 X

A description of this book is available from
the British Library and from the Library of Congress

Typeset by The Midlands Book Typesetting Company
Printed on acid-free paper and bound in
Great Britain by Cambridge University Press.

Contents

Preface

Most edited volumes of this kind are produced in order to honour a prominent scholar who has either recently retired or is on the point of so doing. This volume is something of an exception. Josephine Howie was not a prominent scholar although she had the potential so to be. It has been compiled by a group of her close friends who remember her with affection and to whom her death in 1988, from cancer, came as a great shock. She was a frequent attender and active participant at the fortnightly military history seminars at the University of London Institute of Historical Research, organised jointly by King's College and University College, London, which was where (and afterwards at her home in Chelsea) we all first met. She had almost completed her Ph.D at London University on Britain and the Irish Question during the First World War and she planned to publish a number of articles on the subject before her untimely death. One of these, written jointly by Josephine and her husband, is included in the volume. She is greatly missed.

It was felt apt, therefore, that the essays in this collection should deal with aspects of British policy and strategy during the First World War, in line with her interests, and in which the contributors are either leading experts or are concerned with in their professional work.

Michael Dockrill

David French
August 1994

Acknowledgements

Copyright material from the Public Record Office, Kew, appears by permission of Her Majesty's Stationery Office. Material from the Public Record Office of Northern Ireland appears by permission of the Deputy Keeper of Records. The Council of Trustees of the National Library of Ireland have kindly allowed us to quote copyright material from the Hobson and Moore papers. Extracts from the H.A. Gwynn papers at the Bodleian Library are quoted with the kind permission of Mrs Hogg. Extracts from the private papers of Lord Samuel and David Lloyd George, which are in the custody of the House of Lords Record Office, are reproduced by permission of the Clerk of the Records. The National Army Museum has given us permission to quote from National Army Museum, 7611–23, 'History of 36' (Ulster) Division Sept 1914 to July 1914', by R.H. Stewart. Lord Gainford has kindly given us permission to quote from the papers of J.A. Pease (Lord Gainford Papers). The Trustees of the Liddell Hart Centre for Military Archives, King's College, London have given us permission to examine and reproduce extracts from the papers of Sir Basil Liddell Hart, General Sir William Robertson, General Sir Edward Spears, General Sir Lancelot Kiggell and Colonel Sir Reginald Benson in their possession. Extracts from the A.G. Denniston papers, held at Churchill College, Cambridge, have been reproduced by permission of Mr Robin Denniston. The Bodleian Library have given us permission to reproduce extracts from the papers of H.A.L. Fisher, Christopher Addison and H.H. Asquith. The Trustees of the Imperial War Museum have given us permission to use material from the diary of Field Marshal Sir Henry Wilson and General Sir Walter Kirke. Finally an earlier version of Chapter 8, 'Major General J.F.C. Fuller and the Decline of Generalship: The Lessons of 1914–1918', by Dr Brian Holden Reid, appeared in the December 1988 issue of the *British Army Review*. Material from this is used with the kind permission of the editor. We apologise if we have unwittingly infringed any other copyrights.

Notes on Contributors

Kathleen Burk is professor of history at University College, London. She is the editor of, and contributor to, *War and the State: The Transformation of British Government 1914–1919* (1982). She is the author of *Britain, America and the Sinews of War, 1914–1918* (1985); *The First Privatisation: the Politicians, the City and the Denationalization of Steel* (1988); *Morgan Grenfell, 1838–1988: The Biography of a Merchant Bank* (1989); and (with Sir Alec Cairncross) *'Goodbye Great Britain': The 1976 IMF Crisis* (1991).

Michael Dockrill is Reader in War Studies at King's College, London. He is the author of several books and numerous articles on British foreign policy before 1914 and during the Paris peace conferences of 1919–1920, and on British foreign policy during the early years of the cold war. His recent works are *The Cold War, 1945–1963* (1988) and *British Defence since 1945* (1989). He has co-edited (with John Young) *British Foreign Policy, 1945–1960* (1989). He is also General Editor of the King's College, London/Macmillan series, *Studies in Military and Strategic History*.

John Robert Ferris is Professor of History at the University of Calgary. He is the author of *The Evolution of British Strategic Policy, 1919–1926* and many articles on British secret intelligence.

David French is Reader in History at University College, London, and is the author of two books and numerous articles on the development of British strategic policy in the early twentieth century. In 1988–1989 he was a Fellow of the Woodrow Wilson International Center for Scholars, Washington DC, where he completed work on a book entitled *The British Way in Warfare, 1688–2000*.

Josephine Howie was completing a Ph.D thesis on the Irish Question, 1914–1915, at the London School of Economics before her untimely death in 1988. She published an article on 'Britain's Irish Problem' in *Brassey's Defence Yearbook* in 1984.

Keith Neilson is Professor of History at the Royal Military College of Canada. His numerous works on the First World War include *Strategy and Supply: The Anglo-Russian Alliance, 1914–1917* (1984).

Brian Holden Reid is Senior Lecturer in War Studies at King's College, London and, since 1987, has been Resident Historian at the British Army Staff College, Camberley. He is the first civilian to work on the Directing Staff for over a hundred years and helped set up the Higher Command and Staff Course. A Fellow of the Royal Historical Society and Royal Geographical Society, from 1984 to 1987 Dr Holden Reid was Editor of the *RUSI Journal*. He is the author of *J.F.C. Fuller: Military Thinker* (1987; paperback 1990). He has edited (with John White) *American Studies: Essays in Honour of Marcus Cunliffe* (1991) and (with Colonel Michael Dewar) *Military Strategy in a Changing Europe: Towards the Twenty-First Century* (1991), along with three volumes of contemporary British military thought and numerous essays in British and American history. He is currently working on the origins of the American Civil War.

Chris Wrigley is Professor in Economic History at Nottingham University. His books include *David Lloyd George and the British Labour Movement* (1976); *A History of British Industrial Relations*, i, *1875–1914* (1982); ii, *1914–1939* (1987). He edited *Warfare, Diplomacy and Politics: Essays for A.J.P. Taylor* (1986).

Abbreviations

AA	Anti-Aircraft
ADGB	Air Defence of Great Britain
ASE	Amalgamated Society of Engineers
BEF	British Expeditionary Force
CIR	*Commission Internationale de Ravitaillement*
DMI	Director of Military Intelligence
DMO	Director of Military Operations
DMRS	Director of Munitions Supplies and Statistics
FO	Foreign Office
GFU	General Federation of Trade Unions
GHQ	General Headquarters
GQG	*Grand Quartier-Général*
HLRO	House of Lords Records Office
INV	Irish National Volunteers
IWM	Imperial War Museum
LADA	London Air Defence Area
LHCMA	Liddell Hart Centre for Military Archives
MAF	Ministry of Food
MFGB	Miners Federation of Great Britain
MID	Military Intelligence Department
MUN	Ministry of Munitions
NID	Naval Intelligence Department
NLI	National Library of Ireland
OHL	*Oberste Heeresleitung*
PID	Political Intelligence Department
PRO	Public Record Office
PRONI	Public Record Office of Northern Ireland
RAF	Royal Air Force
RESD	Restriction of Enemy Supplies Department
RFC	Royal Flying Corps
RGC	Russian Government Committee
RN	Royal Navy
RNAS	Royal Naval Air Service
RNVR	Royal Naval Volunteer Reserve
RPC	Russian Purchasing Commission

RSC	Russian Supplies Committee
R/T	Radio Telephone
UVF	Ulster Volunteer Force
WEWNC	War Emergency Workers National Committee
WO	War Office
W/T	Wireless Telegraphy

Introduction

Michael Dockrill and David French

In the aftermath of the First World War British military historians concentrated on the tactical and strategic aspects of that war. Official historians were recruited by the service departments to write authorised versions of the land, sea and air battles. These histories usually extolled the virtues of the British military leaders, and particularly of Field-Marshal Haig, the British Commander on the Western Front after 1915. The official historians often suppressed evidence that might have adversely affected the reputations of British commanders. Inevitably these hagiographies provoked ripostes from other military historians who were bitterly critical of British military leadership during the First World War – Sir Basil Liddell Hart and General J.F.C. Fuller being the most prominent examples. The controversy about Britain's First World War generals is still very much alive today.[1]

Books about aerial warfare between 1914 and 1918 have tended to concentrate on the aerial struggle over the Western Front or bureaucratic intrigues over air policy and have largely neglected the technological and scientific dimension.[2] In the same way naval historians have meticulously examined Admiral Jellicoe's naval dispositions at Jutland; or the defeat of Germany's U-boat challenge.[3] Such histories were largely concerned with the tactical minutiae. This is clearly crucial to any understanding of the conduct of the war but, in the process, other important areas of the war were disregarded, although there were official histories of the civil aspects of the war, such as the blockade, and memoirs by most of the leading war-time politicians.

[1] B.J. Bond, (ed.), *The First World War and British Military History* (Oxford, 1991), examines the historiography of the war.

[2] M. Cooper, *The Birth of Independent Air Power: British Policy in the First World War* (London, 1986) and B.D. Powers *Strategy without Slide-Rule* (London, 1976), are two excellent studies of the development of air power.

[3] See the five-volume study of the Royal Navy and the war at sea by the American historians, A.J. Marder, *From the Dreadnought to Scapa Flow: The Royal Navy in the Fisher Era, 1904–1919* (London Oxford, 1961–1970), and P.G. Halpern, *The Naval War in the Mediterranean, 1914–1918*, (London, 1987). More recently Jon Sumida has pointed towards the role of new maritime technologies in shaping British naval policy. See J.T. Sumida (ed.), *The Pollen Papers: The Privately Circulated Printed Works of Arthur Hungerford Pollen, 1901–1916* (London, 1984); idem, *In Defence of Naval Supremacy: Finance, Technology and British Naval Policy, 1899–1914* (London, 1989).

It was not until the 1960s and 1970s, with the opening of the official British archives on the First World War to researchers, that a number of younger historians began to explore these wider issues in depth. They were united by the fact that their understanding was unclouded by any personal memories of the war. In a war which involved not just the armed services but society as a whole, to an extent hitherto unthinkable, the British government was forced to embark on a thorough reorganisation of the machinery of state – although it was a slow process with much improvisation.[4] The realisation that this was not to be a 'short war' but a long, static war requiring perseverance and steadfastness forced politicians by 1915 to the realisation that the entire resources of the country would have to be mobilised. Furthermore, it was reluctantly accepted that what had become a war of attrition required the production and consumption of huge military resources as well as the expectation of heavy casualties.[5] In these circumstances victory required the British government to perform two tasks: it had to carry out the effective and efficient organisation and management of Britain's own resources; and it had to coordinate Britain's war effort with that of its Allies. One of the major themes of the publications produced since the 1970s concerning the British war effort was the fact that the war was not a duel fought between Britain and Germany. On the contrary, Britain and Germany were members of two competing alliance systems. Ultimately victory would be won by the alliance which could mobilise its resources with the greatest efficiency and direct them towards an agreed goal.[6] By 1918, Britain possessd the most efficient war machine of any of the belligerents.

[4] K.M. Burk (ed.), _War and the State: The Transformation of British Government, 1914–1919_, (London, 1982).

[5] R.J.Q. Adams, _Arms and the Wizard: Lloyd George and the Ministry of Munitions, 1915–1916_ (Texas, 1978); D. French, _British Economic and Strategic Planning, 1905–1915_ (London, 1982); P. Fraser, 'British War Policy and the Crisis of Liberalism in May 1915', _Journal of Modern History_, 54 (1982), pp. 1–26; D. French, 'The Meaning of Attrition, 1914–1916', _English Historical Review_, 103 (1988), pp. 385–405; K. Grieves, _The Politics of Manpower, 1914–1918_ (Manchester, 1988).

[6] There is now a considerable body of literature examining various aspects of Britain's political, strategic and economic relations with its allies. See, for example, C.J. Lowe and M.L. Dockrill, _The Mirage of Power: British Foreign Polocy, 1914–1922_ (London, 1972); W.B. Fowler, _British-American Relations, 1917–1918: The Role of Sir William Wiseman_ (Princeton, 1969); I. Nish, _Alliance in Decline: A Study in Anglo-Japanese Relations, 1908–1923_ (London, 1972); K. Neilson, _Strategy and Supply: The Anglo-Russian Alliance, 1914–1917_, (London, 1984); D. French, _British Strategy and War Aims, 1914–1916_ (London, 1986); K.M. Burk, _Britain, America and the Sinews of War, 1914–1918_, (London, 1984); D. Dutton, 'The Deposition of King Constantine of Greece, June 1917: An Episode in Anglo-French Diplomacy', _Canadian Journal of History_, 12 (1978), pp. 325–45; idem, 'The Balkan Campaign and French War Aims in the Great War', _English Historical Review_, 94 (1979), pp. 97–113; E.B. Parsons, 'Why the British Reduced the Flow of American Troops to Europe in August–October 1918', _Canadian Journal of History_, 12 (1977–78), pp. 173–91; W.J. Philpott, 'British Military Strategy on the Western Front: Independence or Alliance, 1904–1918', (D.Phil., Oxford University, 1991).

Of course, Britain's relative geographical isolation from the continent made this accomplishment possible – unlike her Allies her territory was not occupied by enemy forces. Furthermore her industrial strength and her ability to borrow large sums on the American money market were crucial ingredients in the control she was eventually able to exercise over the allocation of food, raw materials and shipping to her Allies.[7]

The British government's relations with the trade union and labour movement also improved considerably, especially by comparison with the bitter confrontations between labour and industry of the pre-war years. This was the result of a conscious effort by the government to improve industrial relations, conscious as it was of the serious consequences for war production of a demoralised and dissatisfied work force.[8] Relations were by no means always harmonious, of course, but the industrial disputes which did occur were generally free from the political overtones which characterised many of the post-1916 strikes in Germany, or the much more threatening stance of Russian labour during the latter days of the Tsarist autocracy.

The achievements of Britain's scientists, technicians, technologists, industrialists and other experts who were recruited into government service during the war were given little prominence by historians in the immediate post-war years, despite that this was the first war fought by Britain in which such people were employed in large numbers. Many often worked at the outer edge of new technology, for instance in pioneering electronic warfare in the air. Journalists and others were enrolled in the various propaganda organs that were created during the war: a long struggle clearly required that strenuous efforts be made to uphold the morale of the British population and to undermine that of the enemy.[9] For instance the Foreign Office Political Intelligence Department (PID), consisting mostly of ex-Information Ministry officials of considerable ability, was adept at suggesting means by which enemy propaganda could be countered and the effects of British propaganda enhanced. It was not of course all an unremitting success: the PID was as much taken by surprise by the speed and extent of the German collapse in October 1918, as were most observers; and British military intelligence was successfully deceived by its German counter-part in 1917 and 1918 about the dispositions of the Germany army.

The essays in this volume deal with many of the subjects discussed above. They are concerned with administration, organisation and intelligence behind and on the front line, in other words with strategy in its broadest

---

[7] Burk (ed.), *Britain, American and the Sinews of War*, passim.

[8] John Turner has suggested that by mid 1917 the Lloyd George government saw itself as a conscious bulwark against revolution. See J. Turner, *British Politics and the Great War: Coalition and Conflict, 1915–1918*, (London, 1992).

[9] G.S. Maier, *British Propaganda and the State in the First World War* (Manchester, 1992).

sense. Josephine Howie's essay deals with civil–military relations in Ireland during the first few months of the war. The essays by John Ferris and David French deal with the role of intelligence in the air and on the Western Front respectively. The British were successful innovators in the radio detection of incoming German bombers in 1918, but on land in 1917 and 1918 British intelligence was sometimes outwitted by the Germans.[10] The contributions of Keith Neilson and Kathleen Burk are concerned with British strategy in its widest sense – the organisation of economic resources, food and raw materials – crucial to ultimate victory. The essay by Michael Dockrill examines the role of political and diplomatic intelligence in the war. Finally Brian Holden Reid concludes the volume by examining the role of generals in the First World War as seen through the eyes of that iconoclastic soldier 'Boney' Fuller. Fuller was one of the more outspoken critics of Haig as a commander but he also had some interesting views about the art of generalship, which he derived from his experiences as a front line soldier during the First World War.

The first essay, by David and Josephine Howie, examines the bitter relations between the Irish Nationalists and the Ulster Unionists during the early months of the Great War. Contrary to previous assumptions, the authors demonstrate conclusively that 'the outbreak of the European war in August 1914 did not cause Irishmen to forget their past differences when confronted by a common danger'. For its part, the British War Office wanted to recruit as many Irishmen as it could for Kitchener's New Armies. It was neither greatly concerned nor particularly scrupulous about how these recruits were to be obtained. Before the war the Ulster Protestants had formed the Ulster Volunteer Force (UVF) to fight Home Rule, or at least any Home Rule which would include Ulster, while the Nationalists had formed the Irish National Volunteers as a counter to the UVF. Both sides hoped to use the government's urgent need for recruits, who would be mainly raised from these Volunteer forces, to extract concessions from Westminster – the Nationalists wanted Home Rule for the whole of Ireland immediately while the Unionists did not want Home Rule at all. In the end the Asquith administration postponed the issue of Home Rule for the duration of the war, a compromise which satisfied neither side in the long run, but which at least was enough at the time to enable both the Unionist and the Nationalist leaders to encourage their supporters to enlist.

Towards the end of the First World War Britain experienced direct assault on her towns and cities from enemy bombing. The shock of these air raids resulted in much hysteria and scare-mongering by populist MPs,

---

[10] This was not invariably the case. As John Ferris has argued elsewhere, one reason why the British Army in France was victorious during the last hundred days of the war was because of the success of their own signals deception campaign. See J. Ferris, 'The British Army and Signals Intelligence in the Field during the First World War', *Intelligence and National Security*, 3 (1988), pp. 23–48.

who found the seeming inability of the government to find adequate means to protect the defenceless population a useful stick with which to beat the Lloyd George government. Hitherto air historians have suggested that, while British anti-aircraft defences were successful against the Zeppelin menace, they were incapable of dealing with the subsequent Gotha bomber attacks in 1917 and 1918. John Ferris, after careful archival research, has dispelled this myth. His analysis of Britain's command, control communications and intelligence system shows that it was at the cutting edge of radio technology; its work gave Britain's air defences ample forewarning of an imminent attack. By 1918 air intelligence had a reasonably good knowledge of the enemy's bomber strength, of the technical capabilities of its equipment, the personalities of its commanders and the morale of its men. Ten per cent of intruders were shot down in 1918. Both sides invested equivalent resources in the campaign, but the effectiveness of British defences ensured that Germany's losses were much higher. As Ferris points out, all this was largely irrelevant to the real war on the Western Front but it did provide important lessons for the Battle of Britain in 1940.

British intelligence during the First World War by no means enjoyed an unblemished record of success. David French shows that the British were wrong-footed by the German retreat to the Hindenburg Line in February 1917 and by the German offensive against the British Army in March 1918: a result in both cases, of skilful German deception measures. Of course the Germans could hardly disguise the fact in February 1918 that they were planning an offensive in the west: the collapse of Russia and the ensuing German troop movements to the west made this obvious in early 1918. Yet they managed to deceive the Entente as to the time and place of their initial assault in Flanders.

On the civilian side of the war, Keith Neilson examines the various *ad hoc* committees which were set up between 1914 and 1918 to manage British and Allied resources. This is a subject which has hitherto been neglected by historians, to the detriment of our understanding of how the British governmental system actually functioned on a day-to-day basis. His study deals with the various committees which were established to co-ordinate supplies to Russia, the purchase of war material in the United States and elsewhere for British and Allied use and the provision of shipping. This also touches on the difficulties of dealing with allies in wartime. The British were well aware that much of the war material they were sending to Archangel lay mouldering in the depots for the want of an efficient Russian railway system capable of conveying it to the front. However, British efforts to rationalise the purchase and supply of material to Russia met with Russian threats that any reduction in deliveries would adversely affect their war effort. Moreover, Russian War Ministry agents in the United States tended to purchase material without any reference to the inter-allied Commission Internationale de Ravitaillement which the British had set up on 14 August 1914 to act as a clearing house for allied purchases abroad. Eventually the British, after experimenting with a variety of inter-departmental committees, did manage to impose some kind of order on the purchase and supply of material, but by 1918, as far as Russia was concerned, it was too late.

Kathleen Burk also examines the various measures Britain took to organise and mobilise her finances and trade for war. Having started the war on the basis of 'business as usual' – that the war would not be allowed to affect the normal patterns of economic life – the British later embarked on a *dirigiste* policy by which, for instance, the purchase of wheat, for which no provision had been made before 1914, was tightly controlled by a Royal Commission on Wheat Supplies, set up in 1916. Of course the process of rationalisation underwent many vicissitudes – earlier Allied competition for purchases in world wheat markets had led to an unnecessary rise in grain prices.

As Chris Wrigley shows, the war also had a considerable impact on the fortunes of the British labour movement, enhancing its political importance in ways which would have been unthinkable before 1914. As a result 'the Labour Party emerged as a major political force' after 1918. At the same time, the trade union movement experienced a massive expansion in its membership. The government was generally cautious and discrete in its handling of the unions, whose immense industrial strength was crucial to the war effort. Wrigley points out that the unions generally repaid this with a 'degree of patriotic restraint in conditions exceptionally favourable for them'. Labour and trade union leaders were regularly consulted by government agencies on matters of common interest and the Labour leader, Arthur Henderson, served for a time in Lloyd George's government.

Michael Dockrill's essay on the Foreign Office Political Intelligence Department deals with another *ad hoc* body (although the Foreign Office intended the PID to be permanent, it was abolished in 1920) created to meet the immediate needs of the war. The PID was set up to provide the Foreign Office, the War Cabinet and other departments of state with reports and analyses of developments in enemy, neutral and allied countries. Dockrill has examined the PID's reporting on Germany and concludes that, by and large, the PID provided reliable and useful information about economic and political developments in Germany and shrewd assessments of the motives behind so-called German peace offers – mostly bogus before October 1918, given the favourable military situation for Germany down to the summer. The PID was another example of the use of outside specialists in government during the war. Few of its members, apart from its head, were professional diplomats but they all had had a variety of experience in other spheres of activity before the war.

Finally, Brian Holden Reid assesses the lessons that one general gleaned from his experiences on the front during the war. Fuller was a maverick and, to most of his brother officers, a nuisance. But he was a thinking soldier, in an age when intellectual curiosity was not often to be found in the British Army. To Fuller British generalship during the First World War was an object lesson in how not to command in war. In his view Haig and his generals abdicated the crucial role of the commander of managing armies. He attributed this to a lack of imagination and of intellectual ability. Unfortunately, Fuller was somewhat reckless in his judgements and often overstated his case thus alienating those very officers whom he sought to convert.

The theme of this volume is that the achievement of both British military and civilians in organising the nation for victory by 1918, after a long process of improvisation and experimentation, provided important lessons for the next war. While in 1940 the Entente allowed itself to be deceived about the strength and intent of the German armoured thrust across the Ardennes, by 1944 it was the turn of the Allies to use deception methods which confused the Germans about the Normandy landings – the Germany military were persuaded that this was a feint and that the real landings would take place on the Pas de Calais. The Royal Air Force learned valuable lessons in tracking enemy aircraft and in analysing enemy radio traffic in 1918 which, together with the advent of radar, was to stand it in good stead during the battle of Britain. In 1941 the British once more had to organise supplies to Russia in rather more inauspicious circumstances, given the intensity of the U-boat campaign, than in 1917. Problems arising from the blockade and the procurement of foodstuffs and raw materials from the United States and elsewhere had to be overcome once again after 1939. With the outbreak of war the Foreign Office immediately re-established the Political Intelligence Department and many of its members were stalwarts from the 1918 PID. Finally, some Generals, like Montgomery, had reached similar conclusions to Fuller about the shortcomings of British generalship on the Western front. They were determined not to make the same mistakes a second time. Despite its rise to prominence during the First World War, the Labour movement's record between 1919 and 1939 was a chequered one. However in the 1945 election the Labour Party was able to secure for the first time a massive parliamentary majority – clearly public opinion had turned its face against the dreary compromises and social drift of the inter-war period.

Of course many war time lessons were forgotten after 1918 and had to be painfully relearned during the Second World War: the techniques of anti-submarine warfare is a case in point. In any case no one in 1918 would have welcomed the thought that the First World War was a dress rehearsal for the next one. It had been, after all, 'the war to end all wars'. Under the circumstances it was notable that many of the achievements of that war were not forgotten and that the innovations which had then emerged were gradually readopted after 1939.

Michael Dockrill

David French
August 1994

To
the memory
of
Josephine Howie

1

Irish Recruiting and the Home Rule Crisis of August–September 1914

David and Josephine Howie

Both the primary and secondary sources concerning the question of recruiting in Ireland in the opening weeks of the First World War reflected the highly partisan attitudes which existed on both sides of the political divide as each party – Nationalist and Unionist – boasted of its loyalty and achievements at the expense of its political opponents. Typical of the view of many Nationalists was the comment of the *Daily Chronicle* of 16 September 1914 that 'we must observe that whereas Mr Redmond's great speech pledging Nationalist support throughout the Empire was delivered on 3 August, it was not until 3 September that Sir Edward Carson made any equivalent pronouncement upon behalf of the Ulstermen'.[1] More recently a historian of Irish nationalism has suggested that the treatment accorded the Irish Nationalists by the War Office was in marked contrast to that given to the Ulster Volunteer Force, whom, as soon as the war broke out, were allowed to form their own Ulster division within the British Army with its own distinctive badges and emblems.[2] In reality the outbreak of the European war in August 1914 did not cause Irishmen to forget their past differences when confronted by a common danger. On the contrary, in the opening weeks of the war both sides worked hard to exploit the new situation to their own advantage.

The Protestant population of Ulster had no wish to become part of a united Ireland for they feared that if they did so they would be dominated by, and possibly discriminated against, by the majority Catholic population. Their opposition to this fate had hardened in the face of the abortive Home Rule Bills of 1886 and 1893. In March 1905 they had formed the Ulster Unionist Council to unite all Unionist associations against any movements in the direction of Home Rule. It was not until after the two general elections of 1910 that the Irish question once again emerged as the dominant issue in British politics, for the second of those

---

[1] Public Record Office of Northern Ireland [henceforth PRONI], D 1507/3/4/4. *Daily Chronicle*, 16 Sept. 1914.
[2] R. Kee, *The Green Flag, ii, The Bold Fenian Men* (London, 1972), pp. 220–21.

elections left H.H. Asquith's Liberal government dependent upon the votes of the Irish Nationalist Party in the House of Commons for its political survival. In the following year the passage of the Parliament Act, which deprived the Tory-dominated House of Lords of its absolute veto over legislation, opened the way for a third attempt to pass a Home Rule Bill. As a result, in April 1912 Asquith introduced a Bill into Parliament to fulfil the Gladstonian ideal of granting Home Rule to the whole of Ireland. It promised to establish an Irish Parliament and executive in Dublin with powers to control purely Irish domestic affairs; it also promised to ensure that the Imperial Parliament in Westminster would retain responsibility for defence and external policy.[3] He did this despite the often expressed wishes of the Ulster Unionists that they wanted no part of a united Ireland ruled from Dublin. Only in the autumn of 1913 did the government recognise the seriousness of Ulster's opposition to their proposals and by then it was too late. In March 1914 the Curragh crisis robbed the Liberal administration of the opportunity to use the army to impose their own Bill on the Ulstermen.

Even before the Liberal government introduced its Home Rule bill the Ulster Unionists had begun to organise themselves to oppose the imposition of Home Rule on Ulster by force. In November 1910, encouraged by their leading spokesman Sir Edward Carson, they began to collect money to purchase arms. By the autumn of 1911 members of Orange lodges throughout Ulster were beginning to organise themselves on paramilitary lines. In September 1912, after the Bill had been introduced, 218,000 Ulster Protestants signed the 'Solemn League and Covenant', promising to use all necessary means to defeat the proposal to establish a Home Rule Parliament in Ireland. In January 1913 the Ulster Unionist Council decided to form the large number of different bodies which were drilling in Ulster into a single organisation, the Ulster Volunteer Force. (UVF) The council planned that it would consist of 100,000 men between the ages of seventeen to sixty-five who had signed the Covenant and would be organised along military lines. By February 1914 the UVF already had nearly 90,000 men, led by a considerable number of half-pay and reserve officers of the British Army. Most units had received elementary military training and it had its own signalling, medical and commissariat services. Its efficiency was demonstrated on the night of 24–25 April 1914, when it organised the importation through the ports of Bangor, Donaghadee and Larne of 24,000 rifles and 3,000,000 rounds of ammunition purchased in Germany.[4] The result was that by May 1914 the Liberal government depended upon the agreement of the Unionist opposition in Parliament

---

[3] F.S.L. Lyons, *Ireland since the Famine* (London, 1971), pp. 301–2; P. Jalland and J. Stubbs, 'The Irish Question after the Outbreak of war in 1914: Some Unfinished Party Business', *English Historical Review*, 96 (1981), p. 778.

[4] Peter Simpkins, *Kitchener's Army: The Raising of the New Armies, 1914–1916* (Manchester, 1988), pp. 21–22; A.T.Q. Stewart, *The Ulster Crisis* (London, 1967), pp. 41, 69–72, 107.

to achieve a settlement of the Irish question. This was unlikely to be forthcoming as the Unionists in Britain were under increasing pressure from Carson, who was buoyed up by the Curragh and the Larne gun-running, not to compromise.[5]

The Nationalist community had established their own organisation to counter the UVF. On 25 November 1913, at a public meeting in Dublin, the Irish National Volunteers (INV) were established. By the end of 1913 it had only 10,000 members but, following the Curragh crisis, its membership rose rapidly until by May 1914 it equalled and perhaps exceeded the strength of the UVF. Although it was also drilled by former members of the British Army, it possessed far fewer weapons than the UVF and on the eve of the European war could not aspire to its military efficiency.[6]

The unamended Home Rule Bill passed its third reading in the Commons on 25 May. Only the royal assent was required to make it law throughout Ireland. But there was no agreement over Ulster. A separate Amending Bill introduced in the Lords offered six counties in Ulster the chance of exclusion from the Home Rule Bill for six years. In mid July the Unionist-dominated House of Lords transformed this Bill by inserting an amendment to exclude all nine counties of Ulster. In a last-minute effort to secure the agreement of the Unionist opposition the King called an all-party conference at Buckingham Palace between 21 and 24 July. It was a futile attempt. Although the Liberal government and the British Unionists agreed that the time limit might be abandoned, the two Irish parties remained totally intractable. The Nationalists wanted a unified Ireland and the Ulstermen wanted all of Ulster to be permanently excluded from a Home Rule Ireland. A compromise satisfactory to all parties seemed impossible and by early July Ireland appeared to be on the brink of civil war.[7] The Home Rule crisis reached a dangerous crescendo on the eve of war: a platoon of the King's Own Scottish Borderers killed three people when they opened fire, near Dublin on 26 July, on a party of Irish National Volunteers, who had just taken delivery of a consignment of rifles at Howth which had been smuggled into Ireland from Germany.

One Liberal Minister, Herbert Samuel, may have believed that, faced with the prospect of a European war: 'How infinitely small, in the shadow of this awful catastrophe, appear the petty troubles of Ulster . . .', but the Irish crisis, coinciding as it did with the European crisis, caused the cabinet a good deal of concern.[8] On 4 July the Military Members of the Army Council had warned them that, if civil war did break out in Ireland, all six of the regular army's divisions in Britain would be required to keep order

---

[5] Jalland and Stubbs, 'The Irish Question', pp. 778–79.

[6] Kee, *The Green Flag*, pp. 201–2.

[7] Jalland and Stubbs, 'The Irish Question', p. 779; C. Hazlehurst, *Politicians at War August 1914 to May 1915: A Prologue to the Triumph of Lloyd George* (London, 1971), p. 25.

[8] Samuel to his mother, 26 July 1914, HLRO, Samuel Papers, A/156/466.

in Ireland. In the event of an international crisis, it would be impossible to spare any troops for service outside Britain. Britain would thus be unable to give any military assistance to India or Egypt, if they were threatened, and the government would not be able to fulfil any other obligations abroad.[9] Maurice Hankey, the Secretary of the Committee of Imperial Defence and a confidant of Asquith, was worried that the UVF might in some unspecified way take advantage of the situation if Britain went to war.[10] Hankey was only mistaken in failing to recognise that the leaders of both of the Irish parties were determined to pursue this course. On 30 July Captain James Craig, Carson's lieutenant and the leader of the Ulster Unionists, suggested to Carson that they should offer to postpone the Home Rule question. His proposal combined patriotism with a shrewd grasp of how to wrest some political advantage from the circumstances created by the war. Not only would such an offer be 'most patriotic' but it would also 'greatly disconcert . . . the Nationalists. They would find it extremely difficult to follow on with a similar offer from their side; and surely the country would . . . store up that much to our credit when the issue is finally fought out'.[11] On 30 July, after consulting Bonar Law, the leader of the British Unionist Party, they jointly proposed to Asquith that, 'in the interest of the international situation', government and opposition should agree to postpone the second reading of the Amending Bill. Perhaps to encourage the Prime Minister to agree, they threatened that, if the Army was called upon to mobilise, a number of reservists who were also members of the UVF would refuse to rejoin the colours and would remain to defend Ulster. After consulting some of his colleagues, the Prime Minister fell in with their suggestion. That afternoon he told the Commons that he had done so in order to secure national unity in the face of a common danger.[12] Bonar Law welcomed his announcement and suggested that it meant that 'this postponement will not in any way prejudice the interests of any of the parties in the controversy'.[13] Content with the Prime Minister's agreement, Carson then telegraphed to the headquarters of the UVF ordering all reservists who were members of the UVF to answer the call to the colours. On 1 August he went a step further. The *Morning Post* carried a report that Carson had stated that, if required by the government, a large body of Ulster Volunteers would be willing to give their services for home defence; others would be willing to serve anywhere they were required.[14]

Carson and the Ulster Unionists were not the only party intent on

[9] PRO, CAB 37/120/81, Memorandum by the Military Members of the Army Council on the military situation in Ireland, 4 July 1914.

[10] PRONI, D 1295/14B/1, W.B. Spender, 'Ulster and the Outbreak of War', nd.

[11] I. Colvin, *Carson* (London, 1934), ii, p. 422.

[12] Hazlehurst, *Politicians at War*, p. 32.

[13] Jalland and Stubbs, 'The Irish Question', pp. 780–81; 65 HC Deb 5s, cols 1601–2.

[14] PRONI, D 1507/3/4/4, cutting from *Morning Post*, 1 Aug. 1914.

gaining some political advantage from the European crisis. Following Carson's speech and press announcement, Margot Asquith, the Prime Minister's wife, promptly wrote to John Redmond, the leader of the Irish Parliamentary Party urging him to set 'an unforgettable example to the Carsonites' and make a speech in the Commons offering his soldiers to the government.[15] Redmond responded positively. On 3 August, without consulting any members of his own party, or the Provisional Committee of the INV, Redmond told the Commons that he would support Britain in her hour of need: 'I say to the Government', he intoned, 'that they may to-morrow withdraw every one of their troops from Ireland. I say that the coast of Ireland will be defended from foreign invasion by her armed sons, and for this purpose armed Nationalist Catholics in the south will be only too glad to join arms with the armed Protestant Ulstermen in the North.'[16]

At first sight Redmond's declaration seemed to run contrary to the whole tenor of Nationalist policy. During the Boer War Redmondite critics of the war had booed Irish regiments as they embarked from Dublin for South Africa.[17] Redmond made his offer for several reasons. He recognised the part which British public opinion would play in the achievement of Home Rule and that any refusal by the Nationalist community to support the war effort would have an adverse impact on his cause. He was also deeply moved by the plight of Belgium, another small nation like Ireland. His announcement struck a responsive chord amongst a large part of the Nationalist population – in the following weeks he received numerous messages of support from local government bodies and branches of the National, Volunteers throughout Ireland.[18] But it did not extinguish the bitterness felt by many Nationalists in the aftermath of the Howth gun-running.[19] The episode had caused widespread indignation: men had flocked to join the INV and Nationalists were determined not to make any further concessions to the Ulstermen. The INV also offered Redmond a powerful tool for embarrassing the government once war had broken out, as they contained many reservists from Irish regiments. Indeed on 31 July Colonel Maurice Moore, the Inspector-General of the National Volunteers, suggested to Redmond that the 25,000 reservists who were members of the organisation should be told not to rejoin their regiments unless Home Rule was placed immediately on the Statute Book. Instead of adopting this form of overt coercion,

15 M. Asquith, *Autobiography* (London, 1922), ii, p. 124.

16 *Hansard*, House of Commons Debates, 5th series, 65, col. 1821; B. Hobson, *A Short History of the Irish Volunteers* (Dublin, 1918), p. 179.

17 P. Karsten, 'Irish Soldiers in the British army, 1792–1922: Suborned or Subordinate?', *Journal of Social History*, 17 (1983–84), p. 47.

18 Simpkins, *Kitchener's Army*, p. 113.

19 Jalland and Stubbs, 'The Irish Question', p. 782.

Redmond opted for the more indirect and subtle pressure of his speech of 3 August.[20]

In some quarters in Britain Redmond's speech was greeted with a relief which almost amounted to joy. William Bridgeman, a Unionist Party whip, was 'much impressed by this speech at the time, as I thought it was made without any *"arrière pensée"*. . .'[21] The Postmaster General, Sir Charles Hobhouse, who was present in the Commons to hear it, believed that 'Redmond's few words had an immense influence in steadying our people, and perceptibly affected the Tories, while taking the wind out of the sails of the Orangemen'.[22] Some Ministers, including Asquith himself, hoped that Redmond's announcements presaged the end, at least for the time being, of the Irish question. At dinner of 3 August he told his colleague J.A. Pease 'the one bright spot in this hateful war was the settlement of Irish civil strife & the cordial union of forces in Ireland in aiding the government to maintain our supreme national interests, & he added, nearly breaking down: "Jack, God moves in a mysterious way his wonders to perform".'[23] Samuel was 'ever more hopeful than before that we shall reach a settlement. A dramatic ending would be if both the Ulster and National Volunteers were enrolled as Territorials for the defence of the United Kingdom!'[24]

There were a number of obstacles in the way of recruiting in Ireland, obstacles which did not exist on the other side of the Irish Channel. The most significant of these was that the government and the Volunteer movements and their political supporters were in pursuit of different objectives. The government sought tranquillity at home coupled with a search for the largest possible army they could raise to send abroad to fight the Germans. The Volunteers, whilst anxious to be seen to be patriotic by rallying behind the government, were intent on continuing to pursue their own domestic agenda. They had no wish to surrender complete control of their paramilitary organisations to the War Office, for fear that if they did so their standing on the Home Rule issue would be fatally compromised.

Lord Kitchener, who became Secretary of State for War on 5 August, was the main architect of British strategic policy in the opening months of the war. Kitchener regarded both leaders of the Irish community as fractious children. He once remarked brusquely to Carson that: 'If I had been on a platform with you and Redmond I should have knocked your heads together.'[25] But he was particularly suspicious of Redmond, for he

[20] D.R. Gwynn, *Life of John Redmond* (London, 1932), p. 353.

[21] P. Williamson (ed.), *The Modernization of Conservative Politics: The Diaries and Letters of William Bridgeman, 1904–35* (London, 1988), p. 79.

[22] E. David (ed.), *Inside Asquith's Cabinet: From the Diaries of Charles Hobhouse* (London, 1977), p. 180.

[23] J.A. Pease diary, 3 Aug. 1914, Nuffield College, Gainford Papers, box 39.

[24] Samuel to wife, 29 July 1914, HLRO, Samuel Papers, A/157/691.

[25] Quoted in H. Montgomery-Hyde, *Carson: The Life of Sir Edward Carson, Lord Carson of Duncairn* (London, 1976), p. 378.

had been brought up in south-west Ireland in a Protestant family and had been taught to see the Irish as a subject race. As a Unionist, he opposed Home Rule and was sympathetic to Carson's views. He regarded the INV as rebels and remembered that Nationalist volunteers had fought against him during the Boer War. He also feared that if he gave the INV arms they would eventually use them against Britain. [26]

Kitchener's policy towards Irish recruiting was not just conditioned by his attitude towards Home Rule. It was also determined by his strategic policy. He was a professional, soldier of vast experience who had little time for paramilitary forces. His great objective was to raise troops for general service so that he could send an army to the Continent. In 1914 the British Regular Army consisted of approximately 247,000 men. They were divided into an Expeditionary Force based in Britain of six infantry divisions and a single cavalry division. In addition, the equivalent of another four regular divisions were stationed abroad and could be recalled for service in Europe as soon as colonial governments could muster their own troops to replace them. Thanks to the work of the former Liberal Secretary of State for War, R.B. Haldane, Britain also possessed a second-line army of part-time soldiers, the Territorial Force. On paper it could muster a total of fourteen infantry divisions and fourteen Yeomanry brigades, but its real strength of approximately 268,000 men meant that it was nearly 47,000 men below its establishment. They were raised and administered by voluntary organisations known as County Associations. The Territorial Force had been recruited for home defence and its members were not liable to serve abroad. Before the war Ireland did not possess a Territorial Force, as its security was safeguarded by a garrison of two divisions of the Regular Army.[27] Kitchener recognised that this was a small force by the standards of the continental belligerents. He believed that by early 1917 the armies of the continental belligerents would have bled each other dry. In 1914 he wanted to raise a continental-scale army in Britain so that, by early 1917, it would be able to intervene decisively on the Continent, inflicting a final defeat on the Central Powers and so enabling Britain to impose her peace terms on enemies and allies alike.[28] He wanted to ensure that the British Army 'should reach its full strength at the beginning of the third year of the War, just when France is getting into rather low water and Germany is beginning to feel the pinch'.[29] Hence his main objective in Ireland was to raise troops for the Regular Army, not merely for home defence. Consequently he 'strongly deprecated the enlistment of "local forces" to "preserve the peace" and with other such objects'.[30]

[26] Simpkins, *Kitchener's Army*, pp. 274–75.

[27] G.H. Cassar, *Kitchener: Architect of Victory* (London, 1977), p. 195; T. Royle, *The Kitchener Enigma* (London, 1985), pp. 261–62.

[28] D. French, *British Strategy and War Aims, 1914–1916* (London, 1986), pp. 24–25.

[29] Sir G. Arthur, *Life of Lord Kitchener* (London, 1920), iii, p. 244.

[30] PRO, CAB 41/35/30. Asquith to King, 14 Aug. 1914.

Kitchener therefore quickly encountered two major obstacles in Ireland. Despite their public protestations, neither of the leaders of the Irish parties was really willing to sink their differences and make co-operation for home defence a reality; just as neither of them was willing to surrender control of their paramilitary forces to the War Office so that they could be sent to France. On the contrary, both men were intent on using their volunteers to exercise pressure on the government in their own favour. In the same way that Redmond and the Nationalists were reluctant to give their full support to Kitchener's recruiting campaign for general service, until some form of Home Rule was on the statute book, so Carson and the Ulster Unionists had doubts about committing the UVF unless the government agreed to postpone Home Rule, at least until after the war. Redmond had made his speech on 3 August on the assumption that Home Rule would reach the statute book within a matter of a few weeks. On 3 August he had refrained from bargaining with the government before making the speech, in the expectation that Asquith would treat him with similar generosity. After his speech, however, he received a telegram from the Irish Volunteers in Derry City which announced that their members who were reservists had decided not to rejoin the colours until they were assured that the King would sign the Home Rule Bill. Redmond thought such a course of action was potentially ruinous, especially if it was adopted by the Provisional Committee of the Volunteers which was due to meet on 5 August.[31] But he was not above using the episode to put pressure on the government, writing to Churchill and Asquith on 4 August to warn them that if the Home Rule Bill was postponed his supporters 'will consider themselves sold & I will be simply unable to hold them. In that event deplorable things will be said & done in Ireland & the Home Rule cause may be lost for our time'.[32] He wanted the royal assent to be given to the Bill, coupled with promises by the government that they would introduce an Amending Bill in the winter and that, until such a bill was introduced, they would not put the original Bill into operation. Similarly, on 5 August, Carson wrote to Asquith urging him not to use the present crisis to the detriment of the Ulstermen.[33] Caught between these two fires, Asquith tried to ascertain if the two leaders were prepared to co-operate by engineering a meeting between them, only to discover that there was still no likelihood that they could compromise. As Redmond reported to Asquith:

> I spoke to Carson this afternoon in the Speaker's Library in the presence of the Speaker. I found Sir Edward Carson in an absolutely irreconcilable mood about everything. His position was that if the government put the H.R. bill on

[31] Gwynn, *Life of Redmond*, pp. 357–58.

[32] R.S. Churchill (ed.), *Winston S. Churchill: Companion Volume II, Part 3, 1911–1914* (London, 1969), p. 1422; Jalland and Stubbs, 'The Irish Question', pp. 782–83.

[33] Ibid., p. 783.

the statute book he and the Tory party would obstruct the Appropriation Bill and revive all the bitterness of the controversy.[34]

In the face of Carson's intransigence Redmond showed himself equally obdurate, informing the Prime Minister that

I can add very little to my letter of yesterday; but if the Government allow themselves to be bullied in this way by Sir Edward Carson, a position of the most serious difficulty will arise with us. It will be quite impossible for us to abstain from raising a discussion on the Second Reading of the Appropriation Bill, which would have most unfortunate and disastrous results in Ireland, and really would put us and our country in an absolutely cruel position. It would make it quite impossible for me to go to Ireland, as I desire to do, and to translate into action the spirit of my speech the other day. It would revive all the suspicion and bitterness and controversy, all through the South and West of Ireland, and would exhibit us to the world as torn into a hundred fragments, and disaffected with the Government of the day.[35]

The absence of real agreement between the leaders of the two Irish parties extended to Ireland itself. On the same day that Carson and Redmond met in London, the Standing Committee of the Irish Volunteers endorsed Redmond's speech of 3 August and, under the guidance of their president, Eoin MacNeill, declared 'the complete willingness of the Irish Volunteers to take joint action with the Ulster Volunteers for the defence of Ireland'.[36] To give this resolution reality MacNeill then arranged to visit Belfast to discover the attitude of the Ulster Unionist leaders to the proposal. A telegram was sent to Carson suggesting that the meeting should take place on 7 August. MacNeill prepared a letter which he planned to give to Carson on his arrival, explaining that he thought that the proper way to proceed would be for the commanders of the two volunteer forces to meet to discuss arrangements for mutual assistance in the event of a German invasion.[37] Carson acknowledged receipt of MacNeill's telegram but never came to Belfast. Nothing more was heard of co-operation between the two Volunteer movements. Although there is no firm evidence to support MacNeill's suspicion that Carson deliberately cancelled his trip to Belfast to avoid meeting him, it is apparent that Carson had little time for Redmond's proffered co-operation. He was convinced that Redmond's speech was no more than a political move designed to ease the passage of the Home Rule Bill. He was also afraid that Asquith would use the truce to reward Redmond for his speech by giving the Bill the royal assent and he was determined that if he did so co-operation between the UVF and the National Volunteers would be out

[34] R.S. Churchill (ed.), *Winston S. Churchill: Companion Volume II, Part 3, 1911–1914*, (London, 1969), pp. 1423–24.

[35] Ibid., pp. 1423–24.

[36] MacNeill to Carson, 5 Aug. 1914, NLI, Hobson Papers, 13174/4.

[37] MacNeill to Carson, 6 Aug. 1914, NLI, Hobson Papers, 13174/4.

of the question.[38] On 9 August the chief staff officer of the UVF told all regimental commanders that, for the time being, they were to tolerate the presence of Nationalist Volunteers in their districts but that they were to be disarmed if they threatened violence or outrage.[39]

Thus, despite the 'truce' of 30 July, the Prime Minister remained under a good deal of political pressure over Home Rule and could not avoid infuriating one party or the other.[40] He now had two alternatives: he could prorogue Parliament, in which case the Home Rule Bill would automatically be presented for royal assent; or he could adjourn the sitting, in which case the Bill's further passage into law would merely be postponed. The Unionists, whom Asquith knew were afraid 'that we shall make use of the "truce" to spring a trick on them, by suddenly proroguing & putting our Home Rule & Welsh Church Bills on the Statute book as *fait accomplis* before they can say knife', wanted an adjournment.[41] The Nationalists wanted prorogation, so that the Home Rule Bill could be placed on the Statute Book immediately coupled with an Amending Bill in the next session.[42] On 6 August Asquith tried to buy some time with a suggestion which pleased no one. He promised Redmond that he would not allow the truce to interrupt the passage of Home Rule Bill but that to prorogue at this moment would be regarded as a piece of sharp practice by the Unionists and he therefore asked Redmond to accept a brief adjournment. Redmond thought this was a 'fatal' proposal. He counselled that in the present state of public opinion the government should proceed with his own plan. If it hesitated the Nationalist community in Ireland would condemn it for evasion and he would lose control of his supporters in Ireland.[43]

In the meantime the War Office had decided that

> The first thing, and the most important, is for Mr Redmond and Mr Carson to come to some arrangement by which the whole body of volunteers, north and south, should be put under the direct control of the Army Council.[44]

Subsequent discussions between the War Office and the leaders of the Volunteer forces only served to demonstrate that the two sides were pursuing different agenda. On 5 August Sir Horace Plunkett, an Irish Protestant landowner and a leader of the Irish Co-operative Movement, wrote to Moore informing him that he had spoken to General Sir Arthur Paget, the General Officer Commanding in Ireland, asking him to discuss

[38] Carson to Gwynne, 7 Aug. 1914, Bodleian Library H.A. Gwynne Papers, 17.

[39] UVF order no. 158/1914, 9 Aug. 1914.

[40] Jalland and Stubbs, 'The Irish Question', pp. 781–82; Hazlehurst, *Politicians at War*, p. 27.

[41] Asquith to Stanley, 4 Aug. 1914 in M. and E. Brock (eds), *H.H. Asquith*, p. 150.

[42] Asquith to Stanley, 10 Aug. 1914, ibid., p. 163.

[43] Jalland and Stubbs, 'The Irish Question', p. 784.

[44] PRO, 30/57/60, Memo on Irish Volunteers, nd but *c.* 7–8 Aug. 1914.

with Moore the possibility of co-operation between the Army and the two volunteer forces.[45] Moore welcomed the suggestion, for the Army could supply his force with the two things it most lacked: sufficient weapons and the instruction in their use, which had formerly been provided by the reservists who had now rejoined the colours. At Paget's headquarters he was presented with a scheme by which large drafts of Irish Volunteers and Ulster Volunteers would be called up for active service in the defence of Ireland. The men were to serve for three months, during which they would receive barrack square drill and field training, then spend nine weeks on coastal defence duties. Units would not be broken up and mixed with other troops but would retain their own separate organisation and identity.[46] However, when Moore presented the scheme to the Provisional Committee, they rejected it. They were entirely averse to placing volunteer units under War Office control, being suspicious that the proposal contained no safeguard against the inevitable tendency of the military authorities to direct men into the regular army and thus wreck the INV's organisation.[47]

Their suspicions that the War Office wanted to break up the INV's organisation and direct their men into the regular army soon received further confirmation. On 7 August Percy Illingworth, the Liberal Chief Whip, had informed Kitchener that once the Home Rule Bill had been passed 'Redmond will undertake that you will get 100,000 or 200,000 or more recruits from Ireland'.[48] When they met, Redmond explained that 'I hope you don't think, Lord Kitchener, that we are coming here as recruiting sergeants'.[49] But that was just what Kitchener did want him to be, for he wanted help in mounting a straightforward recruiting drive in Ireland for the regular army and hoped that Redmond, who was accompanied by his lieutenant John Dillon, would persuade the INV, or at least part of them, to assist him. The War Office believed that at the moment the military usefulness of the INVs 'is nil' but that 'if about 30 per cent are eliminated, this 30 per cent consisting of the "corner boy" element and "ne'er do weels"' they would make good soldiers. But before that could happen they had to be placed under the discipline and control of the Army Council and then organised, equipped and trained by the army under officers approved by Lord Lieutenants and the Army Council. The result would be just what the leaders of the INV did not want for, if the war lasted for any time, many of the men enlisted in the Irish Volunteers when 'they got a taste of soldiering and were imbued with a military spirit, would drift into Line Regiments'.[50]

45 Plunkett to Moore, 5 Aug. 1914, NLI, Moore Papers, 10561/30.
46 Hobson, *History of the Irish Volunteers*, pp. 185–88.
47 MacNeill to Moore, 1 Nov. 1914, NLI, Moore Papers, 10561/28.
48 PRO, 30/57/60. Illingworth to Kitchener, 7 Aug. 1914.
49 F.S.L. Lyons, *John Dillon* (London, 1968), p. 358.
50 PRO, 30/57/60, Memo on Irish Volunteers, nd but *c*. 7–8 Aug. 1914.

The next day Redmond wrote to Asquith. He explained that if the War Office ignored the INV he would not encourage Nationalists to join the Army and Kitchener's call for recruits for the regular army would meet with little response. He also warned that Kitchener's suggestion that he might send English Territorials to Ireland to replace the two regular divisions garrisoning the country would be deeply offensive to the Nationalist community.[51] Three days later, at a Cabinet meeting, Augustine Birrell, the Liberal Chief Secretary for Ireland, urged that the INV should be accepted as an official military force. Asquith added his voice in support, but Kitchener remained obdurate, insisting that 'recognition should be the vehicle by which arrangement should be reached. His idea of arrangement was the postponement of Home Rule.'[52]

Many southern Unionists had been traditionally suspicious of Nationalist good faith and were bewildered by Redmond's speech of 3 August. Lord Meath, the Lord Lieutenant of Dublin, believed that the great mass of Unionists in Dublin were puzzled as to whether or not they should throw in their lot with the INV. He wrote to Redmond asking for an assurance that the latter were loyal to the Crown. But many southern Unionists, like their cousins in Ulster, never had any such doubts. They saw only sinister motives behind Redmond's support for the war and were as determined as he was to retain control of their own militia.[53] On 7 August the Lord Mayor of Belfast read a letter from Carson to a meeting at the City Hall which had been called to consider how they could best assist the government in the war effort. Carson claimed: 'We will now be prepared to show once more without any bartering of conditions that the cause of Great Britain is our cause and that with our fellow citizens throughout the whole Empire we will make common cause and suffer any sacrifice.'[54] Beneath this stirring rhetoric the bartering for the Ulster Unionist's support had already begun. On 5 August the UVF head-quarters asked its local commanders to ascertain unofficially how many of their units would be willing to volunteer their services for home defence and to forward the information to UVF head-quarters the next day.[55] The initial response seemed to be favourable, so on 7 August General Sir George Richardson, the commander of the UVF, asked all unit commanders to ask each individual member of the UVF whether, if called upon, he was ready to serve anywhere in the United Kingdom, whether he

[51] Gwynn, *Life of John Redmond*, pp. 366–67.

[52] David (ed.), *Inside Asquith's Cabinet*, p. 181; Asquith to Stanley, 11 Aug. 1914 in Brock (ed.), *H.H. Asquith*, pp. 165–66.

[53] P. Buckland, *Irish Unionism*, i, *The Anglo-Irish and the New Ireland, 1885–1922* (London, 1972), pp. 45, 48–49; PRO, 30/57/60, Meath to Kitchener, 14 Aug. 1914; ibid., Meath to Redmond, 15 Aug. 1914.

[54] PRONI, D 1507/3/6/1, Carson to Lord Mayor of Belfast, 7 Aug. 1914.

[55] PRONI, D 1507/3/4/4, Urgent confidential circular memorandum from Col. G. Hackett-Pain, Chief of Staff of UVF to divisional, regimental and battalion commanders, 5 Aug. 1914.

would serve abroad, or whether he was only willing to serve in Ulster.[56] When Carson and Craig met Kitchener on 7 August it is likely that they already had some indication of the numbers of Ulster Volunteers who were ready to serve in the defence of their country. At this meeting, the Unionist leaders made it plain that, if sufficient men were forthcoming for imperial service from the UVF, they expected Kitchener to keep them together as a fighting unit; and that the word 'Ulster' should appear after the number of the division it was proposed to raise. Kitchener demurred and the meeting ended without agreement.[57] Carson then approached Asquith to ask whether, if the UVF were to volunteer for the defence of the United Kingdom, the Prime Minister would give him an assurance that the Home Rule Bill would not become law; and that whilst the volunteers were fighting to save the Empire, those who remained at home would not be massacred by the Nationalists supported by the government in Dublin.[58] Asquith refused to give any such guarantee and on 8 August UVF head-quarters made it clear to the volunteers that they would only be asked to serve outside Ulster on the distinct understanding that Carson told them that he was satisfied with the situation as regarded Ulster.[59]

On 10 August Carson tried to bribe and blackmail Asquith by sending him what the Prime Minister described as a 'rather threatening letter',[60] intimating that if the truce was abrogated he would return to Belfast 'and throw in my lot with my people there in any action they may feel bound to take'. He insisted that the Ulster Unionists were indignant and felt they had been betrayed. He also declared that Asquith could avoid this difficulty by postponing the controversy and, if he did so, the UVF could offer Kitchener two divisions for immediate service abroad and a similar number for home service in Ulster. 'If the controversy goes on of course none of these men will be available, much to my regret.'[61] Stephen Gwynn, a Nationalist MP, warned Asquith and Kitchener that the UVF would hold back unless they were assured that Home Rule would not become law while the war lasted. They would not enlist as individuals because they were determined to keep their organisation intact.[62] In the meantime Craig remained in contact with Kitchener 'so that if a settlement is reached one way or another, the UVF may be utilized to the best advantage at home and abroad . . .'[63]

[56] PRONI, D 1507/3/4/4, Cutting from *Belfast Newsletter*, 8 Aug. 1914.

[57] H. Montgomery-Hyde, *Carson* p. 378.

[58] R.H. Stewart, 36 (Ulster) Division: formation and early training, National Army Museum, MS 7611/23.

[59] PRONI, D 1507/3/4/4, Circular from UVF HQ to all divisional and battalion commanders, 8 Aug. 1914.

[60] Asquith to Stanley, 10 Aug. 1914 in Brocks (ed.), *H.H. Asquith*, p. 163.

[61] Colvin, *Carson*, iii, p. 29.

[62] Gwynn to Asquith, 11 Aug. 1914, Gwynn Papers 14; Gwynn to Kitchener, 11 Aug. 1914, Gwynn Papers, 11 Aug. 1914.

[63] PRONI, D 1295, Craig to Spender, 12 Aug. 1914.

On 14 August, when a UVF battalion commander disclosed to the press the assurance they had been given by their headquarters on 8 August, the tug-of-war between Redmond and the Nationalists and Carson and the Unionists, with Asquith in the middle, became clear to Redmond.[64] Whilst Redmond was holding back from urging the Irish Volunteers to enlist in the British Army until the Home Rule Bill had received the Royal Assent, Carson was holding back from offering the UVF until the Home Rule question had been shelved until after the war.

This impasse was not broken until the last week of August. Asquith was initially content to 'wait and see'. On 8 August he had offered Bonar Law two ways forward. Parliament was due to adjourn on 10 August and they could resume discussion on the Amending Bill when it met again. Or they could introduce a short Bill suspending the operation of the Home Rule Act until an Amending Bill had been dealt with in the next session.[65] When he adjourned the Commons on 10 August, he repeated his promise of 30 July that postponing the Amending Bill 'must be without prejudice to the domestic and political position of any party'. He then announced an adjournment until 25 August and concluded by saying that the government was 'not without hope that in the interval we may be able to make proposals . . . which may meet with something like general acquiescence'.[66] He was too optimistic but fortunately by late August events in France and Belgium helped to break the logjam. On 23 August the Second Corps of the British Expeditionary Force fought a numerically much superior German force at Mons. The British lost 1600 men and joined the French in a headlong retreat which eventually took them to the Marne. Although the British losses were trivial compared to those suffered by the French army, the Germans had apparently succeeded in throwing General Joffre's plan of campaign completely out of gear and were pressing onwards towards Paris.[67]

Asquith was quick to recognise how he could exploit this new national peril. On 24 August he wrote to his confidante Venetia Stanley that 'it seems trivial & futile to be haggling about the boundaries of the six counties, the precise terms of a time limit, and all the other "sticking points", as you so well describe them. So I have sent Birrell to the Irish to say that these are not the urgent matters of the moment and, if the situation abroad does not mend, they must be content with further delay.'[68] By the end of the month Anglo-French military co-operation seemed to be on the point of collapsing. Until Joffre's counterattack on

---

[64] Gwynn, *Life of John Redmond*, p. 368.

[65] Jalland and Stubbs, 'The Irish Question', p. 788.

[66] Quoted in M. and E.Brock (eds), *H.H. Asquith*, p. 164.

[67] Sir James Edmonds, *History of the Great War: Military Operations France and Belgium, 1914. Mons, the Retreat to the Seine, the Marne and the Aisne, August–October 1914* (2nd edn, London, 1933), pp. 71–295.

[68] Asquith to Stanley, 24 Aug. 1914 in Brock (ed.), *H.H. Asquith*, p. 191.

the Marne, which began on 6 September, removed the German threat to Paris, it seemed as if the Germans might indeed succeed in defeating France in a lightning war.

Asquith's demarche was shrewdly calculated to exploit the weakest link in the Unionists' armoury, namely their public protestations of their patriotism. After his speech of 3 August, Redmond had told Churchill that 'in the *present* temper of the Unionist Party after my speech you can afford to take the course I suggest'.[69] He was correct. The war had greatly weakened the Unionists' bargaining position, for their patriotism prevented them from renewing their threat of civil war in Ulster. As Bonar Law admitted: 'We cannot fight the Government now. They have tied our hands by our patriotism.'[70] On 6 August he had written to the Foreign Secretary, Sir Edward Grey, intimating that his party would not divide the House of Commons if Asquith did as the Nationalists wished. They would, however regard his action as dishonourable and they would not co-operate with him.[71] By mid August the best the British Unionist leaders hoped for was an adjournment to postpone the whole issue, so that the Home Rule Bill could be taken up again after the war, by when the balance of power in the Commons might have tilted in their favour following another general election. Asquith therefore knew that he did not have to take the Unionist threat too seriously and that he could rely upon their patriotism.[72] On 25 August he personally described the situation in Belgium to Bonar Law and coupled it with news of his own preferred policy for Ireland, placing Home Rule on the statute book immediately coupled with the exclusion of the six counties for three years. At the end of three years each county was to have the opportunity of voting on whether or not to opt in or out of Home Rule. Bonar Law was sufficiently impressed with the gravity of the military outlook to agree to support the Prime Minister and to impart the offer to Carson.[73]

The Irish Unionists capitulated almost at once. Carson's dilemma was that he had promised his supporters the exclusion of the whole of Ulster, not just part of it. There were UVF units in Fermanagh, Monaghan, Cavan and Donegal who would revolt if they found that their county was to be incorporated into a southern Irish state. There would then be a breakdown of public order and Britain would lose the military support of Ulster in the war against Germany.[74] But Carson, too, was swayed by the news from the Western Front for he was also intent on resisting the Germans. 'I shudder to think what will happen if we have a defeat', he

[69] R. Churchill (ed.), *Winston S. Churchill: Companion Volume II*, p. 1423.

[70] Quoted in D. Dutton, *Austen Chamberlain: Gentleman in Politics* (Bolton, 1985), p. 115.

[71] R. Blake (ed.), *The Unknown Prime Minister. The Life and Times of Andrew Bonar Law, 1858–1923* (London, 1955), p. 228.

[72] Jalland and Stubbs, 'The Irish Question', pp. 784–85.

[73] M. and E.Brock (eds), *H.H. Asquith*, p. 195.

[74] Jalland and Stubbs, 'The Irish Question', p. 793.

wrote on 22 August.[75] Fundamentally he agreed with Craig, who had written to him two days previously that 'however much we curse and damn the P.M. in the House, we must say all the same that we will do our best under the circumstances for the Army and the country; then come over here and face the music.'[76] After a series of meetings with other Unionist MPs, one of their number, Colonel Hickman, the President of the British League for the Defence of Ulster, delivered a copy of a letter from Carson to Kitchener. In this Carson emphasised that he could not commit either the Ulster Unionist Council or the UVF as a body but that he would place his personal support behind any recruiting drive Kitchener mounted amongst the members of the UVF. At a subsequent meeting between Carson, Craig and Kitchener at the War Office, Carson assured the Secretary of State that some 35,000 Ulster Volunteers were willing to enlist for foreign service. Carson attached no conditions to this offer, thus giving Kitchener what he wanted. In return the Secretary of State waived his previous doubts and objections to the formation of an exclusively Ulster unit.[77] On 28 August the War Office instructed the GOC in Ireland to give Carson and Craig every assistance in their efforts to recruit in Ulster and informed him that Craig and Hickman had been appointed as special recruiting officers for the north of Ireland.[78]

On 3 September Carson travelled to Belfast to make a blatant appeal to the patriotism of the Ulster Unionist Council, in a successful effort to persuade them to follow his lead. 'England's difficulty was not Ulster's opportunity', he declared. 'England's difficulty is our difficulty.' Anticipating Asquith's probable action over the Home Rule Bill he insisted that, however unworthily the government might act, in a great national emergency the Ulster Unionists must place their country before party politics and not seek to purchase better terms by selling their patriotism.[79] The Ulstermen's commitment to the British cause was by no means unconditional, for Carson and the Ulster Council were careful to promise those Ulstermen who enlisted that the UVF would be kept in being during the war and would fulfil the purpose for which it had been established, to resist Home Rule and to carry out the Covenant.[80]

Kitchener had dropped his objections to the formation of a distinctive Ulster division once Carson had agreed that those members of the UVF who were eligible should enlist for general service. He had not, however, lost any of his suspicions of armed Nationalists. As late as April 1915 H.J. Tennant, Asquith's brother-in-law and the Parliamentary Under-Secretary

[75] Montgomery-Hyde, *Carson*, p. 379.

[76] Jalland and Stubbs, 'The Irish Question', p. 794.

[77] R.H. Stewart, 36 (Ulster Division): formation and early training, National Army Museum, MS 7611/23; Montgomery-Hyde, *Carson*, p. 380.

[78] PRONI, D 1507/I/1914/31, Cubbitt to GOC, Irish Command, 28 Aug. 1914.

[79] R. McNeill, *Ulster's Stand for Union* (London, 1922), pp. 231–32.

[80] PRONI, D 627/4295/5, memorandum, 'The Ulster Unionist attitude in Face of the Present Circumstances', 22 Sept. 1914.

at the War Office, believed that Kitchener remained opposed to arming the National Volunteers even with obsolete Belgium rifles 'for fear of revolution'.[81] In late August Kitchener recognised that he would have to make some minimal concessions to Irish susceptibilities because recruiting in Ireland, especially outside Ulster, was below what he had hoped to achieve.[82] Kitchener had made his first appeal for 100,000 men on 7 August. Four days later each of the six existing home commands was called upon to organise an infantry division, complete with all arms, for the first of his new armies.[83] The Irish Command's contribution to this effort was to be the 10th (Irish) division formed at Dublin and the Curragh. The volunteers who presented themselves were to be regular soldiers who enlisted for general service. Unlike the Territorials they were to be liable to be sent abroad once they had been trained and equipped. Most of the first six divisions found the recruits they required very rapidly but the 10th division was something of an exception. By the end of August only one of its twelve battalions was recruiting satisfactorily. The War Office recognised that the formation of a projected second division in Ireland, the Sixteenth Division, would not be possible unless recruiting improved dramatically. That would only happen if both the UVF and the Irish National Volunteers were allowed to enlist en bloc.[84]

Despite Kitchener's obvious reluctance, on 10 August Asquith had told the Commons, in reply to a question from Redmond, that Kitchener would do all he could, after consulting with leaders of Nationalist opinion in Ireland, to arrange for the full equipment and organisation of the INV.[85] As his hand had now been forced, the next day Kitchener told the Cabinet that he was sending a general to Ireland to inspect and report upon the INV. The next day Birrell wrote to Redmond that the 'very distinguished Irish officer, Lieutenant-General Sir B.T. Mahon KCVO ... crosses over today from the War Office to confer with the leaders of the National Volunteers. Cocker him up and make his Irish heart glow within him. Much may come of this ...'[86]

Some newspapers thought that Asquith's announcement and Mahon's journey meant that the government was about to take control of the movement. Many Volunteers feared that, following Redmond's meeting with Kitchener, an attempt would be made to hand them over to the War Office as an imperial force.[87] As far as can be ascertained, most

---

81 J. O'Connor to Major Crean, 8 April 1915, NLI, Moore Papers, 10544/2.

82 David (ed.), *Inside Asquith's Cabinet*, p. 190.

83 V.W. Germains, *The Kitchener Armies: The Story of a Great National Achievement* (London, 1930), p. 55.

84 T. Denman, *Ireland's Unknown Soldiers: The 16th (Irish) Division in the Great War, 1914–1918* (Dublin, 1992), pp. 23–24.

85 Hobson, *History of the Irish National Volunteers*, p. 184.

86 PRO, CAB 41/35/86, Asquith to the King, 11 Aug. 1914; Gwynn, *Life of John Redmond*, p. 368.

87 Hobson, *History of the Irish National Volunteers*, pp. 179, 184.

Volunteers had no desire to adopt this course of action. Fairly typical seems to have been the attitude exhibited at a meeting of some 2000 Irish National Volunteers held at Galladuff where a speaker asserted that 'They would ... defend their shores under John Redmond and the Green Flag; but they would not be turned into militiamen to be generalled by Roberts and Kitchener (cries of "Never"). If they sacrificed their independence, and allowed this movement to be controlled by the Government, and the War Office, their national usefulness would be ended for ever.'[88] Throughout August Redmond confined his efforts to appealing to all INVs to co-operate to prepare to repel a German invasion.[89] But rumours that the leadership might be about to permit the War Office to take control of the Volunteers lock, stock and barrel met with such hostility from amongst their ranks that, on 19 August, the Provisional Committee was forced to issue a statement in Dublin insisting that the Volunteers were not about to be placed under War Office control. They desired to inform their members that

> The Irish Volunteers simply consented to carry out the understanding which Mr Redmond made on their behalf in the House of Commons to take joint action with the UVF for the defence of Ireland. The government accordingly, at the suggestion of Mr Redmond have, as the Provisional Committee is pleased to learn, abandoned their intention of drafting English Territorials into Ireland.[90]

On 23 August Kitchener appointed Mahon as the GOC of Tenth (Irish) Division. Far from being an apolitical soldier, Mahon was a Protestant and a Unionist. He had known Moore before the war and called on him to ask for introductions to the Volunteers in the principal centres. Having received them, he immediately set off on a tour of the south and west of Ireland in the company of his staff officer, Colonel Lewis Comyn. On every occasion Mahon inspected an INV unit, he asked them whether they would be willing to enlist in an Irish division in Kitchener's army. On each occasion he received the same answer, that they would do whatever Redmond asked of them. Mahon came away with a poor opinion of the military value of the INV. When he asked Redmond to encourage his followers to enlist for overseas service, the latter replied that he would do so only if he could secure two conditions: that his men were not to be required to take the oath of allegiance to the King; and that they were only to be used to defend Ireland and were not to be sent abroad. Mahon agreed to the former but, knowing Kitchener's determination to secure troops for service abroad, said that, if Redmond wanted his men incorporated into the Army, he could not agree to the second condition.

[88] PRO, 30/57/60, J.M. Wilson to H. Wilson and enc., 19 Aug. 1914.

[89] PRONI, D 1507/3/5/3, cutting from *King's County Independent*, 15 Aug. 1914.

[90] PRONI, D 1507/3/5/3, cutting from the *Northern Whig*, 20 Aug. 1914.

The fate of England and Ireland was being decided on the battlefields of Flanders. If those battles were lost, no amount of soldiers sitting on the coast of Ireland would save Ireland from a German invasion.[91] Before Redmond's supporters would agree to Kitchener's terms they wanted, as the Inspecting Officer for the County Wexford volunteers explained, 'the Bill on the Book'.[92]

Asquith drew the by now obvious conclusion: 'They [the Irish Nationalists] will not flock in until they are sure that their Bill is going to be put on the Statute Book.'[93] On 7 September he presided over a Cabinet committee which consisted of Lloyd George, McKenna (the Home Secretary), Birrell, Grey and Haldane (Lord Chancellor since 1912) to consider two possible solutions: to place Home Rule on the statute book together with an Amending Bill and a Suspensory Bill promised for the next session; or to pass Home Rule with the six counties excluded for three years pending a decision taken by the Imperial Parliament. They quickly agreed on the first alternative, that Home Rule Bill would be placed on the statute book at once, despite the expected Unionist opposition.[94] This was the price Asquith had to pay for Redmond's support for, in a letter to Illingworth on 27 August, Redmond had again threatened if anything less were offered he would lose control of the Irish situation.[95]

On 15 September Asquith announced the Cabinet's decision in the Commons. As a sop to the Unionists he paid a tribute to the 'patriotic and public spirit which had been shown by the Ulster Volunteers' promising that their conduct had made 'the employment of force, any kind of force, for what you call the coercion of Ulster, an absolutely unthinkable thing'.[96] As the Cabinet had predicted, the Unionists were furious. They insisted that Asquith had gone back on his word. Carson condemned the Prime Minister's announcement as a piece of unparalleled treachery. He also insisted that his followers should not therefore slacken their efforts to defeat the Germans. In southern Ireland the Executive Committee of the Irish Unionist alliance, representing Unionists of the three southern provinces, reminded their supporters that, despite the Liberal government's policy, southern Unionists should continue with their efforts to secure recruits for the Army.[97] The Home Rule Bill reached the statute book on 18 September, when the entire Unionist party walked out

91 Denman, *Ireland's Unknown Soldiers*, pp. 24–25; Gwynn, *Life of John Redmond*, p. 359; F.X. Martin (ed.), *The Irish Volunteers* (Dublin, 1963), pp. 146–48.

92 L.G. Edmonde to Moore, 13 Sept. 1914, NLI, Moore Papers, 10545/11.

93 Asquith to Stanley, 6 Sept. 1914 in Brocks (eds), *H.H. Asquith*, p. 223.

94 Jalland and Stubbs, 'The Irish Question', p. 799.

95 Hazlehurst, *Politicians at War*, p. 138.

96 Quoted in MacNeil, *Ulster's Stand for Union*, p. 235.

97 PRONI, D 1507/3/6/3, manifesto by Carson, 'The Betrayal of Ulster', 15 Sept. 1914; Bonar Law to Asquith, 10 Sept. 1914, Bodleian Library, Asquith Papers, 13, fos. 210–11; Jalland and Stubbs, 'The Irish Question', p. 800; W.A. Phillips, *Revolution in Ireland, 1906–23* (London, 1923), p. 83.

of the Commons in protest. The Act was accompanied by a Suspensory Act which postponed the enforcement of Home Rule for twelve months or until the end of the war, whichever was the longer. It was also subject to a new Amending Bill which the government promised to introduce to settle the question of Ulster.

Asquith hoped that, after the Home Rule Act had received the royal assent, 'the Irish [Nationalists would be] breast high for loyalty & recruiting'.[98] The passage of the Act was followed by considerable rejoicing in Ireland, where it was a triumph for Redmond. He quickly issued a new manifesto to the people of Ireland on behalf of the Nationalist Party claiming that, in passing the Bill, Britain had kept faith with Ireland, so Ireland was bound in duty and honour to keep faith with Britain. But he also imposed two conditions on Irish recruiting. Irish recruits for the Expeditionary Force should be kept together as a unit, led as far as possible by Irishmen and formed into an 'Irish Brigade'. Simultaneously the Volunteers remaining in Ireland should be put into a state of efficiency as quickly as possible for the defence of Ireland. In this way, when the war ended Ireland would possess an army of which she could be proud.[99] He then returned to Ireland. On 20 September, while on his way to Aughauanagh, he heard that a parade of Volunteers was taking place at Woodenbridge. As the men were from his own neighbourhood he stopped to deliver an impromptu address in which he declared that it would be a disgrace if Irishmen confined their activities to home defence. He encouraged his followers to enlist for foreign service.[100] Asquith also threw his support behind recruiting in Ireland. On 25 September, in a speech at the Mansion House in Dublin, he made a clear pledge that there would soon be a Southern Irish Division in the British Army on the same lines as the Ulster Division. Five days later, he wrote to Redmond, saying that he had spoken to Kitchener and that the latter had promised to make an announcement that the War Office had sanctioned the formation of an Irish Army Corps. Kitchener however refused to make any such announcement and ensured that the commander of the Sixteenth (Irish) Division put every possible obstacle in the way of the division resembling an 'Irish Brigade'.

The willingness of the leaders of both of the Irish parties to encourage their followers to enlist in the British Army did not mean that by late September all Irishmen had sunk their parochial differences in the face of a common enemy. Amongst the Nationalist community, Redmond's manifesto did not meet with universal approval. Many INVs were Constitutionalists like Redmond but others, like Patrick Pearse, were Republicans. The latter were quite willing to be trained and equipped at the expense of the British Army but had not the slightest intention

[98] Asquith to Stanley, 14 Sept. 1914 in Brocks (eds), *H.H. Asquith*, p. 237.
[99] Gwynn, *Life of John Redmond*, p. 385.
[100] Simpkins, *New Armies*, pp. 113–14.

of serving overseas. They wanted to take over from the British Army the defence of Ireland for, as Pearse wrote on 3 August: 'If the British army is engaged elsewhere, Ireland falls to the Volunteers.'[101] On 24 September twenty members of the Provisional Committee of the INV issued their own manifesto. They claimed that Redmond's announcements were fundamentally at variance with the stated aims of the INVs, and that consequently Redmond and his nominees should have no further say in the course the movement adopted. They repudiated his call to Irishmen to enlist in the British Army.[102] Only about 7 per cent of the total membership of 188,000 refused to follow Redmond's lead and formed a break-away organisation under Pearse and MacNeill. The main body of Volunteers, who continued to follow Redmond continued to be known as the Irish National Volunteers while the secessionists took the title Irish Volunteers, although they were usually known as Sinn Fein Volunteers. In the short term the secession strengthened Redmond's position, because it enabled him to continue his recruiting campaign without having to face hostile criticism from within his own camp. In retrospect this split can be seen as an important step along the road to revolution and the disintegration of the Irish Parliamentary Party.[103]

In November 1914 Birrell wrote a report for the Cabinet on opinion in Ireland. He stated confidently that hostility towards Britain was no longer as marked as it had been before the outbreak of war and that in the Irish Parliamentary Party there was no indication of sedition or opposition to the war. But sedition and opposition to the war was being aroused by two sources. A handful of clergymen were delivering anti-recruiting addresses from the altar and at public meetings while a small number of newspapers, like the *Irish Volunteer*, declared that 'Ireland's national identity, Ireland's national Soul, demands that Ireland should take no part, either through its leaders or through its masses, in promoting this iniquitous war'.[104]

The Unionists remained equally suspicious of their adversaries. In May 1915, on the very eve of his entry into the Coalition government which Asquith was about to form, Carson wrote to Sir George Richardson urging him to keep the UVF's organisation in being, despite the fact that so many of his men had enlisted in the Regular Army. While the war was being fought, he did not expect those who remained in Ulster to show the same energy they had shown before August 1914:

> but I feel bound to remind them that as the Home Rule Bill has been placed upon the statute book and will come into operation the moment the war is over, we must be in such a position as in a very brief time to render ourselves

---

101 Denman, *Ireland's Unknown Soldiers*, p. 26.

102 B. Mac Giolla Choille (ed.), *Intelligence Notes, 1913–1916* (Dublin, 1966), p. 105.

103 Lyons, *John Dillon*, p. 369; Phillips, *Revolution in Ireland*, p. 85.

104 Quoted in J. St Ervine, *Craigavon* (London, 1949), p. 294; Denman, *Ireland's Unknown Soldiers*, p. 32; State Paper Office, *Intelligence Notes, 1913–1916*, p. 119.

effective against all attempts to force the Bill upon us, and I should strongly advise that members should pay particular attention to the very grave and hostile speeches that were made by Mr Dillon and others in Dublin.[105]

Redmond's speech of 3 August did not 'pledge Nationalist support throughout the Empire', for it was not until after the Home Rule Bill had received the royal assent that he was prepared to do that. Similarly, Carson's announcement of 7 September that Ulster would 'without any bartering of conditions' support Britain and the Empire was equally hollow. Throughout August both of the contending parties in Ireland had jockeyed for position and attempted to extract every ounce of political advantage from the new political situation created by the war. For them the war was, quite literally, the continuation of politics by other means.

[105] PRONI, D 1327/3/21, Carson to Richardson, 19 May 1915.

2

Airbandit: C³I and Strategic Air Defence during the First Battle of Britain, 1915–18

John Ferris

The first battle of Britain scarcely affected the outcome of the First World War.[1] This event and its interpretation, however, did spark the rise of independent airpower. That was particularly true in Britain. Between 1919 and 1939, the arguments for and development of strategic bombers by the Royal Air Force (RAF) rested on the experiences of the Great War. Its air defence system of 1940 stemmed directly from that of 1918.[2] During 1915–18, three German forces – the Zeppelins of the Navy and the airships and aeroplanes of the Army fought a campaign in the skies above Britain and on the leading edges of contemporary tactics and technology. Commanders and their men were the pioneers in unprecedented forms of warfare. The air war lay at the intersection

[1] I am grateful to Eric Ash, Sebastian Cox, Christina Goulter and Holger Herwig for comments on earlier drafts of this essay. The best recent works on the British and German air forces before and during the First World War are Matthew Cooper, *The Birth of Independent Airpower: British Air Policy in the First World War* (London, 1986); Alfred Gollin, *No Longer an Island: Britain and the Wright Brothers, 1902–1909* (London, 1984); Matthew Paris, *Winged Warfare: The Literature and Theory of Aerial Warfare in Britain, 1859–1917* (Manchester, 1992); and J.H. Morrow, *German Air Power in World War One* (Lincoln, 1982). The best modern accounts of the first battle of Britain are Christopher Cole and E.F. Cheesman, *The Air Defence of Britain, 1914–1918* (London, 1984); Douglas H. Robinson, *The Zeppelin in Combat: A History of the German Naval Airship Division, 1912–1918* (Sun Valley, 1966); G.W. Haddow and Peter M. Grosz, *The German Giants: The Story of the R-Planes, 1914–1919* (London, 1969); and Raymond H. Fredette, *The Sky on Fire: The First Battle of Britain, 1917–1918, and the Birth of the Royal Air Force* (London, 1966). Several older works are still of fundamental significance: Joseph Morris, *The German Air Raids on Great Britain, 1914–1918* (London, 1925); E.B. Ashmore, *Air Defence* (London, 1929); T.E. Winslow, *Forewarned is Forearmed: A History of the Royal Observer Corps* (London, 1948); and the relevant sections of H.A. Jones, *The War in the Air: Being the Story of the Part Played in the Great War by the Royal Air Force*, iii (Oxford, 1931), v (Oxford, 1935). John Bushby, *Air Defence of Great Britain* (London, 1973), offers a good introduction to the topic.

[2] Useful accounts of RAF policy during the 1920s are the relevant sections of John Robert Ferris, *Men, Money and Diplomacy: The Evolution of British Strategic Policy, 1919–1926* (London and New York, 1989) and 'The Theory of a "French Air Menace", Anglo-French Relations and the British Home Defence Air Force Programmes of 1921–1925', *The Journal of Strategic Studies*, 10 (1987), and Neil Young, 'British Home Air Defence Planning in the 1920s', *Journal of Strategic Studies*, 11 (1988); and, for the 1930s, Malcolm Smith, *British Air Strategy between the Wars* (Oxford, 1984).

between the learning curves of two competitors aiming to kill each other, and able opponents at that. By autumn 1918, for example, British officers on the ground possessed the organisational and technical means, within a ninety-second period, to collect information from thousands of observers over 10,000 square miles and use it to direct fighter aircraft onto specific targets at 20,000 feet. Aeronautical and electrical engineers, pilots and wireless operators, were simultaneously fighting a war, conducting fundamental research into physical phenomena and serving as guinea pigs in experiments.[3] German strategic bombers strained against the leading edge of aeronautical engineering. Sometimes they smashed on it. By 1917 Zeppelins, flying over 20,000 feet above the earth to evade fighters, entered parts of the atmosphere which scientists did not understand. The Riesenflugzeuge ('Giant' bombers) had a wingspan of 138 feet, close to that of Boeing 747s. Not surprisingly, bad landings claimed twelve of the fifteen Giants lost in the war.[4] One fact illustrates how far the first battle of Britain pressed the state of the art. Accidents rather than engagements claimed two thirds of the losses to attackers and every one of the downed defenders.

At the heart of the first battle of Britain were command, control, communication and intelligence (C^3I) systems. C^3I has not been ignored by writers. On the contrary, many of them have discussed some parts of the topic with accuracy and detail. Overall, however, C^3I has not received the attention it deserves and its significance has been obscured by the focus on ephemera. Far too many works place less emphasis on C^3I than on Rankin darts. Contemporaries did not make such errors. On 7 January 1915, for example, the Prime Minister received his first briefing on strategic air defence. Herbert Asquith immediately and correctly appreciated two fundamental issues – the need to coordinate departmental action and to create 'a complete system of intelligence and communication'.[5] General E.B. Ashmore, architect of the first strategic air defence system ever to reach maturity, the London Air Defence Area (LADA), placed at its core C^3I – 'a highly centralized intelligence and command system', 'a highly centralized system of control and communications'.[6]

Historians have particularly misconstrued the issue of intelligence in air defence. Recently, for example, many works have assumed that 'in the First World War, attacks by airships or aeroplane upon Britain came with almost no warning'.[7] Such views ignore facts known since 1919. In the decade

[3] The best short introduction to the relationship between science, technology and the war in the air is Guy Hartcup, *The War of Invention, Scientific Developments, 1914–1918* (London, 1988).

[4] Haddow and Grosz, *German Giants*, p. 61.

[5] Captain S.W. Roskill, *Documents relating to the Naval Air Service*, i, *1908-1918* (Navy Records Society, 1969), p. 192.

[6] Ashmore, *Air Defence*, pp. 92, 110.

[7] Norman Franks, *RAF Fighter Command, 1936–1945* (Yeovil, 1992), p. 14; Bushby, *Air Defence*, p. 62.

after the Armistice, several veterans revealed that signals intelligence had provided ample forewarning of Zeppelin raids. During the interwar years the RAF's Official History of the First World War amply discussed these issues as, subsequently, did the leading students of British home defence, Christopher Cole and E.F. Cheesman; and of the Zeppelins, Douglas Robinson.[8] Such writers, however, have made errors of their own. They have rightly identified the Naval Intelligence Division (NID) as a source for wireless intelligence against Zeppelins. They have wrongly identified it as the only source, even though Ashmore publicly stated that a 'highly efficient' section of the Military Intelligence Department (MID) had done the same.[9] Historians have virtually ignored the role of intelligence against Gothas and Riesenflugzeuge. These errors and omissions have occurred because, until recently, important documents were kept from the public record while British intelligence was veiled in mystery. A good historian like Douglas Robinson did not have access to much relevant material and misunderstood the organisation of British intelligence. Where his evidence on the topic was good so was his account, but the many gaps in the evidence available to him hampered his assessment. Thus, he bolstered his suggestion that Britain had spies in the naval airship service with the argument that the NID had reconstructed the Zeppelin call sign system 'by means that are not clear'.[10] He clearly did not realise how easily traffic analysts could do so. One need not disparage scholars in order to determine the limits to scholarship.

Intelligence was fundamental to the first Battle of Britain; its nature and its role have been fundamentally misunderstood. This essay will address that problem by examining the evidence on the topic, which still remains fragmentary in places. From that basis, this study will reconsider a broader topic – the nature, origins, development and influence of C³I and air defence systems during the first Battle of Britain. That, in turn, will contribute to the history of signals intelligence and of RAF doctrine. It will help to determine the relative significance of all the components of air defence, especially of radio-telephones (R/T) and radar. This essay will illuminate an air war and air warfare. It will show that effective command systems and intelligence have been central to strategic air warfare since its inception. They must also be central to its study.

Since the 1960s, intelligence has conventionally been broken down into

[8] Jones, *War in the Air*, iii, pp. 129 and passim; Robinson, *Combat*, p. 3 and passim; and Cole and Cheesman, *Air Defence*, p. 32 and passim. For some of the many other references to the topic, see John R. Cuneo, *The Air Weapon, 1914–1916* (Harrisburg, 1947), pp. 364, 452; and the popular account by Kenneth Poolman, *Zeppelins over England* (London, 1960), pp. 54–56.

[9] Ashmore, *Air Defence*, p. 16. A similar statement is made in H.T. Sutton, *Raiders Approach! The Fighting Tradition of Royal Air Force Station Hornchurch and Sutton's Farm* (Aldershot, 1956), p. 5.

[10] Robinson, *Combat*, pp. 3, 271; idem, 'Zeppelin Intelligence', *Aerospace Historian* (March, 1974), p. 2.

the categories of 'strategic', 'operational' and 'tactical'. These categories cannot easily be applied to air warfare and they were not always used by contemporary air forces. In 1930, for example, the RAF distinguished two kinds of intelligence: what 'may be termed "Pure Intelligence"' on background issues from that 'which may be termed "Fighting Intelligence"' for specific battles.[11] When carefully defined, however, the conventional categories are useful tools for the study of intelligence in air war. In this essay, 'strategic' refers to air strength built and building, deployment in and transfers between theatres, policy, doctrine, industrial and techno-logical capabilities. 'Operational' refers to capabilities at specific bases and to the intention to conduct particular actions at given times and places – most specifically, to the period between a squadron's initial preparation for action to the moment it enters defended airspace. 'Tactical' refers to all the different aspects of combat during an air mission.

Many sources provided intelligence on these needs during the first Battle of Britain. Prisoners, captured documents, signals intelligence and wrecked aircraft all offered strategic intelligence of first-rate quality on Zeppelins and, to a lesser degree, aeroplanes.[12] The role of agents in that process is less certain and more controversial. Robinson argued that British agents had penetrated the Zeppelin service, a view shared by many veterans of that service. In 1921, moreover, the American Naval Attaché in Berlin reported that, according to a senior German naval officer, during the war,

> the British Admiralty obtained advance information regarding proposed movements of the German vessels, through a German Naval officer in the German Admiralty. This officer had been bribed by English secret agents. The point unexplained as yet as [sic] how the information was transmitted to London in such a short time. The Germans even suspected an unknown cable from Wilhelmshaven to Denmark, one terminus of which was supposedly in a private house. Another solution being the use of carrier pigeons. As far as can be definitely ascertained, the Germans do not yet know how the information was relayed to London so quickly.

Such statements were not necessarily correct – after all, for thirty years following 1945, German officers credited nonexistent British spies for the hidden triumphs of Ultra. Similar British cover stories might have tainted German views in 1921, and through an obvious means. As Robinson demonstrated, during the war British interrogators attempted to impress their infallibility on captured airshipcrew. They did so by offering these men detailed accounts of the most trivial and recent events in the lives

---

[11] 'Handbook (Provisional) on the Air Defence of Great Britain', Air Defence of Great Britain, April 1930, PRO, AIR 5/768.

[12] Memorandum by War Office, 87/611, 16 April 1916, PRO, AIR 1/910/204/5/827; Robinson, 'Zeppelin Intelligence' and 'Secret Intelligence: The Destruction and Salvage of the Zeppelin L 70', *Cross and Cockade Journal*, 4/4, Winter 1963.

of their services, which the interrogators often credited to spies. After the war, British officers told their German counterparts similar tales. These stories became accepted and reported as truth by airship veterans. In fact, the details in question could easily have been acquired through competent interrogation of prisoners of war.[13]

On the other hand, significant evidence does support these accounts of British spies in the German Navy. At the turn of 1915, the Kriegsmarine was preparing (but had not yet presented) its case to convince Kaiser Wilhelm II that Zeppelins should attack London. At precisely this point, on 1 January 1915, the British Admiralty told the Cabinet that according to 'a trustworthy source . . . the Germans intend to make an attack on London by airships on a great scale at any early opportunity'. This report does not seem to have stemmed from codebreaking. It may have been nothing more than rumour but it might equally well have come from agents. Again, in 1917 George MacDonogh, the Director of Military Intelligence, held that if necessary Britain could detect Zeppelin attacks 'by various measures which do not necessarily involve the use of Wireless D.F. Stations'. Meanwhile Hugh Trenchard, the commander of the RFC on the Western Front, believed that under certain circumstances agents could provide operational intelligence on enemy aircraft.[14] Above all stand two important pieces of evidence. In May 1916, some messages from agents received by the British Legation in Copenhagen did in fact 'refer to movements of Zeppelins' while there is a strong possibility that, shortly afterward, the Admiralty did procure genuine copies of Admiral Sheer's two assessments of the battle of Jutland.[15] Neither of these documents, however, are absolutely conclusive – the Zeppelin reports

[13] Report, Naval Attaché, Berlin, 25 Nov. 1921, serial no. 200, file no. 911/500, RG-38, E-3-f/9420. National Archives, Washington D.C. Robinson, 'Zeppelin Intelligence'; Ernst Lehmann with Leonhard Adelt, *Zeppelin: The Story of Lighter-than-Air Craft* (New York, 1937), pp. 174–75; A.P. Scotland, *The London Cage* (London, 1957), offers an authoritative account of prisoner of war interrogation during the Great War.

[14] Roskill, *Naval Air Service*, p. 188; DAO to DMI, 9 Nov. 1917, DMI to DAO, 21 Nov. 1917, PRO, AIR 2/163 M.R. 1184; Jones, *War in the Air*, v, p. 30.

[15] Nicholson to Lowther, 10 May 1916, PRO, FO 211/381; NID 086 (undated), Lloyd George Papers, E/8/5, House of Lords Record Office. I am indebted to my colleague, Professor Holger Herwig, for confirming the authenticity of the documents from the Lloyd George Papers. These pose especially complex problems as evidence. Their authenticity is certain but not their provenance. Lloyd George received them from the British NID, but at an unknown date, while the source from which they received it is unclear. These reports are found in the First World War section of the Lloyd George Papers, which as a general rule includes only documents he received during that time. Sheer's reports, moreover, were not available for official British access in Germany until years after the war, nor were they published in English or in German during Lloyd George's lifetime. It is possible that after the war, perhaps when writing his memoirs, Lloyd George received copies of Sheer's reports, but improbable. The most likely explanation is that at some unknown stage during the Great War, British agents procured copies of these documents from some source in Germany, which were received by the most senior British decision-makers of the day. What use they made of that material is unclear.

from Copenhagen may have been inaccurate or have been delivered too late to matter . . . while the other evidence is fragmentary in the extreme. This material does not prove that British agents had penetrated the airship service, although it does suggest that they might have had access to the highest levels of decision making in the German Navy, a point of some significance. This evidence is indicative rather than conclusive, and Robinson's suggestion must be treated as unproven, but possible.

In any case, many sources provided good strategic intelligence during the first battle of Britain. With one exception, the daylight raids by Gotha bombers, no new phase of the air war caught Britain by surprise. It had a good grasp of the enemy's deployed strength in and redeployments to the theatre, of the technical capabilities of its equipment, of training regimes, the personalities of commanders and the morale of men. British strategic intelligence was not perfect, but it was good enough. In practical terms, however, that knowledge was of little significance. The first Battle of Britain was a sideshow to which neither side committed more than a tiny fraction of its power. It was a matter of operations rather than strategy.

Operational intelligence had greater importance for air defence during the first Battle of Britain. It was also dauntingly difficult to acquire. Aircraft could attack Britain from the Heligoland Bight and from or over Belgium. Airships could strike the United Kingdom anywhere, aeroplanes could hit any target on the south-east coast or inland between Dover and London. German aircraft might attack any day or night of the war, yet they did so rarely. To cover all of Britain every hour of every day against this danger could easily become expensive and, at some stage, cost would equal a defeat. In order to be of use, any system of operational intelligence would have to help strategic air defence manage that threat effectively and inexpensively. It would have to show precisely, and with sufficient forewarning, that a given twenty-four-hour period would be among the roughly 20 per cent between 19 January 1915 and 11 November 1918 where raids were launched (and in half of these cases, one aircraft attacked one coastal target); and indicate which part of the United Kingdom would be raided in time to let the home defence system function with effect. The time in question was substantial. In 1918, at best a seasoned squadron on alert took thirty seconds to act on an order to launch a patrol. Some took five minutes. In 1915 this process often required thirty minutes. The standard height for interception was 10–12,000 feet. In 1915, British aircraft required forty-five to sixty minutes to reach that altitude and twenty to twenty-five minutes in 1917–18. Hence, anywhere between twenty-five to ninety minutes warning was needed to give fighters any chance to intercept an incoming intruder.[16] With any shorter forewarning, one could intercept an intruder only as it left British airspace, if ever. Again, in 1915 much

---

[16] See below, no. 88.

of London's anti-aircraft system was provided by guns borne on trucks. An hour was required to deploy them.[17] The permanent system of 1918 still required several minutes forewarning to function. Only a powerful and precise source could meet the needs of operational intelligence. Most of the sources of military intelligence, such as prisoners and spies, could not meet these needs – their main contribution, and an important one, was to determine the enemy's deployed strength in specific bases. During the Great War, however, one source could meet these needs – signals intelligence, or material derived from the interception of the enemy's radio traffic.

Strategic air warfare and signals intelligence emerged at the same time: in the first months of the Great War. They grew together like children: they also fought, which led to the creation of the world's first electronic war. This campaign used the best technology and science and electrical engineers of the day; but it was early days. Any contemporary radio set, especially one of the dominant spark type, used a large part of a small section of the electromagnetic spectrum. Hence, nothing was easier than the accidental or intentional jamming of frequencies, while fundamental decisions of policy turned on the scarcity of airwaves. During 1916–17, for example, the Royal Flying Corps (RFC) tried to develop R/T for fighter aircraft. In hindsight, this was essential for efficient air defence. Until 1918, however, the Admiralty blocked these proposals because it wished to reserve those frequencies for its own immediate and, of course, imperative uses. As a result, R/T was never actually used against German bombers during the first Battle of Britain.[18]

Similarly, in 1917 technical experts throughout Europe considered the adoption of wireless beacons to guide bombers. Under such 'silent' direction finding systems, stations in known locations emitted radio messages from which crews in the air drew cross bearings and determined their position. British technical experts agreed that such a system would require the dedicated use of a large waveband and jam adjacent frequencies. Meanwhile, Zeppelins and U-boats might use it for their own purposes. The leading British intelligence authorities, both able men, split over the balance of compromises at stake. The Director of Naval Intelligence, Admiral Hall, opposed any system that would block operational frequencies used by Britain – or Germany. 'If it is urged that the enemy will be jammed as badly as we are, I consider it preferable that the enemy should use wireless as much as possible rather than that he should be hindered.' Only then could the NID locate U-boats and intercept enemy traffic. MacDonogh, conversely, favoured the proposal, because it would support offensive operations and could be arranged so not to jam allied or enemy stations. None the less, Hall's arguments prevailed and Britain

---

[17] A. Rawlinson, *The Defence of London, 1915–1918* (London, 1923), p. 52.

[18] Jones, *War in the Air*, v, p. 23; Cole and Cheesman, *Air Defence*, pp. 154–60; Graham Wallace, *RAF Biggin Hill* (London, 1957), pp. 15–30.

rejected the system. As proof of the complexity of the situation, at exactly this time other sections of the Admiralty wished to adopt a similar wireless direction finding system for aircraft, which their opposite numbers in the War Office blocked.[19] The Zeppelin service, however, adopted such a procedure. In September 1918 the RAF also resurrected the idea and perfected it two months later; by then, the war was over.[20]

Similar technical problems affected signals intelligence. One intercept station could search only a tiny part of the electromagnetic spectrum at any time, and switching wavelengths was a laborious process. When examining overlapping frequencies, sets miles apart might howl with feedback. All this happened because the equipment was primitive and clumsy. One veteran described an early version of the rotating frame direction finder, standard issue for British signals intelligence, thus: an '8 foot square wooden frame aerial on a scaffolding pole . . . rotated mainly by a motor car wheel and brute force'.[21] To find a bearing, operators had to determine the point of equilibrium in the strength of the signal intercepted by two aerials. They swung the aerials, varying their physical angle, adjusted valves and condensers and judged equilibrium by ear. Atmospherics and cliffs, overhead wires or drain pipes, produced errors in bearings. Inland wireless stations sometimes were located at sea and the High Seas Fleet in Hanover.

Ultimately, developments in technology and organisation reduced the scale of these problems. The NID and the MID created two self-contained interception systems, each internally linked by landlines. Within each system, stations were organised into groups which coordinated the search of wavelengths and the monitoring of stations. In 1919 H.J. Round, the leading electrical engineer working on signals intelligence in Britain and perhaps the world, noted that

> With a position-finding group of three or more stations, one station acted as a kind of censor. All bearings were sent to and were plotted at this station, and it was only when the bearings from all stations intersected at a point that they were allowed to pass. It was contended that if four directions intersected at a point or a close approximation to one, the readings were reliable. This censorship also tended to eliminate operators' errors both in reading the direction and on the land line.

---

[19] DAO to DMI, 9 Nov. 1917; DMI to DAO, 21 Nov. 1917, PRO, AIR 2/163 M.R. 1184; Christina Jean Munro Goulter, *A Forgotten Offensive: Royal Air Force Coastal Command's Anti-Shipping Campaign, 1940–'45* (unpublished Ph.D. thesis, University of London, 1993), pp. 45–46.

[20] DAO to CAS, 11 Nov. 1918, passim, PRO, AIR 2/97 B. 847. Further material on this topic may be found in Wallace, *Biggin Hill*.

[21] Unsigned and undated memo, 'An Intelligence Section of the First World War', post-1969, presumably by Sir Ronald Nesbitt Hawes, Intelligence Corps Museum, accession no. 198.

The accuracy of bearings became surprisingly good. By November 1918 RAF wireless intelligence personnel claimed an accuracy of 1.75 degrees on a moving aeroplane. Round held that readings in daylight usually were accurate to 1 degree.

> when signals come over-sea from moderate distances, and practically no land intervenes, results are then the most reliable and can be relied upon for the greater part of the time. If, however, there is land anywhere near either the transmitter or the receiver, or between the two, results become very troublesome.[22]

These facts were fundamental to the accuracy and effect of operational intelligence in air defence. The Zeppelins were ideally suited for the contemporary capabilities of British signals intelligence. Aeroplane bases in Belgium were not. All this was further complicated by the phenomenon of increased errors in bearings taken at night. Round noted, 'when Zeppelins were well at sea, night errors were not usually serious, but aeroplanes nearly always gave trouble'.[23] All told, wireless intelligence was most successful against airships above the North Sea in the day and least so against airplanes flying from Belgium at night.

Nor was equipment alone primitive during this dawn of signals intelligence. The techniques of attack and even more those of defence were equally so. One veteran of the wireless war against Zeppelins commented that 'the ordinary Teutonic mind was especially suited for devising schemes which any child could unravel'. German signals intelligence personnel criticised British minds in similar terms.[24] In fact, superiority pertained not to nations but to occupations. Hunting was easy, defence was difficult. As radio unexpectedly became a major mode for communication, codebreaking achieved pre-eminence among the sources of operational intelligence while entirely new arts rose from nowhere. This was particularly true of traffic analysis, which derived information from the structure and characteristics of communication systems. Starting from elementary techniques, like locating stations through direction finding and linking them to formations through the observation of the unique key-signature of operators, one could reconstruct the order of battle of entire armies.

---

[22] Captain H.J. Round, 'Direction and Position Finding', *Journal of the Institution of Electrical Engineers* 58, (1920), pp. 236–38 passim. Useful accounts of the technological, scientific and organisational background to wireless during this period are Hartcup, *War of Invention*, pp. 123–27 passim; Hugh G.J. Aitken, *The Continuous Wave: Technology and American Radio, 1900–1932* (Princeton, 1985); and Daniel R. Headrick, *The Invisible Weapon: Telecommunications and International Politics, 1851–1945* (Oxford, 1991).

[23] Round, 'Position Finding', p. 236.

[24] E.W.B. Gill, *War, Wireless and Wangles* (Oxford, 1934), pp. 19–26; John Ferris (ed.), *The British Army and Signals Intelligence during the First World War* (Army Records Society, 1992), pp. 78–84.

Intelligence officers systematically recorded and analysed this material and then displayed their deductions in a visually effective way for use in operations. At the War Office, 'little pins with flag heads' on a chart of the North Sea represented the wireless fixes of U-boats.[25] At the intelligence office of British airships working against U-boats in 1917–18, tickets pinned to a squared chart of the North Sea showed the time and bearings of wireless intelligence on U-boats. A bearing provided by one station made a vector and two or more a cross-bearing, which was determined and demonstrated by running threads across the chart.[26] The personnel of all nations used pins and threads for direction finding in the same manner. Such material was not merely charted but logged. Several surviving log-books show the techniques by which wireless intelligence was recorded for analysis and use in strategic air defence. These logs were arranged so that officers could scan quickly all the most recent information. Specific entries showed precisely whether an aircraft was located by a vector or a cross-bearing, where and when; the dates when new call signs were first heard and changes in or uncertainty about them; and details of standard operating procedures and patterns of intercommunication. Sometimes 39 call signs of aircraft or ground stations were reported on a single day. Elaborate indices correlated each call sign with its first date of interception and its frequency of recurrence.[27]

All this illustrates a fundamental point – air defence centred on an information processing network. This reached its apex in LADA where, one witness noted:

> A large map was laid out on a table and a number of operators sat round the table receiving the information on telephone handsets as it came in. This information was plotted on the map and thus it was possible for the GOC to see the position of a raid at any moment by a glance.[28]

Counters placed on a squared map of south-east England represented all the information reported by thousands of observers sixty seconds before. False or unconfirmed material was filtered out through cross-reference by experts in the seconds before pieces were placed down. The counters were coloured so as to distinguish current reports from those three or five minutes old – thus a rainbow spilled across the map along the trajectory of intruders. As Ashmore put it, 'I sat overlooking

[25] Ferdinand Touhy, *Crater of Mars* (London, 1929), pp. 92–93.

[26] 'Report on Submarine Intelligence Department now in Practice at Mullion Airship Station', Squadron-Leader Maitland, 26 Jan. 1918, PRO, AIR 1/308/15/226/194.

[27] The logs in PRO, AIR 1/567/16/15/122 to 125 presumably stem from MI1e, both because of the dates and of the focus on Gothas and Riesenflugzeuge, which were irrelevant to the NID. Two logs from Room 40 are 'Airship Directionals', July–November 1916, ADM 137/4536 and 'Zeppelin Movements', June–October 1918, AIR 1/296/15/226/146.

[28] 'Personal Narrative', by Squadron-Leader P. Babington, undated but presumably mid 1920s, AIR 1/2393/229/1.

the map from a raised gallery; in effect, I could follow the course of all aircraft flying over the country, as the counters crept across the map'.[29] Alongside such sophisticated procedures for the representation of information stood primitive ones. In particular, the absence of R/T crippled the communication of information from the ground to the air. During daylight raids over Britain in 1917, the otherwise unemployed crews of searchlights swung large arrows so to point pilots toward enemy aircraft observed from the ground. On the Western Front, arrows were augmented with coloured flares and long white strips which indicated the height of enemy aircraft.[30]

None of these things had even been conceptualised before the outbreak of war. During the decade before the July crisis, the War Office always intended to create a signals intelligence service in case of war; before the outbreak of hostilities the Admiralty may have reached the same decision.[31] In any case, during August 1914 both did so, creating code-breaking bureaus which became best known under the names 'Room 40' and 'MI1b'. In their early days these bureaus co-operated closely. Soon, however, differences emerged between their masters, their personnel and their work. These bureaus attacked unrelated German cryptographic systems and, in September–October 1914, each suddenly began to do so with success. As a result, for thirty months Room 40 and MI1b ceased to co-operate and began to duplicate each other's work, in a wasteful and damaging way. Each, for example, independently broke American diplomatic codes and located U-boats in and airships over the North Sea.[32] Only during the spring of 1917 did this relationship improve. In the interim, these signals intelligence services particularly competed about issues related to strategic air defence. So did their parent departments.

During the autumn of 1914, in co-operation with the Marconi Corporation and the General Post Office but not with each other, the Army and the Navy began to establish wireless interception services.[33] The issue of strategic air defence did not shape these decisions but it was shaped by them. No sooner had each service established capabilities for codebreaking and direction-finding than German airships began to attack Britain. This threat sucked the service departments and their signals

[29] Ashmore, *Air Defence*, p. 93.

[30] Ibid., p. 42; Ferris, *Signals Intelligence*, pp. 94, 99.

[31] John Ferris, '"Before Room 40": The British Empire and Signals Intelligence, 1898–1914', *Journal of Strategic Studies*, 12 (1989); Nicholas Hiley, 'The Strategic Origins of Room 40', *Intelligence and National Security*, 2 (1987).

[32] Ferris, 'Before Room 40'; Patrick Beesley, *Room 40: British Naval Intelligence, 1914–18* (London, 1982); Christopher Andrew, *Secret Service: The Making of the British Intelligence Community* (London, 1987), pp. 139–85; Memorandum by A.G. Denniston on the origins of Room 40, Alastair Denniston papers, 1/3, Churchill College, Cambridge; Charles Hardinge to Lloyd George, 14 and 15 Dec. 1916, F/3/2, and Robertson to Lloyd George, 14 Dec. 1916, F/44/3, David Lloyd George Papers, HLRO; Ferdinand Touhy, *Crater of Mars*, pp. 92–93.

[33] The best sources are ADM 116/1454; ADM 137/986; PRO, T 173/428 and 429.

intelligence services into a complex and confused relationship. Between the autumn of 1914 and the spring of 1916, the Admiralty took primary responsibility for the air defence of Great Britain but the War Office also became increasingly involved in the task. Similarly, in 1916–17 the Army controlled home defence, but the Royal Navy Air Service (RNAS) still served in the campaign. By 1917 the continual bickering between these departments, combined with the effects of the German strategic bombing campaign, caused the government to merge the RNAS and the Royal Flying Corps (RFC) into the Royal Air Force. Ironically, this confused the issue of bureaucratic and operational responsibility for strategic air defence more than ever. In effect, the older services were stripped of the air forces involved in home defence and then immediately given complete operational, control over precisely the same squadrons, which now belonged to a third service with separate but subordinate functions.[34]

In the spring of 1915, the War Office and the Admiralty wished to acquire intelligence on the German air threat. Their signals intelligence services could easily provide it. By virtue of breaking the cryptographic systems of the Kriegsmarine, Room 40 automatically uncovered material about German airships. By virtue of tracking German wireless traffic, the direction-finding stations of both services did the same. Between early 1915 and the Armistice, Room 40 continually worked in this area and, so it appears, did the MID's signals intelligence services. While no direct evidence survives about MI1b and airships during 1915, in that year half of its strength of eight officers specialised in wireless intelligence and they controlled as many direction finding stations as Room 40. The memoirs of two veterans of MI1b indicate that it was tracking German airships during 1915. So do two other pieces of evidence. A report by MI1b written in April 1916, a time when it was not co-operating with the NID, describes the wireless practices of German naval airships during 1915. The MID's signals intelligence services also published their material about enemy strategic bombing in so-called 'WTS' reports. While the publicly available run of these documents is incomplete, they were published on average every two weeks. The earliest volume known to survive is no. 18 of 9 March 1916. Reading backwards, this would place the first volume of the series in May 1915, about that time when the Zeppelins began to use a radio direction finding system, the War Office became concerned with air defence and the RFC component of the British Expeditionary Force (BEF)

---

[34] The most useful older sources on this topic are Jones, *War in the Air*, v, pp. 34–45, 487–93 and Roskill, *Naval Air Service*. The most useful modern accounts are Matthew Cooper, 'Blueprint for Confusion: The Administrative Background to the Formation of the Royal Air Force, 1912–1919', *Journal of Contemporary History*, 22 (1987); John Sweetman, 'The Smuts Report of 1917: Merely Political Window Dressing?', *Journal of Strategic Studies*, 4, (1981); and Alfred Gollin, 'A Flawed Strategy: Early British Air Defence Arrangements', in R.J.Q. Adams, *The Great War, 1914–1918: Essays on the Military, Political and Social History of the First World War* (London, 1990), pp. 31–38.

in France began to practise traffic analysis against German aeroplanes, as MI1b would have known. Indeed, in June 1915 the War Office actually sent that RFC component an assessment by a Belgian intercept operator of Zeppelin wireless practice.[35] The accuracy, the extent and the use of MI1b's reports of 1915, however, remains unclear.

During the spring of 1916, the War Office took over responsibility for strategic air defence. This immediately affected its signals intelligence service. Between April to July 1916, 'owing to increase of work and requirements in connection with defence against air raids', the wireless intelligence personnel within MI1b were formed into a new section. MI1e oversaw the War Office's interception service in Europe and the Middle East and, in particular, controlled wireless intelligence against Zeppelins. As the MID's official history put it, MI1e 'became the main source of information regarding air raids. It deciphered the special codes employed by the German Air Service, plotted the courses of German air raiders and transmitted information by direct wire to the Anti-Aircraft Section of GHQ Home Forces at the Horse Guards'. By 1917, so one veteran of MI1e recalled, six direction finding stations in the United Kingdom were primarily ordered to 'pinpoint anything moving – naval aircraft and Zeppelins. If they could take a bearing whilst the station was sending its call-signs, they might be able to record the messages as well'. Other interception stations in Britain did similar work on a part-time basis. Initially, MI1e had four officers, two of whom collated Zeppelin messages and attacked the daily changes in their 'cipher keys'. The nature of these 'keys' and 'ciphers' is unclear; presumably these were used for operations or weather reports.[36] MI1e's final strength is unclear but undoubtedly was larger than that with which it started. Between May 1916 and November 1918, every other signals intelligence organisation of the Army increased in size roughly by a factor of ten. Meanwhile Ie, the codebreaking section of the BEF, assigned seven personnel, augmented by others during operations, to handle work parallel to that of MI1e.[37] In any case, MI1e was not overmanned – before May 1918, it lacked the strength in officers to maintain a routine twenty-four hour duty roster.[38]

Until the Armistice, MI1e remained the central signals intelligence service for strategic air defence, but not the only one. Two others also

[35] WTS no. 18, 9 March 1916, ADM 137/4355; War Office to RFC, 1 June 1915, PRO, AIR 1/754/204/4/71; Touhy, *Crater of Mars*; Gill, *Wireless*.

[36] Unsigned and undated memo, 'An Intelligence Section of the First World War', post-1969, presumably by Sir Ronald Nesbitt Hawes, Intelligence Corps Museum, accession no. 198; 'Historical Sketch of the Directorate of Military Intelligence During the Great War, 1914–1919', (undated, but 1919 according to internal evidence), PRO, WO 32/10776; Lt. Col. W.R.V. Isaac, 6 Nov. 1957, 'The History of the Development of the Directorate of Military Intelligence: The War Office, 1855–1939', p. 31, copy in the Ministry of Defence Library; War Office to Treasury, 15 April 1916, PRO, T1/11937/15727.

[37] PRO, WO 32/10776; Ferris, *Signals Intelligence*, pp. 22–23, 195–208.

[38] Colonel Samson, MI1e, to DAAI, 14 May 1918, PRO, AIR 1/2420/305/8.

had to cover such work in order to handle their own. The NID needed material on Zeppelins, which often operated with the High Seas Fleet. It did so because of its success against Kriegsmarine traffic. Meanwhile, Riesenflugzeuge and Gothas threatened the BEF and thus concerned Ie. The NID may have given the MID no help against airship traffic in 1916 but the cold war between the bureaus ended in 1917. A 'private line' was installed between Admiral Hall and the chief of MI1b, Malcolm Hay, while Room 40 began to share its material with the intelligence branch at GHQ, Home Forces. In 1917–18, these services, Ie and French bureaus routinely exchanged operational intelligence on German strategic bombing in real time. Ironically, the RAF was the only fighting service without a wireless intelligence bureau for strategic air defence.[39]

British signals intelligence services for strategic air defence developed in a haphazard fashion, but they quickly became proficient at their work. Previous commentators have mentioned only three aspects of this issue: Room 40's exploitation of the Handelsschiffverkehrsbuch (HVB); and of the radio-direction finding system used by the Zeppelins; combined with the argument that wireless intelligence never provided any material about the Army airships. More remains to be said about these issues. Everything remains to be said about others.

By the middle of 1915, British wireless intelligence began to reconstruct the call sign systems of both German airship services, almost as soon as the latter began to attack Britain and to rely on radio. That work rested on the observation of external procedures of wireless traffic, the interrogation of prisoners and the capture of a notebook showing the current call signs of naval Zeppelins.[40] It offered sizeable rewards in this era of primitive security procedures. When a station used only one and the same sign for months on end, imperfect knowledge of call sign systems – of the number of calls in use but of nothing else – would still reveal the enemy's operational strength in specific areas. Perfect knowledge would uncover with precision its order of battle, dispositions and command structure. This might even let one predict matters such as how a given captain was likely to act, by reference to his known past behaviour.

As ever in the Great War, British intelligence was assisted by the childish signals security of the Kriegsmarine. The German Navy used radio far more frequently than necessary and far less securely than possible. Its security procedures were primitive and frequently ignored. During operations, for example, Zeppelin crews were ordered to carry no personal

---

[39] Unsigned and undated letter, *c.* March 1917 and by Hall according to internal evidence, to de Watteville, GHQ Home Forces, PRO, ADM 137/4305; Alice Ivy Hay, *Valiant for Truth: Malcolm Hay of Seaton* (London, 1971), p. 62; Air Ministry to Admiralty, 12 Feb. 1918, PRO, AIR 1/273/15/226/124.

[40] Memorandum, unsigned and undated, but 1915 by internal evidence, by Squadron-Leader 9, PRO, AIR 1/607/16/15/257.

or official documents and only one codebook for communications with Germany, the HVB. In September 1916, however, a Zeppelin destroyed over Britain carried a copy of the Allgemeinefunkspruchbuch, a system widely used by German shore establishments, U-boats and smaller craft. In June 1917 the L-48, destroyed over Britain, carried unauthorised if relatively insignificant cryptographic material. In October another airship destroyed over France carried a codebook and an index to the call signs in use by the entire Zeppelin service over the next three months. All these documents were captured, as were many others of significance. Similar compromises happened when the last Zeppelin was destroyed over Britain, in August 1918.[41]

The signals security of the Naval Airship Division was bad even by the standards of the Kriegsmarine. This allowed Britain to acquire a letter-perfect knowledge of the order of battle of that service. In 1915–16, for example, naval Zeppelins used two-letter call signs which followed exactly the same sequence as their official service numerals. These signs were changed every four months in a primitive fashion – 'LA' and 'LB' became 'MB' and 'MC' and so forth. Even when this system was altered in October 1916 and January 1917, and each Zeppelin was assigned two different call signs, Britain always knew the value of at least half the call signs. It usually knew all of the active ones.[42] During May 1917, Zeppelins adopted a three-letter system which avoided obvious connections between call signs and individual airships and instituted frequent random changes in calls. British signals intelligence found this procedure somewhat more difficult to reconstruct but still possible. By then, in any case, the Zeppelin campaign was broken.[43]

This happened largely because of another failure in signals security. Several overlapping errors compromised the time and place of every naval airship attack launched between 1915 and 1918. According to MI1b, throughout 1915 'the practice prior to a raid [was] for the flagship at Wilhelmshaven to hold a sort of wireless roll-call of the airships. A general call was sent to the airship squadron and this was acknowledged by each airship in turn'.[44] By early 1916 the Naval Airship Division

[41] Robinson, *Combat*, p. 189; Beesley, *Room 40*, p. 145, shows, contrary to Robinson and Arthur Marder, *From the Dreadnaught to Scapa Flow: The Royal Navy in the Fisher Era*, iii (London, 1966), p. 220, that by the time this copy of the AFB was captured, Room 40 had already reconstructed most of the system; British Mission to Director of Military Intelligence, 24 Oct. 1917, PRO, ADM 137/4305 (the identity of the codebook in this case is unknown: it may have been a copy of the HVB); Robinson, 'Secret Intelligence'.

[42] Robinson, 'Zeppelin Intelligence', p. 2; Gill, *Wireless*; reports in PRO, AIR 1/295/15/226/143; MI1e, WTS 43, 31 March 1917, PRO, ADM 137/4305; memoranda by MI1e, no. 39, 1 Nov. 1916; 'Analysis and Consideration', and 29 Dec. 1916, PRO, ADM 137/4355.

[43] GHQ Home Forces, 'Wireless Calls during May 1917', 'German Naval Airships', 5 August 1918, PRO, ADM 137/4305.

[44] MI1b, WTS no. 20, *c*. April 1916, PRO, ADM 137/4355.

ended this dangerous practice, but not others. In particular, when leaving for a mission over Britain, Zeppelins were ordered to signal by radio 'Naval Airship — taking off for distant scouting, course —, only HVB on board'.[45] While this regulation was reasonable in general, the insistence on a report by radio was infantile. Even had the HVB system remained unreadable, competent traffic analysts could be expected to link this stereotyped procedure to Zeppelin raids. That would be certain if the HVB system was compromised, which the Kriegsmarine knew it was. Room 40 almost immediately determined the meaning of these particular messages.[46] Similarly, on days when the enemy planned to launch Zeppelin raids, weather reports were sent by radio, wireless sets were tested and frequencies were checked in stereotyped fashions. The head of French military codebreaking, General Cartier, wrote that the despatch of a weather report from the radio station at Bruges 'was nearly always the announcement that these dirigibles were going toward the west to make a raid upon England'.[47] The NID, MI1b and MI1e each exploited several or all of these indicators, any one of which would have compromised an operation before a single Zeppelin lifted off.

Another failing allowed every British wireless intelligence service to track the course of every Zeppelin toward the United Kingdom. Naval airships generally flew west-south-west from Wilhelmshaven along the German and Dutch coasts and then, near the Hook of Holland, made an eighty-mile run westward across the North Sea to Britain. They returned from their mission across open water. Zeppelins might spend twenty-four hours over the North Sea or hostile territory, often unable to determine any of the fundamentals of navigation – location, direction or airspeed. They overcame these problems by emitting regular requests for bearings over the radio. This was done through a highly disciplined and centralised system. Individual Zeppelins would request permission to call for bearings from the 'Directing Station: Wireless Command Post' on board the *Kaiser Wilhelm II* in Wilhelmshaven harbour. This post would respond by ordering a Zeppelin either to wait or to call. After a call was authorised, three German direction-finding stations each would take a bearing on it and send the reports back by wireless, where the aircrew used the vectors to fix their position. British interception stations could also exploit that opportunity but with even greater accuracy. Deployed over a range of 49 to 57 degrees latitude, they had a better base for triangulation than German stations on 51 to 55 degrees. If the station at Bruges failed, as frequently occurred, the other German stations, bunched on the narrow line between the Dutch and Danish frontiers,

[45] Robinson, 'Zeppelin Intelligence', p. 2.

[46] See n. 8 above; Beesley, *Room 40*, p. 26.

[47] 'Personal Narrative' by Squadron-Leader P. Babington, undated but presumably mid 1920s, PRO, AIR 1/2393/229/1; General Cartier, 'Le service d'écoute pendant la guerre', *Radioeléctricité*, iv, 15 Nov. 1923, p. 491.

could not provide useful bearings at all. This system of direction-finding had another flaw. It worked well if one airship at a time requested bearings. It collapsed during what Zeppelin crews called 'the battle of the wireless'. When several airships called for bearings simultaneously, using one dedicated frequency which British stations were jamming, then the hammering of morse keys from spark sets made a 'terrible drum fire that raged over hundreds of knots' on the airwaves.[48]

All this allowed British wireless intelligence to forewarn of attacks in particular places at specific times. During the raid of 31 March/1 April 1916, MI1b located four airships fifty to ninety miles (two to three hours) away from the coast and followed them in. An unusual weather report at 10.15 was MI1e's 'first intimation' of a raid on 23 May 1917. A second such report at 16.35 made MI1e 'certain' that a raid was imminent. The first call for bearings by an airship were detected eighty miles east of Lowescroft at 20.45 and subsequently three Zeppelins were tracked to the coast.[49] This power declined in late 1917, when MI1e noted that Zeppelins rarely used wireless over Britain, which they had done as a matter of routine earlier in the war, and even more so in 1918, when the Zeppelins adopted the 'silent' direction-finding system. None the less, wireless intelligence provided three to four hours advance warning of the only two airship raids actually to enter British airspace during 1918.[50]

Their success affected the psychology of wireless intelligence personnel. They came to think they knew the men they were helping to kill. There was an affectionate ring to the NID's use of woman's names to identify individual Zeppelins and to its code phrase for wireless intelligence, 'the Little Woman at Borkum'. Similarly, Round reported:

> One general feeling amongst the Naval Intelligence operators, I know, is to meet the one operator who controlled the German Zeppelins and warships. They always imagined it was one particular man who was a super-operator. On several occasions with nine or ten Zeppelins in a raid, all frantically trying to communicate with home for bearings or otherwise, wireless occasionally got into a horrible tangle. At that moment the super-man would arrive, take control, and in a twinkling all would be peace and order.[51]

Sometimes more than a twinkling was required to achieve this end. During the disastrous 'silent raid' of 17–18 October 1917, catastrophic and

---

[48] Two brief accounts of the work against Zeppelins by French signals intelligence services are ibid., pp. 491–92; and Colonel Calvel, 'Intercept Service and Radiogoniometry in the Armies', pp. 106–11, RG-165, 8280-C-83, National Archives, Washington.

[49] Rolf Marben, *Zeppelin Adventures* (trans. Claud W. Sykes, London, 1934), pp. 104–10.

[50] WTS no. 20, April 1916, by MI1b, PRO, ADM 137/4355; WTS no. 44, 31 May 1917, ADM 137/4305; GHQ, Home Forces – Air Board, 28 Nov. 1917, PRO, AIR 1/36, 13 March 1918 and 6 August 1918, e.g. MI1e 13 April 1918, 'Zeppelin Raid', PRO, WO 158/960; Cole and Cheesman, *Air Defence*, p. 409.

[51] Round, 'Position Finding', p. 242.

unexpected winds produced deadly navigational problems for Zeppelins flying at high altitudes and outside the area in which their ground based direction finding stations could provide useful reports. Their radio discipline simply collapsed. As one surviving German officer noted,

> all trace of organisation in wireless intercourse had disappeared – it was simply impossible to get a wireless message through. The airships were wirelessing pell-mell and quite regardless of each other. One ship even sent out an SOS .... There was no doubt that various ships were in distress and a dread foreboding filled us all.[52]

Here, flawed systems of signals and signals security were fatal against experienced wireless intelligence personnel. Referring to this raid, a veteran of MI1e wrote 'On one famous occasion in bad weather the incpt [sic] service learned from the Zeppelin transmissions that the bombing fleet tho [sic] over our East Coast was badly off track and hopelessly lost. The AA guns and searchlights round London were silenced as a calculated risk' by home defence authorities, so to deny the airships any chance to reorient themselves.[53] Over the next day five Zeppelins, 30 per cent of the existing fleet, were blown off course and wrecked by accident and the Allies. In this most elegant of instances, signals intelligence allowed strategic air defence to kill without moving a muscle.

Initially, Army airships also had weak signals security. In 1915, they used call signs which consisted of the first three letters of the last name of their commanding officer. The NID understood the system but could not link every call to a specific ship because it did not know the names of all their commanders.[54] In March 1916, however, the Army's service adopted a new system, marked by frequent and random changes in call signs. British wireless intelligence found this difficult to reconstruct, and hence could no longer use that means to acquire much certain knowledge about the enemy's strength and dispositions.[55] Meanwhile, Army airships avoided the elementary errors in wireless security which compromised Zeppelin raids. This occurred in large part, as MI1e observed, because they faced fewer problems of navigation and therefore had less need to use radio. Army airships generally flew within German-controlled territory

---

[52] C.F. Snowden Gamble, *The Story of a North Sea Air Station* (London, 1928), p. 276; Treusch von Buttlar Brandenfels, *Zeppelins over England* (trans. Huntley Paterson, London, 1931), pp. 118–19.

[53] Unsigned and undated memo, 'An Intelligence Section of the First World War', post-1969, presumably by Sir Ronald Nesbitt Hawes, Intelligence Corps Museum, accession no. 198; memorandum by Ie, Ie/1692, 22 Oct. 1917, 'Movements of 11 German Airships during the Raid of 19th–20th October, 1917, PRO, WO 158/960; Calvel, 'Intercept Service', pp 109–111, 'Raid of the German Dirigibles during the Night of the 19th of October, 1917'.

[54] Robinson, 'Zeppelin Intelligence', p. 2.

[55] MI1e, no. 39, 1 Nov. 1916, 'Analysis and Consideration', and memorandum by MI1e, 29 Dec. 1916, PRO, ADM 137/4355.

to the Belgian coast, then due west to the United Kingdom, returning along the same route. In February 1917 MI1e emphasised that 'military airship raids will in the future, as in the past, be proceeded by few if any wireless indications'.[56] MI1e and the NID both found it difficult to handle the Army airship service until it was abolished and absorbed by the Navy in 1917. On the other hand, Army airships which attacked targets in France during 1915–16 did call for bearings precisely as did Zeppelins operating against Britain, and were easily tracked by French signals intelligence.[57]

The technical success of wireless intelligence against the airships and its effect on British operations are easy to determine. This is not true of the campaign launched by the Gothas of Bombengeschwader 3, assisted by the Riesenflugzeuge of Rfa-501. Although the evidence is incomplete and often in conflict, one thing is clear – some airplane raids did achieve complete surprise. This was especially true of the initial ones. The Chief of the Imperial General Staff, William Robertson, noted that Gothas had attacked three times between 25 May and 13 June 1917:

> We never know the raiders are coming until they appear on the coast and the distance in time from the coast to important places like London is less than the time required by most of the machines we have got to ascend to the necessary height. Consequently, before they can get up the enemy has done his job and is on his way home.[58]

On 21 November 1917 George MacDonogh, held that 'wireless methods' could not 'foretell' aeroplane raids.[59] These are good sources but not unchallenged ones. After the war, knowledgeable veterans claimed that wireless intelligence often had foretold airplane raids. In particular Philip Babington, commander of 141 Squadron, a central part of the home defence system during 1917–18, wrote that wireless intelligence had warned of most raids 'the minute the aircraft left their aerodromes'. Similarly, General Cartier claimed 'that as soon as [Gothas] began to transmit their presence in the air and their evolutions were detected by our radiogoniometric service'.[60] Several other pieces of contemporary evidence support such statements.

This conflict between sources of evidence can be clarified by considering how and why German bombers used wireless. Every Riesenflugzeug carried radio and used it as a matter of routine. Gothas, conversely, were always capable of carrying radio but they did not do so during

---

[56] GHQ Home Forces, 'Wireless Calls during February 1917', ADM 137/4305.

[57] GHQ Home Forces, 'Wireless Calls during August 1917', PRO, ADM 137/4305; Calvel, 'Intercept Service', p. 107, RG-165, 8280-C-83, National Archives, Washington.

[58] Robertson to Haig, 15 June 1917, Robertson Papers, 1/23, Liddell Hart Centre for Military Archives.

[59] DMI to DAO, 21 Nov. 1917, PRO, AIR 2/163 M.R. 1184.

[60] 'Personal Narrative', by Squadron-Leader P. Babington, undated but presumably mid 1920s, PRO, AIR 1/2393/229/1; Cartier, 'Le service d'écoute', p. 491.

the first months of the campaign.[61] Nor, in fact, was radio needed during the daylight raids conducted by formations of bombers of May through August 1917, or for the attacks which individual aeroplanes launched against coastal towns in daylight until the end of the war. These Gothas located their targets visually. Broad daylight solved any problems of navigation but it also solved the problem of tactical intelligence for fighters on the defence. Once the home defence system was recalibrated to focus on aeroplanes, daylight raids against inland targets became suicide. After suffering 30 per cent losses in such a raid on 22 August 1917, Bombengeschwader 3 changed its tactics.

Between September 1917 and May 1918, it turned to night raids conducted by bombers operating as individuals, most often against London. These aircraft generally attacked on moonlit nights and followed a direct course from Ghent to Kent, where they used the Thames to determine their location. None the less, they still needed extraordinary accuracy in navigation. Given their limited endurance – London was near the extreme end of their operating range – Gothas had to find their targets with maximum efficiency. Unlike airships, they could not spend hours perambulating in search of a target. Giants had a far greater operational range but they also played a more peripheral role in the campaign and were guided by radio direction finding in any case. These problems were most notable when Gothas crossed a forty-mile expanse of the North Sea at the start of a raid. Riesenflugzeuge and Gothas could have used the silent direction-finding system, as British Handley-Page 0/400 bombers proved, but they never did so. Hence, their only means to overcome these navigational problems was to call for bearings while in the air. This was always standard procedure for Rfa 501. Gothas, however, did not begin to use wireless or radio direction finding on missions until December 1917. Thereafter this was common practice.[62] Since Gothas and Giants flew individually, such requests were frequent; since these were made only during attacks, they warned that one was imminent. Once bombers came to rely on wireless, they had to test their instruments before operations, while specialised controlling and bearing stations on the ground had to serve the campaign. These stations and aircraft adopted a normal style of communications, which highlighted the abnormal traffic patterns preceding an operation. Above all, from December 1917, whenever raids were projected Rumpler reconnaissance aircraft off the English coast delivered weather reports by wireless before Gothas took off.[63] This practice, along with the radio procedure of Riesenflugzeuge and of ground stations, were the three means by which

---

[61] Haddow and Grosz, *German Giants*, p. 3, passim.

[62] Fredette, *Sky on Fire*, see n. 68 below.

[63] Cole and Cheesman, *Air Defence*, p. 320; Haddow and Grosz, *German Giants*, pp. 33–34, 42.

British wireless intelligence acquired forewarning during the aeroplane raids.

The question is when MI1e began to do so. While the evidence is fragmentary, it does offer clear indications for an answer. After the war, Ashmore noted that in August 1917 'special intelligence' provided advance warning 'that the 3rd Bombing Squadron were busy practising night flying'.[64] While 'special' often was a euphamism for 'wireless', and may have been so used in this instance, that cannot be demonstrated to have been the case. The surviving evidence from the autumn of 1917 shows that British signals intelligence provided nothing about Gothas but was surprisingly accurate about Giants, even though the latter rarely attacked the United Kingdom. In September 1917 MI1e precisely tracked the first deployment of Riesenflugzeuge from Germany to Belgium. From this, Horse Guards correctly concluded that the Giants would attack Britain. That knowledge was not useful because it was not used: initially, Horse Guards did not even inform its subordinates that Riesenflugzeuge existed. Hence, on 1/2 October 1917, one intercept station which detected signals from a Giant acting in support of a Gotha raid interpreted them as meaning that a Zeppelin was nearby.[65]

On 14 December 1917, in a retrospective analysis based exclusively on wireless intelligence, MI1e correctly dated three of the four Riesen-flugzeuge raids on Britain (counting the abortive one of 1/2 October). It underestimated the numbers of aircraft involved in two of these raids by 33 per cent and 50 per cent and did not realise that Giants had participated in another attack, presumably because some of them had not used wireless. This analysis shows the care with which MI1e searched for precise and reliable wireless indicators of imminent raids. It had observed the traffic of aeroplanes with receiving and transmitting gear twenty-one times between 1 September and 11 December:

> On three occasions only has this W/T activity been manifested around midnight and in each of these it has been synchronized as to date and roughly also as to time with raids on England. The raiders are known to have been principally GOTHA machines which do not actually carry wireless, though they are constructed to enable it to be installed if required. It would appear probable that the wireless activity emanated from giant machines of the Riesenflugzeuge type .... It does not necessarily follow that all or any of these machines actually raided.[66]

On 31 December 1917, MI1e produced another retrospective analysis, based primarily on signals intelligence acquired by itself and by Ie at the

---

[64] Ashmore, *Air Defence*, p. 48.

[65] 'Airship and Wireless Intelligence', Sept. 1917, WTS, no. 51, 30 Sept. 1917, PRO, ADM 137/4355; Cole and Cheesman, *Air Defence*, p. 310; Haddow and Grosz, *German Giants*, p. 29.

[66] GHQ Home Forces, 14 Dec. 1917, 'Participation in Raids', PRO, AIR 1/611/16/15/283.

BEF, augmented by the interrogation of prisoners of war. MI1e noted that during operations, two stations called to Riesenflugzeuge (for purposes of direction finding) while Giants communicated 'almost entirely' with a single radio station in Ghent. That station had also emitted a stereotyped pattern of wireless traffic before every Gotha raid yet launched against Great Britain, whether the bombers had used radio or not. MI1e had intercepted forty-one different radio messages from Giants between 27 September and 29 December.[67] After a raid of 18 December 1917, for the first time British signals intelligence recorded that Gothas had determined their position in the air by calling for wireless bearings. In January 1918, wireless intelligence provided two to four hours advance warning of three Gotha raids. It allowed MI1e to determine their airspeed during operations and offered some indications that Bombengeschwader 3 was receiving replacements. Meanwhile, at the BEF from February 1918 Ie devoted increasing attention to the Gothas and Riesenflugzeuge, with some success. A new branch of Ie was established specifically to process and distribute current effective intelligence about raids on the western front. Notably, Ie itself was charged with issuing direct warnings to the BEF of such raids, rather than going through the chain of command of the intelligence and operations branches at General Headquarters. This reflected experience that only organisational structures which worked with unusual speed could handle the task.[68]

Knowledge of this sort no doubt was used to forecast impending raids on Britain and show when they began and from where. This process became routine in December 1917, when Riesenflugzeuge participated in every raid launched against Britain while the Gothas also began to use radio as standard operating procedure. Whether by coincidence or not, precisely this period marked a turning-point in the night campaign. Before 6 December 1917, British night defences had destroyed not one Gotha. Throughout the rest of the campaign, they destroyed in combat an average of 10 per cent of the bombers involved in every mission. Compared to Zeppelins, however, wireless sources had one notable limitation for operational intelligence against aeroplanes. They could show that a raid was imminent and detect the moment it began. Once Gothas and Riesenflugzeuge took off, their position and direction in the air could rarely be determined. As Round noted, 'In the later stages of the war, night errors from Gothas were extremely troublesome, the only satisfactory times being when they were flying either towards or, preferably, away from the observer'.[69]

Throughout the first Battle of Britain, wireless sources provided virt-

---

[67] MI1e, WTS no. 55, 31 Dec. 1917, PRO, ADM 137/4305.

[68] Naval Staff Operations, 19 Dec. 1917, PRO, AIR 1/296/15/226/143; 'Airship and Giant Aeroplane Intelligence', Jan. 1918, PRO, ADM 137/4355; Ferris, *Signals Intelligence*, pp. 197–202.

[69] Round, 'Position Finding', p. 237.

ually the only operational intelligence available to British air defence. This material was of first-rate quality. It was also provided to commanders and units in real time and through effective means. During 1915–16, all material from the Navy's wireless intelligence sections went directly to the head of the Operations Division of the Naval Staff, Admiral Oliver. His role as the main analyst of intelligence, and the sole filter for its dissemination, generally crippled the value of Room 40 but all this was well suited for defence against Zeppelins. The intelligence involved was easy to understand. It went directly to the heart of the Admiralty and was immediately disseminated through normal channels.[70] These channels worked quickly and efficiently in the case of seagoing forces; not so with the RNAS. Until the spring of 1917, wireless intelligence about Zeppelins and U-boats went to coastal air squadrons through what some RNAS officers later called the 'tortuous channels' of the Admiral Commanding Coast Guards and Reserves.[71] Fortunately, the forewarning provided by signals intelligence allowed this creaky C³I mechanism to function.

The Horse Guards also integrated wireless intelligence effectively into its strategic air defence system. At its heart during the Zeppelin era was MI1e, a 'very secret wireless room', where wireless reports of airship positions were entered on charts hour by hour.[72] According to the only surviving inside account of MI1e, written fifty years after the event, interception stations were connected

by direct lines to the War Office telegraph room, and thence by pneumatic tubes to the main plotting centre in Room 417. This was the nerve centre of the organisation and was DMI's responsibility. As plots of raiding aircraft came through, warning was passed out via GHQ Home Forces at Horse Guards, to all Home Commands. Four plotting tables were maintained and bearings were usually received within about 90 seconds of the original transmission, Plotting officers wore headphones and microphones connected to Home Forces and Admiralty, and they talked as they plotted. The plotting maps covered England and Scotland. There was a hole in the map at each DF site with a cord passing through it and a degree protractor printed round each DF. When a plot was made from two or more DF bearings, a light was switched on below the map and the appropriate map square could be read out. Different Zeppelins were tracked on the various plotting tables and a master map was maintained to follow the whole raid.

An example of the work done was to pick up the German daily weather reports to Zeppelins from Bruges. As Zeppelin raids increased, this traffic of weather reports plus the number of Zeppelins active and their movements during the forenoon indicated the likelihood of a raid the same night. Flying very slowly, at some 30 knots or so, and emitting streams of radio messages,

[70] Beesley, *Room 40*.

[71] 'RNAS/Home Waters, 1917–1918. Part 2. Submarine Campaign', PRO, AIR 1/677/21/13/1902.

[72] Memorandum by 'B.W.', 15 May 1917, PRO, WO 95/5454.

the approaching Zeppelins gave ample warning to the War Office MI1(e) to organise duties and reliefs before nightfall.[73]

The Horse Guards issued orders based on such intelligence direct to RFC units. In the early days, this process was marked by informality. A staff officer might call directly an individual pilot awaiting action on a camp bed beside his aircraft. Thus, on the evening of 13 October 1915, a family friend and officer at Horse Guards told John Slessor

> that four or five Zeppelins had crossed the coast and were in the neighbourhood of Thetford, making for London. There was a touch of avuncular anxiety in his voice as he told me I was on no account to go up unless I was quite sure the weather was all right – it didn't look at all good to him in Whitehall.[74]

The weather looked better from the runway at Sutton's Farm and so Slessor ordered the engine of his BE2c to be warmed up. Despite this delay in taking off, the call had been timed so that he could reach an appropriate altitude before the airship arrived.

Between late 1915 and early 1916, the Horse Guards improved its use of the forewarning provided by signals intelligence. It issued orders not directly to pilots but through a regular chain of command. While each RFC squadron in the midlands remained under the immediate direction of Horse Guards, a Wing-Commander controlled all those south of Watford, the centre of the strategic air defence system. When informed of approaching airships, he determined how to deploy his aircraft and commanded them.[75] Standard procedure was to issue a warning order, at which time each base readied an aeroplane for action. They were ordered to launch when wireless intelligence or ground observation showed that an airship was approaching a given part of Britain, though this order sometimes was given on extrapolations from direction finding.[76] The aim was to place an aircraft at the desired altitude for interception before airships arrived. Aeroplanes were to take off exactly at the minute ordered. This was computed to place a BE2c at 8000 feet before a Zeppelin arrived. That required about forty-five minutes, leaving time for a patrol of forty-five minutes.[77]

Under LADA in 1917–18, the situation became more elaborate and less personal still. On receipt of a warning order, squadrons prepared

[73] Unsigned and undated memo, 'An Intelligence Section of the First World War', post-1969, presumably by Sir Ronald Nesbitt Hawes, Intelligence Corps Museum, accession no. 198.

[74] John Slessor, *The Central Blue: The Autobiography of Sir John Slessor, Marshall of the RAF* (New York, 1957), pp. 11–12.

[75] Ashmore, *Air Defence*, pp. 15–16.

[76] Cole and Cheesman, *Air Defence*, p. 85.

[77] Sutton, *Raiders Approach!*, pp. 12–13.

patrols for immediate take-off.[78] As one pilot, Cecil Lewis, described the process,

> Each squadron had a telephone operator constantly on duty. When raid warnings came through, he pressed a Morse key close to hand sounding three large Klaxon horns set up on the roof of the men's quarters and the officers' Mess. The men swarmed into the sheds and rushed out the machines, the pilots struggled into their kit and warmed up their engines. If the raid warning was followed by the action signal, machines were off the ground within a minute.[79]

Between 1915 and 1918, wireless intelligence offered no material whatsoever about Army airship raids or daylight attacks by aeroplanes. Conversely, it did provide effective warning of the two most important categories of strategic bombing: four or more hours in the case of all Zeppelins and two to four hours for most airplane raids at night. Through negative evidence, signals intelligence also offered a high probability that attacks of these sorts would not be launched in specific periods. Army airships, moreover, often operated in conjection with Zeppelins, and then encountered a home defence system which was on alert in any case. In 1916 the Navy's poor security contributed to the death of the Army's airship service. This material was fundamental to strategic air defence as a source of forewarning and as a force-multiplier. These contributions were linked. Only with forewarning could air defence be effective and efficient. Then, instead of being random and constant, patrols could be launched solely when the enemy was approaching. A contemporary estimate allows one to compute the significance of these factors. In 1917, from his experiences on the Western Front, where intelligence could not provide forewarning, Hugh Trenchard estimated the strength required to defend London against air attack. He concluded that only 'constant patrols' could do so and only in an inefficient fashion. They would 'lock up a very large number of machines and pilots on a purely defensive plan which would never stop an aggressive enemy'. Trenchard believed that 'To keep one machine in the air all day requires five machines and five pilots at least'.[80] If so, signals intelligence reduced by 80 per cent – or by 800 – the number of aircraft and pilots needed for strategic air defence.

So routine and powerful was the forewarning provided by signals intelligence that it was built into the mechanism of home defence. Two statements made after the war demonstrate that forewarning turned on the ignition which set the machine into motion. Babington noted

> in case of Zeppelin raids and in most of the aeroplane raids, warning of an impending attack was usually obtained the minute the aircraft left their

[78] Jones, *The War in the Air*, v, pp. 493–504, describes the standard operating procedure.
[79] Cecil Lewis, *Sagittarius Rising* (London, 1936), p. 202.
[80] Jones, *War in the Air*, v, pp. 479–81.

aerodromes as the Directional wireless picked up cypher messages, which were sent to test instruments, etc., and often en route to establish positions. A preliminary warning was then given to all HD units both air and ground.

Similarly Ashmore wrote that the

> system of control at my Headquarters was as follows: The first indication of raid, generally before the enemy crossed our coast-line, was reported to the duty officer; he had the delicate task of deciding whether the information was true or not. If the report was accepted, the staff and telephone operators on duty were summoned to their 'action' positions. As they were always present in the building, this only took half a minute or so. The code word 'Readiness' was then issued on the direct lines, to warn for action all guns, searchlights, aerodromes, etc. . . . . As soon as 'Readiness' was received, the fighter squadrons would have their machines lined up, and the pilots dressed and waiting in them.
>
> When the approach of the enemy was confirmed, the order to patrol was sent out.[81]

Only effective forewarning allowed strategic air defence to work. Surprise attacks short-circuited it. In such cases, bombers reached the coast before British forces began to react. Warning orders caught commanders ten miles from their headquarters. Horse Guards and its units took several minutes to bring their personnel to battle stations, co-ordinate incoming reports, order counter-measures and put them in effect. During the initial surprise attacks by Gothas, fighters did not begin to take off until fifteen minutes after the bombers were first sighted on the coast.[82] Once launched, depending on the period, fighters needed twenty to fifty minutes to reach their patrolling altitude. By this time German aeroplanes would be over London or airships somewhere over Great Britain. Wireless intelligence, then, did not just influence specific actions – it was a precondition for any and every action. Its operational significance must be gauged by two different criteria: whether the home defence system deployed its standard procedures; and whether any intruders were destroyed or driven off. These criteria also mark the intersection between operations and tactics in air defence.

For the defence in the first Battle of Britain, intelligence was as weak at the tactical level as it was strong at the operational one. This produced the most inefficient possible of efficient air defence systems, or vice-versa. Perfection in interception requires precise material about the height, speed, number and vector of intruders; and the minute and mile of their entry into defended airspace. In 1940, radar did not entirely reach this standard. No source of the Great War even began to approach it. At

---

[81] 'Personal Narrative', by Squadron-Leader P. Babington, undated but presumably mid 1920s, PRO, AIR 1/2393/229/1; Ashmore, *Air Defence*, pp. 49–51.

[82] Ibid., pp. 37–38; Rawlinson, *Defence of London*, pp. 182–83.

best, wireless intelligence might define the number of incoming airships and show that each would enter a given twenty-five mile long section of the coast in a twenty-minute period, but it could not define their altitudes and could only approximately estimate speed and direction. Signals intelligence could not even meet this standard for airplanes – it could only determine that raids had been launched at a specific moment from a given base. The only other relevant sources were a sound locator on the coast of Kent and observers on the coast and ships. These sources frequently gave ten and, rarely, fifteen to twenty minutes warning that aircraft were approaching specific parts of the British coast.[83] They offered little about numbers, speed, height or direction but, together with wireless intelligence, these sources guaranteed that in most raids, ground defences would be at battle stations and aircraft from inland bases would be rising toward 12,000 feet as the enemy crossed the British coast. It was here that problems began to emerge.

As bombers entered British airspace, the main sources of information became the visual and aural observations of personnel in the air and on the ground. These sources provided accurate and useful facts and sometimes became the target acquisition components of weapons systems. Visual and aural observers directed searchlights to illuminate specific areas, which in turn guided gunfire and fighters toward bombers. So too, from 1916, did sound detectors. These used a primitive variant of the technique of sound ranging, by which the analysis of sound waves located the firing position of guns.[84] Each ear of an observer was attached through tubes and stethoscopes to one of a pair of megaphones, each at the end of a long pole. This observer, often blind or blindfolded, manipulated the poles until he received a sound from the sky through both ears at the same time. His actions, in turn, moved the indicator on a compass card from which the bearing of the noise could be computed. Adjacent searchlights then illuminated that position and anti-aircraft guns fired at it. On the Western Front, sound-ranging not only guided specific batteries, it also provided the information needed to direct mass predictive fire against unseen targets and generally pinpointed enemy forces. In air defence, similarly, sound detectors directed predictive anti-aircraft barrages and traced the path of unseen bombers.[85] Nor were these mean contributions. The combination of searchlight, BE2c and Buckingham bullet killed the airship campaign in 1916. Anti-aircraft barrages forced the enemy

[83] Ashmore, *Air Defence*, pp. 37–38; Cole and Cheesman, *Air Defence*, p. 313; Jones, *War in the Air*, v, p. 23; Hartcup, *War of Invention*, pp. 63–64.

[84] John R. Innes, *Flash Spotters and Sound Rangers: How They Lived, Worked and Fought in the Great War* (London, 1935); Sir Lawrence Bragg, 'Sound Ranging', pp. 31–41, in Sir Lawrence Bragg, Major-General A.H. Dowson and Lieutenant-Colonel H.H. Hemming, *Artillery Survey in the First World War* (London, 1971); Hartcup, *War of Invention*, pp. 68–75.

[85] Rawlinson, *Defence of London*, pp. 110–11; Jones, *War in the Air*, v, pp. 73–75; Wallace, *Biggin Hill*, pp. 44–45.

to avoid certain areas or altitudes and allowed fighters to concentrate elsewhere. While guns damaged few airships, they did down half the German airplanes destroyed in combat and probably contributed to some of those lost in accidents.

The great weakness in strategic air defence was the combination of tactical intelligence and tactical communication for fighter aircraft. The difficulty in air-to-ground communication during the day and its virtual impossibility at night denied pilots access to the information which was plentiful on the ground. It left them to rely on their eyes alone. Ashmore defined this as 'the main problem of air defence'.

> Owing to the difficulty of picking up one aeroplane from another in the air, it is essential to give information from the ground, where observation is easier and aircraft can be seen at far greater distances. And, to render this information timely and effective, a great system of ground observation, communication and control is required.[86]

The two Battles of Britain illustrate this point. In 1940, with radar and R/T for tactical intelligence and communication, a good air defence system could deploy every fighter as it wished against any part of the enemy anywhere in defended airspace. In 1917 air defence was equally well organised, almost identically so, but far less efficient. That it lacked radar was a secondary problem. Even had radar existed in 1917, it would have been useless to fighters unless R/T was available for ground-to-air communication. Conversely, had R/T but not radar been available, the ability to transfer tactical intelligence from the ground to air would have increased the ratio of interceptions in a dramatic fashion – in Ashmore's view, fourfold.[87]

In any case, the problems with tactical communication and intelligence served as a force divider. During 1917–18 they cost fighter defence perhaps half of the potential advantage offered by operational fore-warning. In principle, the latter allowed fighters to take off almost as soon as German bombers did and to intercept them on the British coast. In practice, this opportunity had to be foresworn. A fighter in the air was a fighter out of command: they had to be held in hand until senior authorities knew where and when the enemy was entering British airspace. This, in turn, meant that the zone of interception began not over the English Channel but halfway between London and Dover. Nor was this the only division of potential power. Once launched, night fighters had to operate without any advantage of concentration or economy of force. They were driven into a cordon defence, deployed individually at every area and altitude through which bombers might move, unable to reinforce any friend who did encounter the foe. Pilots flew an 'allotted beat' on

[86] Ashmore, *Air Defence*, pp. 13, 38.
[87] Ibid., p. 95.

patrol lines 30 to 100 miles long, at altitudes 500 to 1000 feet apart, most commonly at 10,000, 11,000 and 12,000 feet. In 1915 squadrons would send up one aeroplane for a single ninety-minute patrol. By 1917 they would despatch 33 per cent or 50 per cent of their strength on two-hour patrols, flight after flight sweeping in relief until the skies were clear of the enemy.[88] All this was unavoidable but undesirable. The aim in fighter defence was elementary – as Ashmore wrote, 'to ensure that our pilots have the best possible chance of meeting hostile machines'.[89] The best possible chance was a small one. On an average mission at night during the war, only 1–3 per cent of home defence fighters saw an enemy bomber. Even fewer destroyed one. This significance of this problem varied with the bomber. Cordon defence was better suited to annihilate airships, relatively slow and vulnerable, than Gothas and Riesenflugzeuge, with combat power to match any British fighter. In any case, the inefficiency of this system is clear. Had R/T been available during the strategic bombing campaign, fifty fighters would have achieved results equal to that which 200 achieved without it. Had radar also been available, twelve fighters might well have been able to achieve equivalent results.

Even this low order of tactical efficiency could be achieved only by air defence with a high level of organisational efficiency. That took many years to develop, in a process marked alternately by confusion and imagination. During the autumn of 1914, before any airship raid had been launched, the Admiralty established the first air defence system in British history. It had two components, which combined local with forward defence. The first, several groups of anti-aircraft guns and searchlights, defended government installations in central London. According to the Admirals who created it, 'The whole problem has many points in common with the night defence of the Fleet at anchor. The same general principles are largely applicable'; 'The whole system was modelled on that of the night defence system employed in a battleship'. A dedicated net of telephones linked all units within groups and all layers of command. A Central Control Officer commanded all actions of the system – no combat could be initiated without his approval. He was also in direct contact with the Admiralty. Within the second component, an RNAS flight on the Continent disrupted German airforces and airbases in Belgium, and through a dedicated signals link provided early warning of raids to other flights around London.[90] This system was sophisticated in schematic terms but it also was shaped to meet one specific threat – airship attacks from Belgium to London. It was so successful at this task that it contributed to the creation of a new danger. The RNAS destroyed several German airships on the ground in Belgium and forced them to

---

[88] Ibid., p. 50; Sutton, *Raiders Approach!*, pp. 12–13; Lewis, *Sagittarius Rising*, pp. 202–3.
[89] Ashmore, *Air Defence*, p. 112.
[90] Roskill, *Naval Air Service*, pp. 173–74, 177, 183, 250; Jones, *War in the Air*, iii, p. 83.

abandon bases there. The airship raids of 1915–16 came from across the Heligoland Bight or from the Rhineland over Belgium, and struck throughout all of Great Britain. In order to be effective, the strategic air defence system had to be expanded to central England as well as central London. This caused organisational confusion, as Asquith had predicted. That was not overcome for eighteen months.

The Admiralty, the War Office and civil authorities at local and national levels responded to an unprecedented threat by following the precedents of bureaucratic politics. As a result, strategic air defence simultaneously faced technical and political problems. The fighting services had no choice but to create defence and observation networks throughout Britain. They chose to create two overlapping, convoluted and unco-ordinated networks. Seven control centres loosely co-ordinated anti-aircraft guns and searchlights within London, assisted by a mobile and independent anti-aircraft brigade. Fighters of the RNAS and RFC were scattered in penny packets throughout the country. Meanwhile, local police and civil authorities throughout Britain reported independently any aircraft seen or heard to both the Admiralty and the War Office. These departments and local Chief Constables then immediately informed every civil authority in the country of raids. Those offices and forces communicated over the public telephone system. Other traffic was cleared with the phrase 'Anti-Aircraft, London', later replaced by 'Airbandit'. Individual units made contact by dialling each other and then broke it after the communication was complete so to free the line. This congested structure of signals and command did not always work. It and the defensive system alike collapsed during the first Zeppelin raid of 19/20 January 1915. Communications to specific units failed during raids in April 1915 and 31 January 1916.[91]

From the spring of 1915, the Navy and the Army received ample forewarning of airship raids and tried to act on them. Since material, tactics and organisation were inadequate, virtually the only reward was to make airships avoid low altitudes and broad daylight. Anti-aircraft guns had little effect on airships above 10,000 feet. Airships were difficult for pilots to see and could easily soar above British fighters and survive their useless ordnance.[92] These weaknesses were magnified by haphazard or misguided organisation. Half of the aircraft involved, the RNAS flights, had the virtually impossible task of patrolling for airships on the coast in the dark. Given the technical circumstances of the day,

[91] Morris, *German Air Raids*, pp. 105–10; Rawlinson, *Defence of London*, pp. 52–53; Ashmore, *Air Defence*, pp. 4, 14–19; Jones, *War in the Air*, iii, pp. 84–86. An excellent account of the development of the civilian air-raid warning system is Marian McKenna, 'The Development of Air Raid Precautions in Britain During the First World War', in Timothy Travers and Christon Archer (eds), *Men at War, Politics, Technology and Innovation in the Twentieth Century* (Chicago, 1982).

[92] Roskill, *Naval Air Service*, pp. 249–51; Gamble, *North Sea Air Station*, pp. 143–44; Winslow, *Forewarned is Forearmed*, pp. 22–23; and Ashmore, *Air Defence*, pp. 4–5.

this was as futile as relying on offensive patrols rather than convoy for anti-submarine work. The two approaches probably stemmed from the same simplistic application of a doctrine which emphasised advance and offensive interception of enemy forces. Meanwhile penny-packet deployment hampered command and maintenance, and air defence units were not ready to fight at a moment's notice. In order to be deployed, the mobile anti-aircraft brigade had to speed down London streets, forcing civilian traffic off the roads. The pilots at Great Yarmouth, a main RNAS station in home defence, lived one and a half miles from their airplanes. One pilot wrote

> On about five successive nights now, just as we were sitting down to dinner, a Zeppelin would be reported approaching the coast somewhere on our beat. Result – a general 'hoo-doo'. All the pilots jump into cars and dash down to the sheds, closely followed by the mechanics in lorries. As our way is right along the [water]front, several cars and two 4-ton lorries loaded with men hurtling down to the air station frighten the whole of Yarmouth.[93]

Between late 1915 and early 1916, the air defence system improved in a remarkable fashion and largely because of a change in organisation. Though the RNAS still patrolled the coast while the NID acquired intelligence, otherwise the War Office took over air defence. This simplified bureaucratic lines of demarcation and produced a great if subterranean change in institutional ethos. Naval personnel for air defence had come from three sources: gunnery experts who exaggerated the power of anti-aircraft guns and worshipped range tables; and the RNAS and RNVR, both marked by a privateering approach toward organisation and a trust in strategies of distant interception rather than the point defence of dispersed but valuable targets. The Army's air defence personnel came from its most professional branches – engineers, gunners and intelligence officers, who operated within a tradition of hardening valuable points and then defending them. An 'Operations Room' at the Horse Guards co-ordinated all combat forces and observers throughout the country, working through local control centres. It was served by a dedicated signals intelligence bureau and observation personnel. Observers were posted along the coast and in cordons thirty miles out from major centres. At different times London had a double and triple cordon. The observers reported to control centres which collated their reports and sent them to the Operations Room. Horse Guards also concentrated its scattered flights at central bases under a more effective system of command. So to warn threatened areas while minimising dislocation elsewhere, Britain was divided into eight 'Warning Controls' on the basis of the telephone trunk lines. Local anti-aircraft commanders told trunk managers which districts were to be warned of air raids. Telephone operators then informed the

93 Gamble, *North Sea Air Station*, p. 162.

appropriate local authorities.[94] This system worked effectively enough, though sometimes lines remained congested and reports confused.

Meanwhile, military energies turned from a thin coastal cordon to a thick point defence of the targets which the enemy intended to attack. The skies above the major cities became a killing ground. A cordon defence of the approaches to towns provided a good interception ratio against airships and any interception offered a good chance for a kill. Home defence received BE2c fighters, which could match the speed and height of airships, and also, finally, effective ordnance. Each squadron served as a local centre of command – it received observers' reports and used them to direct adjacent searchlights, which in turn guided fighters onto airships. This broke the airship campaign. Six airships went down in the last five raids of 1916, an average loss rate of 14 per cent per mission. As a result the German Army abolished its airship service while the Navy adopted heroic measures. It developed Zeppelins fit to operate above 20,000 feet. This was a wonder of technology and a failure as tactics. After 1916, more Zeppelin aircrew than civilians died in airship attacks on Britain. By the spring of 1917 Britain shut down much of its strategic defence system because the airships had been beaten.

Zeppelins were not merely driven from Britain but hunted over the North Sea. By the spring of 1917, Room 40 fell under the complete control of Admiral Hall and the Admiralty improved its work against airships. Through a system named 'Tracing "Z"', which involved a code and map chart, the Naval Staff issued wireless intelligence over the public telephone system direct to RNAS flights. A flight commander would be informed, "'We are told by the Little Woman at Borkum that Anna is at so and so". Anna being the first Zeppelin, Bertha the second, Clara the third and so on'. With this, a flight would be ordered to prepare a patrol. If a Zeppelin came within 150 miles of British shores, the Naval Staff would order an attack and guide the interceptor to the target before and during its flight.[95] Three times RNAS aircraft using wireless fixes caught airships by surprise at low altitudes off the German coast and destroyed them. Other Zeppelins narrowly escaped destruction.

However successful against airships, the home defence system of 1917 was ramshackle in structure. It had two separate operational intelligence centres which were barely beginning to co-operate. Each communicated directly with every intelligence and observation station under its control, and often with individual squadrons. Neither could handle a large volume of communications nor function quickly. This sufficed against airships because of their vulnerability and the lengthy forewarning provided by

[94] Ashmore, *Air Defence*, pp. 18–19; Jones, *War in the Air*, iii, pp. 171–82; Morris, *German Air Raids*, p. 111.

[95] 'P.I.X' (pseud. H.D. Hallan), *The Spider Web* (London, 1919), p. 82; Roskill, *Naval Air Service*, pp. 477, 686; 'RNAS/Home Waters, 1917–1918. Part 2. Submarine Campaign', PRO, AIR 1/677/21/13/1902.

wireless intelligence. The same systems collapsed against large numbers of fast moving and heavily armed aeroplanes. The speed and surprise of the German attack brought them into the defensive system before it began to react. Then too much information came in and too many orders had to go out too quickly for the C³I system to function, and its old military drills failed. Horse Guards, for example, directly controlled every anti-aircraft gun in London, so to guide predictive barrages toward individual airships. This prevented anti-aircraft guns from damaging Gothas even at low altitudes in daylight. Meanwhile, formations of Gothas swamped the single fighters which encountered them on their beats. Ashmore, the commander of the newly created LADA, concluded that 'aeroplane patrols are impotent in defence unless they are helped by an elaborate and far-reaching system of observation and control on the ground'.[96] This was precisely what he set out to create.

Defence against Zeppelins north of Watford was left to the existing systems of the Horse Guards and the Admiralty. Against the Gothas in south-east England, Ashmore retooled the engine of strategic air defence and placed an integrated and centralised C³I system at the wheel. In effect, he combined the best characteristics of two different air defence systems – that of the Zeppelin era in the United Kingdom and of the British Army on the Western Front. The latter organisation passed information with extraordinary speed, power and precision. Wireless intelligence, for example, routinely guided fighters onto enemy spotting aircraft and provided effective warning to the targets of enemy artillery bombardments.[97] Ashmore came to LADA after serving as a divisional artillery commander in Flanders. Many of his reforms and much of his terminology came directly from that front – the use of 'Artillery Wireless Machines' to track enemy bombers and to direct and correct anti-aircraft fire, for example, and the swinging of giant arrows on the ground to guide pilots toward observed enemy aircraft. More generally, the increased emphasis on sound locators for anti-aircraft fire was natural in a gunner who had witnessed sound ranging in counter-battery work. The development of flexible systems for switching anti-aircraft guns from independent work to centrally controlled shoots and back again, and the elaborate schemes for predictive fire, mark a scientific gunner determined to demonstrate his prowess. Similarly, the obstinate faith in balloon aprons as a physical obstacle in the sky seems derived from experiences on the trench lines since 1914. The structure of C³I for ground forces in LADA was similar to that for corps artillery. Where admirals had conceptualised the defence of London in terms of a fleet at anchor, Ashmore saw it as a corp defended area.[98]

---

96 Ashmore, *Air Defence*, p. 51.
97 Jones, *War in the Air*, iii, pp. 319–20; Ferris, *Signals Intelligence*, pp. 14–15, 85–114.
98 Jones, *War in the Air*, v, pp. 66–69; Cole and Cheesman, *Air Defence*, p. 420.

LADA was the most sophisticated C³I system of the Great War and the template for every strategic air defence organisation ever since. It was a cybernetic structure. Its communication and command systems were identical – a community on a party line. Officers were distinguished from their men not by carrying swords but by wearing headphones. LADA could carry a huge volume of communications while simultaneously identifying and acting on the important ones. It was able to collect and collate information from thousands of sources over a 10,000 square mile area, despatch it to Ashmore within sixty seconds, and then direct the actions of every combat unit at his disposal in even less time. 286 guns and 200 aircraft could act within two minutes on the report of an observer fifty miles away. At a moment's notice each unit could switch from independent operations to fighting under Ashmore's order and back again.

LADA integrated three layers of organisation – intelligence and observation personnel, combat units and command structures.[99] Twenty-five 'sub-controls' commanded every observer and anti-aircraft unit in a given area. Simultaneously they collected and collated local reports of hostile aircraft and passed them to 'the central control in the Horse Guards' (the 'Lada control').[100] Each sub-control was in contact with fifty or more subordinate units/sources of information, as Lada control was with twenty-five sub-controls, MI1e, the NID and observers on the coast. Each sub-control could receive reports from 100 different subordinate, lateral and superior sources. Lada control could receive raw or processed reports from thousands of pairs of eyes and ears. A simple but powerful C³I system with 300 personnel prevented it from being overwhelmed by information.

Sub-controls served as a filter for passing information up to Lada control and as a megaphone for passing its orders and assessments down. Each sub-control had an operations room with telephones linked directly to subordinates and superiors. During operations, every observer and combat unit reported its sightings of aircraft to sub-controls every thirty seconds. Their reports were entered onto maps and, where appropriate, guided immediate local actions. Simultaneously, a 'teller' at each sub-control reported to ten 'plotters' at Lada control. Each plotter was connected to two or three sub-controls and placed counters on a map to represent the teller's reports. Ashmore could cut into any line between plotter and teller so to clarify uncertainties while his officers passed down information and orders to the staff and commanders at sub-controls.

Ashmore and his RAF Wing-Commander, T.C.R. Higgins, sat on

---

[99] There are three fundamental and basically independent accounts of this issue: Ashmore, *Air Defence*, pp. 92–93; Morris, *German Air Raids*, p. 238; and 'Personal Narrative', by Squadron-Leader Philip Babington, undated but presumably mid 1920s, AIR 1/2393/229/1. Winslow, *Forewarned is Forearmed*, pp. 24–25 and Bushby, *Air Defence*, pp. 73–74, among others, offer accurate but derivative accounts.

[100] Ashmore, *Air Defence*, p. 92.

a raised gallery overlooking a map which thoroughly and accurately represented the current tactical situation, in real time communication with all units. This system produced the inevitable play on Ashmore's nickname. According to Babington:

> The peculiar sing-song reception of messages in-coming and out-going at Horseguards, together with the fact that the GOC [General Ashmore] stood on a raised platform overlooking the whole scene with an array of switches and telephones, gave birth to the title 'Splash's Litany', which was the name usually applied to the scene at Horseguards during a raid.[101]

Ashmore and Higgins could order fighters to concentrate 'at a given locality, height, etc. to intercept the hostile aircraft'. On 12 August 1917, for example, Ashmore held a squadron in reserve at the place and altitude which he expected – mistakenly – a Gotha formation would use when returning home.[102] A year later, squadron commanders or their deputies were expected to 'control their machines by wireless telephone from their operations room, and order concentrations etc., as required by the tactical situation'.[103] Every gun in LADA could fire barrages at specific areas and altitudes under central control or else act at the discretion of the sub-control.

Every sub-control and squadron ran a self-contained defence area. Each had its own target acquisition systems and co-ordinated information as Lada control did, but on a smaller scale. 141 Squadron at Biggin Hill, for example, covered the edge of the approach to London through Kent. It received an unusual mass of material which had to be collated and used with a unique degree of speed. Its operations room received material from observers, coastguards and sixteen sound detectors, which it used to determine areas and altitudes for interception. These were transmitted to fighters in the air, since, in the spring of 1918, 141 Squadron was used to test R/T in home defence. In the operations room, the commanders of 141 Squadron and of a Searchlight Company 'work side by side at adjacent tables with their maps, plotting arrangements and telephones (line and wireless) in order to direct defensive aeroplanes on the path of attack'. Several officers, 'croupier-wise', represented reports with counters on these map tables. Initially, all of this material came through one plotter who passed it on in the form of written messages. That system collapsed under the load of information during the first heavy raid. Subsequently,

---

[101] 'Personal Narrative', by Squadron-Leader P. Babington, undated but presumably mid 1920s, PRO, AIR 1/2393/229/1.

[102] Ibid.

[103] Jones, *War in the Air*, v, p. 495; 'Personal Narrative' by Squadron-Leader P. Babington, undated but presumably mid 1920s, PRO, AIR 1/2393/229/1.

these officers functioned like plotters at Lada control, each attached by headsets to a few sound locators.[104]

The pattern of C³I at the Western Sub-Command mirrored in miniature that of LADA as a whole. This command controlled nineteen gun and thirty-six searchlight positions scattered over a 500 square mile area. The gun-posts were the basic nodes of command and communications within the sub-control. Each was the centre of a defensive system served by searchlights and observers. Each had two sets of dedicated telephone lines for simultaneous communication with searchlights and sub-controls. Searchlights normally communicated only with their gun-station but the sub-control could contact them directly whenever it wished. Tellers at every gun-post had direct lines to the operations room of the sub-control. This room was filled with telephones of two sorts – one to carry information and the other orders. Each plotter was connected to three gun-stations in different areas, so that no plotter would be overwhelmed by material while his fellows sat idle. Each wrote down incoming messages, which orderlies immediately took to the operations table. Here officers weeded out discrepancies from the material, using their own judgement regarding the reliability of individual observers, and represented material about the height, speed, direction and numbers of intruders on a squared map. On the map were representations of the prepared concentrations of fire and light which could be triggered within seconds by uttering a codeword. Through a headset, the sub-control's commander was in contact with Lada control. Through a microphone, he could speak to every unit under his command.[105]

Signals were the nervous system of this structure for the processing and use of information. Under the 'Airbandit' procedure, three minutes – sometimes ten – were required to pass an individual message from an observer through a Warning Centre to Horse Guards.[106] Such delays were acceptable in the Zeppelin era. They were intolerable in 1917, given the speed of German airplanes and the limited degree of forewarning. LADA required a small but dedicated communication system. By May 1918 it had one. Direct landlines linked every unit and command, while R/T and wireless provided ground-to-air communication. Landlines connected Lada control to squadron headquarters and to a WT transmitter near Biggin Hill, which could contact squadron leaders in the air. R/T linked all fighters in the sky. From Ashmore's order that any squadron despatch a patrol to the time that one took off, anywhere between thirty seconds to five minutes passed (on average two minutes) – as against the fifteen minutes required for the purpose in May 1917. Meanwhile, 'wireless trackers' were intended to observe intruders and report their course

---

[104] Wallace, *Biggin Hill*, pp. 43–46; Cole and Cheesman, *Air Defence*, pp. 421–23; minute by Major Simon, 31 Jan. 1920, PRO, WO 32/3120.

[105] Rawlinson, *Defence of London*, pp. 158–62, 167–87.

[106] Fredette, *Sky on Fire*, p. 180.

to Lada control, sub-controls and squadrons. Although this idea never worked, the system of communications was sophisticated and sufficient to the task.[107]

Ashmore's system of air defence grew like a child – unevenly: some characteristics mature, others infantile. LADA easily quashed daylight raids but had mixed success against night attacks. In order to match the heaviest blows Bombengeschwader 3 could strike, LADA turned the skies over London into an elaborate killing zone. Searchlights and balloon aprons covered certain areas and altitudes while an elaborate procedure could guide anti-aircraft barrages onto others. The aim was to force night raiders to abandon formations – which, in fact, did not exist in the first place. Moreover, the difficulty in replacing losses often reduced the enemy's heaviest blows to mere pinpricks. A grand total of sixteen aircraft attacked Britain between 30 January–18 May 1918. Hence, LADA sometimes was bound to strain after a gnat. On 17 February 1918, sixty-nine fighters and 286 guns responded to an attack by one Riesenflugzeug. Germany, however, planned to start another and more dangerous bombing offensive. This had to be matched and LADA did so.

LADA did not destroy a single German raider during the first three months of the night campaign. From 6 December 1917 to 7/8 March 1918, however, 6 of the 53 aircraft (or 11 per cent) which bombed Britain were shot down. The next and last raid, of 19 May 1918, the only large one launched after LADA achieved maturity, was a defensive triumph – 14 per cent of the forth-three raiders (six) were lost in action and another 7 per cent (three) in accidents.[108] During a major exercise of September 1918, LADA's C³I system worked remarkably well. Only thirty seconds passed between any ground observation of an aircraft and the moment it was reported to Ashmore. Aeroplanes took off within a few minutes of his order and within twenty minutes reached 10,000 feet, the standard height for interception. The best of them, Sopwith Camels and Bristol Fighters, reached 20,000 feet in fifty and seventy-five minutes. Higgins was considering how to organise ground-directed interceptions at that altitude, which in technical terms would have been a simple problem. R/T worked well: through a simple code, pilots were directed to fly at a given altitude toward a specific position along their patrol line. Ashmore concluded that R/T would increase fourfold the interception ratio of his aircraft, which seems plausible. That is, about 10 per cent of fighters launched would encounter intruders and 25 per cent of the enemy would be intercepted. All other things remaining equal, this probably would have tripled the enemy's wastage from combat. Together with accidents, that

---

[107] Memo by ADGB, April 1930, PRO, AIR 5/768; Ashmore, *Air Defence*, pp. 92–93; Cole and Cheesman, *Air Defence*, pp. 92–96, passim; Wallace, *Biggin Hill*, p. 24.

[108] The figures are derived from Ashmore, *Air Defence*, pp. 172–74, corrected by reference to Cole and Cheesman, *Air Defence*.

would have doubled their loss rate per mission.[109] This system was never tested in anger; perhaps it would not have worked with perfect efficiency. But it clearly would have worked well. This mixture of performance and promise was a fitting end to the first Battle of Britain.

Air historians often argue that this battle significantly affected the war and did so heavily in Germany's favour.[110] These arguments are dubious. Throughout the entire campaign, Britain lost forty-five airplanes and twenty-eight aircrew, all to accidents. German losses were far higher – almost thirty times more aircrew, to take the extreme example. 40 per cent of airshipcrew, or 369 men, died in action, two thirds of whom were a victim of British defences (including those destroyed over France in the aftermath of the 'silent raid'). Of seventy-three airships, 33 per cent were scraped for obsolescence (an indirect victim of British defences), seventeen were destroyed in air combat and twenty-one wrecked through other causes, most of which involved the indirect effect of combat damage. Barely ten airships survived to see the Armistice. Bombengeschwader 3 was destroyed twice over against Britain. Sixty-one of its Gothas – 16 per cent of every one which took off against Britain – were destroyed, twenty-four in action and thirty-seven through accident. 225 of its aircrew died or went missing, though part of these losses were incurred over the Western Front. Two Riesenflugzeuge were destroyed in accidents linked to operations against Britain. By the spring of 1918 German strategic bombing ended, because Germany was running out of strategic bombers.[111]

These sacrifices were incurred for little gain, whether calculated in absolute or relative terms. Between 1915–18, 270 tons of bombs fell on Britain. These killed 1414 people, mostly civilians, and damaged morale

---

[109] Cole and Cheesman, *Air Defence*, p. 417, passim; Ashmore, *Air Defence*, pp. 95, 110–12; Sutton, *Raiders Approach!*, p. 57.

[110] For examples of this approach, see Jones, *War in the Air*, v, pp. 153–59 passim; Bushby, *Air Defence*, pp. 74–75; Cuneo, *Air Weapon*, pp. 360–61; and Sydney Wise, 'The Royal Air Force and the Origins of Strategic Bombing', in Travers and Archer (eds), *Men at War*, pp. 151–58. Unlike other accounts, Cole and Cheesman, *Air Defence*, pp. 446–51, and Robinson, *Combat*, pp. 345–50, carefully compute the balance of profit and loss in the airship and airplane campaigns. Various technical factors, however, make such comparisons difficult. Virtually all British human losses were pilots, while only 33 per cent of Gotha aircrew had that status, and the value of airship crew was radically different from that of aeroplanes. The strength in equipment and personnel of units involved in the campaign varied significantly month to month. Similarly, the difference between establishment and efficient strength of squadrons, is sometimes staggering: on 8 June 1918, for example, air defence forces throughout Britain had 376 fighter aircraft on establishment of which only 166 were efficient. H.A. Jones, *The War in the Air: Being the Story of the Part Played in the Great War by the Royal Air Force. Appendices* (Oxford, 1937), pp. 171–72. The best indicators, and those used in this analysis, are efficient aircraft and aircrew possessed by squadrons, and personnel and equipment in ground crew or ground defences.

[111] Cole and Cheesman, *Air Defence*; Robinson, 'Zeppelin Intelligence'; Fredette, *Sky on Fire*, p. 218; and Haddow and Grosz, *German Giants*, p. 61, are the best sources for German losses.

and production in an insignificant manner.[112] The bombers also tied down British resources, but the balance between attacker and defender in what Winston Churchill called the cost to 'national life-energy' was closely drawn.[113] This issue merits greater discussion than it conventionally receives.

Germany devoted its best aircrew and equipment to the campaign. Throughout 1917–18, counting replacements, perhaps a hundred Gothas, fifteen Riesenflugzeuge and thirty Zeppelins conducted strategic bombing. Against them, Britain committed to air defence 225 experienced but not outstanding aircrew flying 200 small aircraft, with a handful of replacements. Given the greater structure weight of its aircraft, Germany may have devoted five times the resources of aeronautical industry to the campaign than Britain. It certainly devoted twice the strength in aircrew. On average during 1917–18, 340 German aircrew served in seventeen Zeppelins, eighty in ten Riesenflugzeuge and 117 in thirty-nine Gothas.[114] Germany also committed more ground crew to the campaign. The Riesenflugzeuge absorbed 1750 support personnel – 50 per cent of the entire strength in ground crew for home defence. The Zeppelins used even more. Of course, other aspects of air defence, such as anti-aircraft and searchlight units, required 14,000 men on average during 1917–18, about the engineer and artillery establishments for two divisions. Yet roughly half of these men were medically unfit for service overseas.

Granted, these British units were completely absorbed in home defence while the German ones handled both strategic bombing and other tasks which did tie down further British forces. Still, the material investment in the Battle of Britain must be seen as a tie, which for Germany in a war of attrition was a loss. Above all, this investment was minor. Home defence absorbed as many anti-aircraft guns as the BEF possessed, but then the Army had no particular need for more. Air historians often note that after its advances of August 1918, the BEF requested additional anti-aircraft guns to defend occupied areas and did not receive them because they were used in home defence. This was true. It was also irrelevant to the war. Similarly, air defence absorbed twelve squadrons which might have served elsewhere, while the RAF had 100 squadrons in France. This figure seems impressive, but air defence was far cheaper than might seem to be the case. Losses among its personnel were minuscule – on the Western Front the RAF frequently lost 225 pilots per month. Every pilot involved in home defence during 1917–18 would have sufficed to maintain one RAF squadron for continual service on the Western Front. Accounting for the issue of replacement of losses, the strategic air campaign may

---

[112] The best sources for damage on British civilians and industry are Jones, *War in the Air*, iii, pp. 382–83; v, pp. 474–79.

[113] Jones, *War in the Air: Appendices*, pp. 18–19.

[114] Ibid., pp. 154, 172, 160–65, is the best source for the British side. See n. 111 above for the German side.

have absorbed the British resources needed to maintain the aircrew of one RAF squadron and the groundcrew of twelve squadrons and the engineering and artillery strength of perhaps one half of one division; and the equivalent of the aircrew of two German squadrons and the groundcrew of fifteen squadrons. In material terms this was a draw. It was irrelevant to a war which turned on the ability to deploy millions of soldiers and millions of tons of steel on the battlefield.

Air defence did its duty during the first Battle of Britain, and this shaped victory during the second and more celebrated one. LADA in 1918 was structurally identical to Fighter Command in 1940 with but a few exceptions: two new features, radar and the filtering room to eliminate discrepancies and duplications in reports sent to the commander, alongside better equipment for R/T and sound location and some reorganisation in Operations Rooms. Historians have recognised that the model of LADA influenced Fighter Command. They have not adequately described the process of this influence.[115] That was most simple in the realm of command, control and communications. Whenever the Air Staff considered these issues, it followed solutions pioneered by LADA, though of course technology and organisational details often varied significantly. The Air Ministry first considered this issue in 1924. It was then suggested that landlines should bind together signals intelligence services, direction finding stations (descendants of the 'silent' system, to guide defending fighters), Air Defence Command, Groups, squadrons and other government departments. Fighting Area Headquarters would have direct R/T communication to squadrons while all fighters would be equipped with R/T. This was simply a variant of LADA. Though no immediate decision was taken on these proposals, over the next decade they were adopted in a piecemeal fashion. In particular, after the issue had been relegated to the backburner since 1919, R/T gradually became standard issue for fighter aircraft. This was a more fundamental step than the development of radar, although admittedly both of these devices were essential for British survival during 1940.[116]

In other areas, LADA's influence on Fighter Command was more peculiar. LADA's organisation was well known, and described in several books, including the RAF's official history. The War Office adopted this system for the ground components of air defence – indeed, for several years Ashmore controlled that organisation. With some reluctance, the Air Ministry also adopted LADA as the technical model for fighter

[115] Fredette, *Sky on Fire*, p. 8; Bushby, *Air Defence*, p. 74; Winslow, *Forewarned is Forearmed*, pp. 19–24. An exception to this rule is the useful account in Sutton, *Raiders Approach!*, pp. 71–83.

[116] Memorandum by MacNeece, 9 May 1924, and minutes by Blandy (21 May 1924) and Trenchard (27 July 1924), PRO, AIR 5/371. Material on the development of the communication system for Fighter Command can be found in AIR 2/2643, AIR 16/837–38; PRO, T 161/1103; and Sutton, *Raiders Approach!*, pp. 70–83.

defence, and this fact was ultimately of fundamental significance. As a staff officer in Air Defence Great Britain (ADGB) during 1926–27, Keith Park acquired expert tuition in the techniques of the topic from both Ashmore and H.V. Holt, Higgins' predecessor as Wing-Commander in strategic air defence during 1916–17. A decade later Park became a main craftsman in the creation of Fighter Command. LADA was the model in his mind and it was also the basis for the organisation he inherited.[117]

In a broader sense, conversely, until the later 1930s the Air Ministry ignored the lessons and the promise of LADA. These contradicted its doctrine, of which Ashmore was a public critic. In particular, he argued that the RAF's main figures misunderstood strategic air defence because they viewed it through the prism of operations on the narrow Western Front. The dominant civilian official within the Air Ministry, Christopher Bullock, privately shared that view.[118] In any case, from the same inconclusive base of evidence, RAF officers extrapolated greater things for the attack than the defence. During 1923–24, all senior officers of the RAF debated the theory and practice of strategic air warfare. A fair consensus emerged among them. Virtually alone on one extreme, the Chief of the Air Staff, Hugh Trenchard, harnessed his older view that air defence was impossible to a newfound belief that strategic bombing could single handedly win a war. On the other end a middle level officer, J.A. Chamier, offered this remarkably prescient view:

> To my mind in an air war if it comes five to ten years hence the improvements in sound locating and W/T or R/T will cause all enemy's attacks to be closely followed and aircraft of the defence concentrated to meet them. There will be less and less evasion and more and more fighting to reach one's objective . . . I do not deny that the objective may well be something which is not the enemy air force as a matter of the first importance, but the enemy air force and the importance of air superiority is in the picture [very much so!]. . .

Two important figures, Bullock and Geoffrey Salmond, the Air Member for Supply and Research, held similar if less strong views. Salmond, for example, argued that 'developments in R/T should make it feasible for all [fighter] machines in the air to concentrate at whatever height the enemy's formations are found within two or three minutes'. By 1932, as commander of ADGB, Salmond held that R/T and other technical improvements would allow an interception ratio of 50 per cent. This was not an insubstantial degree of success – indeed, it roughly equalled the

---

[117] Vincent Orange, *A Biography of Air Chief Marshal Sir Keith Park* (London, 1984), pp. 49–50. See also PRO, CID, paper 118-A, CAB 3/4 and Neil Young; cf. AIR 16/195.

[118] Ashmore, *Air Defence*, pp. 147–48; minute to Game, undated and unsigned but July 23 and by Bullock, according to internal evidence, AIR 19/92.

interception ratios achieved in Fighter Command exercises during 1939 with the advantage of radar.[119]

Neither of these extremes, however, dominated RAF doctrine about strategic air defence. That was formulated by the RAF's expert in the topic and Ashmore's RAF commander, T.C.R. Higgins. While developments in R/T and sound locators would help air defence, Higgins concluded, it could never achieve efficiency, effectiveness, economy or concentration of force. Air defence would inflict a slow and low rate of attrition rather than catastrophic losses for the attacker. In particular, Higgins made this central point:

> The nature of Air Warfare makes it impossible to 'stage' a set piece battle between the two opposing fleets of fighting aeroplanes, but all the same a daily and nightly battle would be fought somewhere in the vicinity of the respective capitals with the probable result that one or the other would eventually obtain a fighting superiority and consequently a bombing superiority.[120]

Higgins' views resounded through the RAF over the next fifteen years. In 1924 the Air Staff concluded, 'it may be stated as a principle that the bombing squadrons should be as numerous as possible and the fighters as few as popular opinion and the necessity for defending vital objectives will permit'.[121] This is not to say that the Air Ministry ignored the need for fighters – far from it. Throughout the inter-war years British fighter aircraft and their equipment always lay at the state of the art and in great numbers. Expansion of that quantity and quality figured in all of the RAF's schemes for air rearmament. The point is that the Air Ministry significantly misunderstood the power of strategic air defence and the value of fighters against bombers and thus failed to allocate its resources with full efficiency.

One might argue that these views were essentially correct: that only the advent of radar allowed strategic air defence to be effective.[122] There is some truth to this argument but not the whole truth. In 1918, after all, LADA routinely downed 10 per cent of intruders in British airspace on every mission. Chamier, Ashmore and Salmond argued that the addition of R/T to the equation would increase the power of air defence, and

[119] Meeting in CAS's Room, 26 July 1923, minute to Game, undated and unsigned but July 23 and by Bullock, according to internal evidence, PRO, AIR 19/92; Chamier to Steel, 10 Jan. 1924, AIR 5/328; Sutton, *Raiders Approach!*, p. 71; Orange, *Sir Keith Park*, p. 75.

[120] Higgins to DCAS, 12 June 1923, AIR 5/328; Higgins to AMSR, 25 Jan. 1924; and memorandum, undated, 'Lecture to RAF Staff College', PRO, AIR 5/954; memo by ADGB, April 1930, AIR 5/768.

[121] Air Staff Memorandum, 11 A of 1924, PRO, AIR 5/328. For an important discussion of the formulation and transmission of doctrine, cf. Allan D. English, 'The RAF Staff College and the Evolution of British Strategic Bombing Policy, 1922–1929', *Journal of Strategic Studies*, 16 (1993), pp. 408–31.

[122] Malcolm Smith, *British Air Strategy*; and Ferris, 'French Air Menace', p. 69, both make statements of this sort.

precisely that did happen in British air exercises between the late 1920s and mid 1930s. These exercises were, of course, notoriously unrealistic, nor is interception the only factor in air defence. None the less, it is an indicative fact; and the interception rate against individual night raiders during these manoeuvres was far higher than had been true during 1917–18: 57 per cent during the 1931 exercises and 79 per cent in those of 1932. Daylight raiders operating both individually and in formation were also intercepted with remarkable ease.[123]

Nor should one distort the role of radar in strategic air defence. Ground observation provided good tactical intelligence during the first and the second Battles of Britain, though less than radar. At the operational level, radar never matched the value of signals intelligence. In 1946 'Beppo' Schmidt, chief of German night fighter defences during 1943–45, held that because of its unique ability to provide forewarning, signals and electronic intelligence had surpassed radar in value for German air defence.[124] Between the wars, however, the RAF underestimated the value of ground observation and wireless intelligence in air warfare. In particular, it recognised the use of signals intelligence as a source for strategic but not for operational information. From the middle 1930s, traffic analysis and the penetration of low-grade codes allowed the RAF to reconstruct the strength and order of battle of the Luftwaffe.[125] Against this, the RAF did misunderstand the operational value of wireless intelligence, and for one reason. It believed that bombers could maintain complete wireless silence before and during any raid.[126] Significantly, in 1923, when Higgins lectured on intelligence in strategic air defence to the RAF Staff College, he did not even mention signals intelligence.[127]

Such views were wrong and they had costs. They left the RAF unready for signals intelligence in 1939 and woefully unprepared for signals security. Gradually in 1940, the RAF discovered that simple forms of signals intelligence provided better strategic and operational material than had been true during the Great War; fortunately it learned these lessons in time to bring wireless intelligence alongside radar and ground observation

[123] US Military Attaché, London, report no. 30913, 31 July 1931, RG 168/2083–1280; National Archives, Washington DC; *The Times*, 'Trade and Engineering Supplement', 13 Aug. 1932, 'Mass Bombing Attacks: Brief Experiment of the Air Exercises'.

[124] ADI (K), report no. 416/1945, PRO, AIR 4/1394. Winslow, *Forewarned is Forearmed*, pp. 21–48, offers a useful account of the Royal Observer Corps between the wars. It outlines generally the usually overlooked value of ground observation as an intelligence source.

[125] F.H. Hinsley, E.E. Thomas, C.F.G. Ransom and R.C. Knight, *British Intelligence in the Second World War: Its Influence on Strategy and Operations*, i (London, 1979), pp. 14–15, 23.

[126] ADGB to OC Wessex Bombing Area, 23 March 1931, PRO, AIR 16/193.

[127] Higgins to AMSR, 25 Jan. 1924, and memorandum undated 'Lecture to RAF Staff College', PRO, AIR 5/954.

to the aid of air defence during the second Battle of Britain.[128] By the spring of 1941, the RAF's Y station at Cheadle reported: 'The enemy employs a rigid W/T procedure and his operators carry a great deal of information in the air, from which our "Y" Service have been able to work out the whole of his operational W/T procedure – i.e. he relies on a code which we have broken'.[129] In these instances, luck saved Britain in time: this did not happen elsewhere. Wireless silence was impossible for air forces, and failings in the RAF's signals security gave fundamental advantages to German air defence until 1944.[130]

During the interwar years, the RAF stood far from perfection in strategic air defence; but still it stood ahead of any other air force. However close the shave, moreover, all was right on the night. In 1937, acting primarily for financial reasons, civilians forced the Air Ministry to assign preparations for defence in strategic air warfare priority over those for offence. When ordered to allocate resources in favour of fighters and to strengthen its system of strategic air defence, the RAF knew what to do and did it well. Air defence between 1938–40 was not simply a matter of gallant pilots, good machines and wizard boffins, but, above all, of effective organisation and C³I. In this sphere, Fighter Command acted on the well known model of LADA. Hugh Dowding and Keith Park simply picked up from where Ashmore had left off. LADA's greatest victory occurred not in 1918 but 1940.

---

[128] 'RAF Wireless Intelligence Service Periodical Summary', 6 March 1940, PRO, AIR 20/411. The best account of intelligence and air defence in 1940 is Sebastian Cox, 'A Comparative Analysis of RAF and Luftwaffe Intelligence in the Battle of Britain, 1940', in Michael Handel (ed.), *Intelligence and Military Operations* (London, 1990), pp. 425–43.

[129] 'Notes on 2 Group Cheadle Organisation', undated but spring 1941, PRO, AIR 20/411.

[130] 'Security of RAF Signal Communication', no author cited and undated but *c.* December 1944 according to internal evidence, PRO, AIR 20/1531. Two useful accounts of the intelligence sources of the Luftwaffe, especially against the Allied strategic bombing campaign, are memorandum by A.1.12/USAFE, 21 Dec. 1945, AIR 40/2249; and Horst Boog, 'German Air Intelligence in the Second World War', in Handel (ed.), *Intelligence and Military Operations*, pp. 350–424.

3

Failures of Intelligence: The Retreat to the Hindenburg Line and the March 1918 Offensive

David French

During the last fifteen years the publication of various official and unofficial histories of the achievements of British intelligence during the Second World War has caused historians of that conflict to begin a major reassessment of the British war effort between 1939 and 1945.[1] This reassessment has included a series of path-breaking studies of the ways in which the British employed operational and strategic deception.[2] In contrast, the history of British intelligence during the First World War and its impact upon British strategy still remains largely, although not entirely, unwritten. Following the release of documents to the Public Record Office in the 1970s, Patrick Beesly was able to write an excellent history of the work of the Admiralty's signals intelligence system, Michael Occleshaw has analysed the bureaucratic structures of military intelligence on the Western Front and John Ferris has published a collection of documents with a scholarly commentary illuminating the work of the British Army's signals intelligence units.[3] Little, however, has been published about the way in which the British used deception as a way of masking their

---

[1] F.H. Hinsley et al., *British Intelligence in the Second World War* (London, 1979, 1981, 1984), vols i–iii; R. Bennett, *Ultra in the West: The Normandy Campaign of 1944–45* (London, 1979); P. Beesly, *Very Special Intelligence: The Story of the Admiralty's Operational Intelligence Centre, 1939–1945* (London, 1977).

[2] M. Howard, *British Intelligence in the Second World War, v, Strategic Deception* (London, 1990); J.P. Campbell, 'Operation Starkey 1943: "A Piece of Harmless Playacting"', in M. Handel (ed.), *Strategic and Operational Deception in the Second World War* (London, 1987), pp. 92–113; T.L. Cubbage, 'The Success of Operation Fortitude: Hesketh's History of Strategic Deception', ibid., pp. 327–46; C.G. Cruickshank, *Deception in World War Two* (Oxford, 1979).

[3] P. Beesly, *Room 40: British Naval Intelligence, 1914–1918* (London, 1982); M.E. Occleshaw, *Armour against Fate: British Military Intelligence in the First World War* (London, 1989); M.E. Occleshaw, 'The "Stab in the Back": Myth or Reality?', *Journal of the Royal United Services Institute for Defence Studies*, 130 (1985), pp. 49–54; J. Ferris (ed.), *The British Army and Signals Intelligence during the First World War* (London, 1992). See also R. Popplewell, 'British Intelligence in Mesopotamia, 1914–1916', in M. Handel (ed.), *Intelligence and Military Operations* (London, 1990), pp. 139–72.

intentions from their enemies.[4] Perhaps historians have not been drawn to this subject because it runs so much counter to the still all-too-popular notion that the British Army was led by 'donkeys' who were too lacking in subtlety to devise such measures.

The purpose of this essay is to examine an area of historical investigation which has received even less exploration by recent historians of the First World War, namely those occasions on which the British themselves were deceived by deceptions perpetrated by their enemies. The two examples which have been chosen are the retreat which the German Army began in February 1917 to the 'Hindenburg Line', or more properly the *Siegfriedstellung* and the mounting by the Germans of their Spring Offensive in March 1918. They have been chosen both because of their strategic significance and because the official history of the war on the Western Front presents a partial and incomplete account of the failure of the British to predict the German's intentions.

At the end of February 1917 the German Army conducted an un-expected and voluntary retreat on the Western Front, abandoning the old Somme battlefield and withdrawing to a shorter and more powerful defensive position which was in places as much as twenty miles behind their former front line. In doing so they pre-empted the Spring Offensive which the Anglo-French Armies had hoped to mount. When he wrote his *War Memoirs* David Lloyd George was icily contemptuous of the inability of the Allied generals to predict the Germans' actions. 'It is', he wrote, 'a reflexion on the French and British Staffs that the Germans were able to complete the tremendous arrangements necessary for such a withdrawal [to the Hindenburg line] without any apprehension of the move on the part of their opponents.'[5] In 1940 Captain Cyril Falls, author of the volume of the official history which examined events on the Western Front in the opening months of 1917, tried to defend the British Staff by claiming that as early as October and November 1916 reports from the Royal Flying Corps (RFC) and escaped prisoners-of-war had indicated that the Germans were constructing a strong new defensive position some miles behind their existing front line. But he had to admit that 'it was months before anything definite was known of the remainder of its course'.[6] In exculpation he claimed that two of the reasons for their

[4] Some significant exceptions are Ferris (ed.), *The British Army and Signals Intelligence*, ch. 5, passim; J. Ferris, 'The British Army and Signals Intelligence in the Field during the First World War', *Intelligence and National Security*, 3 (1988), pp. 41–42; Y. Sheffy, 'Institutionalized Deception and Perception Reinforcement: Allenby's Campaigns in Palestine, 1917–1918', in M. Handel (ed.), *Intelligence and Military Operations* (London, 1990), pp. 173–238; R. Prior and T. Wilson, *Command on the Western Front: The Military Career of Sir Henry Rawlinson, 1914–1918* (Oxford, 1992), p. 304.

[5] D. Lloyd George, *War Memoirs* (London, 1938), ii, p. 898.

[6] C. Falls, *History of the Great War: Military Operations France and Belgium, 1917. The German Retreat to the Hindenburg Line and the Battle of Arras* (London, 1940), p. 87.

ignorance were beyond the control of the British staff. Exceptionally wet and foggy weather in the winter of 1916/17 hampered long-range aerial reconnaissance and the work of those aircraft which were despatched was hampered by the superiority which the German Flying Corps enjoyed in the six months to April 1917, thanks to the possession of better machines than their British counterparts.[7] Even Falls had to admit that the third reason why the British were slow to discover the full extent and purpose of the new line was because they were not looking for it. 'There was', he concluded, 'no evidence that any special urgency was attributed by GHQ or the Armies concerned to the discovery of the exact course of the Hindenburg line.'[8] As a result Sir Hubert Gough's biographer could record that when the German withdrawal began on the front of the British Fifth Army 'Gough did not know what the enemy was doing'.[9] It was not until 25 February 1917, when the Germans had actually begun their withdrawal, that the British were able to plot the full extent of the new defensive system. More recent studies of British operations on the Western Front, whilst exploring the strategic significance of the German withdrawal, have passed over in silence the failure of British intelligence to predict the German operation before it began.[10]

The French Commander-in-Chief in the spring of 1917, General Nivelle, stubbornly refused to alter his plans and in April insisted on attacking along the Chemin des Dames. The outcome was that the French Army suffered another 100,000 casualties and a large part of the French Army, strainedd beyond endurance after nearly three years of heavy losses, mutinied. The collapse of Nivelle's plan, which had been strongly supported by Lloyd George, allowed Haig to revert to his long-cherished plan for an offensive at Ypres designed to drive the Germans away from the Belgium coast. By the end of 1917 the Germans were still in occupation of the Belgium coast, Haig's army had suffered over 400,000 casualties and the Germans were preparing for their own offensive in the west which began on 21 March 1918. The initial German offensive fell most fiercely upon the southernmost part of Haig's line, destroying Sir Hubert Gough's Fifth Army and threatening at one point to break the link between the British and French Armies. So close did the Germans come to success that by June 1918 the British naval and military authorities were

---

[7] This argument was repeated by the official historian of the war in the air. See H.A. Jones, *The War in the Air: Being the Story of the Part Played in the Great War by the Royal Air Force* (Oxford, 1931), iii, p. 305.

[8] Falls, *History of the Great War: Military Operations France and Belgium, 1917)*, p. 88.

[9] A. Farrar-Hockley, *Goughie* (London, 1975), p. 204.

[10] J. Terraine, *Douglas Haig: The Educated Soldier* (London, 1963), pp. 264–65; G. de Groot, *Douglas Haig, 1861–1928* (London, 1988), pp. 306–7.

preparing secret contingency plans to evacuate the British Expeditionary Force (BEF) from Dunkirk.[11]

The principal scapegoat for the British defeat was Gough, who was dismissed from command of the Fifth Army shortly after the offensive began. Writing in 1954 and still bitter at his dismissal he insisted that all the indications were that when the German offensive came, it would be against the fronts of his own army and that of Sir Julian Byng's Third Army to his north.[12] He argued that GHQ had given him too few troops because they refused to accept the evidence presented to them by his own intelligence staff and were deceived by a clever German deception plan.

> The false rumours and the mistaken fear that Ludendorff was planning either to attack the British left and the Channel ports, or that he intended to drive in the French right, violating the neutrality of Switzerland if necessary, should not have deceived anyone. However, they led both Pétain and Haig to wrong conclusions.[13]

In his volume in the official history series dealing with early months of 1918, Fall's superior and the head of the Historical Section of the Committee of Imperial Defence, Sir James Edmonds, dismissed this explanation in a footnote.[14] On the contrary, he argued that British intelligence had been much more successful in discerning German intentions in the spring of 1918 than they had been in the spring of 1917. He claimed that they recognised that, following the Russian collapse and the Bolshevik Revolution in November 1917, the Germans were bound to concentrate the maximum possible number of divisions in the west and mount a major offensive against the Anglo-French forces holding the line in France and Flanders. Haig disposed of his troops in the way he did because of geography and the expectation of French assistance. North of the River Scarpe, where his front line was only 5 miles from the coast, Haig could not afford to follow a policy of elastic defence and fight a series of delaying actions. If the Channel ports fell to the Germans it would 'be disastrous for the British Armies, and, moreover, would give the enemy such a measure of control over the English Channel as might go far towards crippling the sea-borne traffic on which the existence of England depended'.[15] But south of the Scarpe, provided the

---

[11] PRO, ADM 116/1603. HHDT, naval aspects of evacuating the BEF from France, 20 June 1918; PRO, ADM 116/1603. Geddes to Lloyd George, 16 July 1918.

[12] Sir J.E. Edmonds, *History of the Great War: Military Operations France and Belgium, 1918* (London, 1936), i, pp. 96–97, 109-110.

[13] Sir H. Gough, *Soldiering On: Being the Memoirs of General Sir Hubert Gough* (London, 1954), p. 149.

[14] Edmonds, *History of the Great War: Military Operations France and Belgium, 1918* i, p. 106, n. 3.

[15] Ibid., i, pp. 93–94.

Germans did not advance so far as to capture the vital railway junction of Amiens, the BEF could afford to give ground without uncovering anything vital. Consequently, whilst Haig concentrated a comparatively large number of divisions on the fronts of his First and Second Armies holding the northern portion of the line, the divisions holding the lines of the Third and particularly the Fifth Armies to the south, were more thinly spread.[16] Only as an afterthought did he mention: 'The only questions still in doubt on the eve of the offensive were whether the first attack would be the main effort or merely a preparatory one, and whether or not the French would be attacked simultaneously.'[17] Sir Julian Byng's biographer was equally in no doubt that by January 1918 it was 'obvious to all' that the Germans planned a major offensive against the British in the spring. A recent history of British military intelligence on the Western Front was equally certain that the Director of Military Intelligence at the War Office predicted precisely the date, time and location of the offensive.[18]

Successfully predicting the German's intentions depended upon three things. It rested upon the ability of intelligence collecting agencies to provide sufficient raw data to form the basis of a balanced assessment of the situation. It depended upon the ability of intelligence analysts to distinguish between false information ('noise') and accurate information ('signals'). And it depended upon the willingness of British policy-makers to accept and act upon the estimates of the German's intentions which were fed to them by their intelligence staffs.[19] By 1917–18 the British had developed a plethora of intelligence collecting agencies.

In France a great deal of raw intelligence was collected at corps level and below. Intelligence officers at the front tapped a number of sources in order to create a picture of the German's capabilities and intentions. These included the interrogation of prisoners and deserters, the examination of captured documents, reconnaissance and observation both from the ground and from aircraft and aerial photography.[20] For example, troops serving in the trenches were encouraged to forward reports to their battalion and divisional intelligence officers on every small

[16] Terraine, *Douglas Haig*, p. 400.

[17] Edmonds, *History of the Great War: Military Operations France and Belgium, 1918*, i, p. 110.

[18] J. Williams, *Byng of Vimy: General and Governor General* (London, 1983), p. 213; Occleshaw, *Armour against Fate*, p. 246.

[19] M. Handel, 'The Politics of intelligence', in M. Handel, *War, Strategy and Intelligence*, pp. 187–89.

[20] PRO, WO 106/1550. Brigadier-General Mitchell to DMI, 30 May 1919; Cavalry Corps – Syllabus of First Intelligence course, *c.* 18 Nov. 1916, LHCMA, Benson Papers, A/1/8; Occleshaw, *Armour against Fate*, pp. 35–143.

detail they could glean about the German units serving opposite them.[21] Intelligence officers interrogating prisoners were enjoined to do so as soon after they were captured as possible in the hope that, dazed from the battlefield, they would give away valuable information. In an ideal situation all prisoners were interrogated on two or three separate occasions to discover not only their name and rank but also their battalion, regiment and division and the position of neighbouring units, their equipment and future plans.[22] Each of these sources had its drawback. Observations made from the air and photographs taken from aircraft had the advantage of providing very timely information, providing that observers and analysts were not deceived by enemy camouflage. Experience in France suggested that prisoners were generally a reliable source of information and usually answered questions truthfully if they were questioned by an officer, because of the strict discipline they were used to in their own army.[23] German prisoners were likely to be better informed about their own units than were the British troops facing them but any information they might provide would probably be at least twelve hours out of date. Captured documents usually provided accurate information but were liable to be even more out of date – it was rare to find corps or army orders as far forward as captured battalion headquarters.[24]

Other intelligence gathering agencies were organised at a higher level. Behind the German lines the British had several, often competing, networks of secret agents. The Secret Service which was established in 1909 had a triple allegiance – to the Foreign Office, the War Office and the Admiralty. In 1914 for practical and administrative purposes it was placed under the Directorate of Military Operations at the War Office. According to Sir Eric Drummond, who as the Foreign Secretary's private secretary also acted as the official point of contact between the Foreign Office and the Secret Service, 'There is complete co-ordination between "C" [ummings, the head of the Secret Service] and the Foreign Office' and '"C"'s instructions are generally framed as wide as possible.'[25] Cummings' organisation ran in parallel, and frequently in competition, with similar

[21] 59 (North Midland) Division, 'Some Notes on Intelligence Regulations and Duties', 15 Sept. 1915, LHCMA, Benson Papers, A1/1.

[22] Intelligence Section, Home Defence Directorate, War Office, instructions regarding examination of prisoners by staff officers, intelligence Corps officers or other selected officers, Sept. 1915. LHCMA, Benson Papers, A/1/2.

[23] PRO, WO 106/1550. Brigadier-General H.C. Mitchell, BG (I), British Expeditionary Force, Italy, to DMI, War Office, 30 May 1919.

[24] Cavalry Corps, syllabus of first intelligence course, 18–25 Nov. 1916, LHCMA, Benson Papers, A/1/8; PRO, WO 106/1550. Brigadier-General H.C. Mitchell, BG (I), British Expeditionary Force, Italy, to DMI, War Office, 30 May 1919.

[25] PRO, FO 800/212, Drummond to Balfour, 19 Nov. 1917.

networks organised by GHQ.[26] It was not until February 1917 that the danger that the British might receive the same information from two or more networks was obviated when GHQ Intelligence and the War Office agreed that henceforth all reports, whatever their origin, must pass through a single clearing-house. Some effort was also made to prevent overlap by laying down the geographical limits for each organisation. The War Office reserved for itself the right to operate networks east of a line Antwerp–Brussels–Namur whilst GHQ had the right to operate networks in the rest of Belgium.[27]

Before the war Military Attachés had been forbidden to engage openly in espionage. But their subservience to the Foreign Office dwindled as the war progressed. In April 1915 Kitchener successfully insisted that attachés must have the right to communicate directly with the War Office. They no longer had to despatch their reports through their ambassadors and they began to develop their own intelligence networks.[28] The Foreign Office could only grit its teeth. In May 1917 Lord Hardinge, the Permanent Undersecretary at the Foreign Office, confessed that 'Military and Naval attachés are everywhere rather difficult to manage just now, and we are having trouble with them elsewhere'.[29] The British legations in Holland, Denmark, Switzerland and Norway became listening-posts busy gleaning every scrap of information they could gather from the Central Powers. Lloyd George described The Hague as 'one of the keyholes of Germany'.[30] Some of their methods were fairly innocuous. In Copenhagen Lieutenant-Colonel A.L.H. Wade frequently questioned neutral travellers about conditions in Germany.[31] The Military Attaché at The Hague learnt of large-scale German troop movements to the Russian Front in April 1917 from a Dutch doctor recently returned from Germany.[32] Lieutenant-Colonel Wyndham, the Military Attaché in Berne maintained contact with the head of the Swiss General Staff, who sometimes gave him information supplied by his 'very complete system of secret service in Germany'.[33] Attachés also exchanged information with their Allied counterparts. In 1918 Wade also gathered reliable information from 'Max' who 'is head of Zionist organization in Copenhagen'.[34] But

[26] Occleshaw, *Armour against Fate*, pp. 146–47; D. French, 'Sir John French's Secret Service in France, 1914–1915', *Journal of Strategic Studies*, 7 (1984), pp. 423–40.

[27] PRO, WO 106/45. Colonel Drake, Intelligence, (B) BEF, France, from January 1917 to April 1919, 5 May 1919.

[28] PRO, FO 800/175/Misc/15/2, Grey to Bertie, 22 April 1915.

[29] PRO, FO 800/191/17/42, Hardinge to Bertie, 21 May 1917.

[30] Lloyd George to Balfour, 29 Dec. 1916, H[ouse of] L[ords] R[ecord] O[ffice] Lloyd George Papers, F/3/1/6.

[31] See, for example, PRO, FO 371/3078/27817. Paget to FO, 4 Feb. 1917.

[32] PRO, FO 371/3079/81204. Townley to FO, 19 April 1917.

[33] PRO, FO 371/3039/7148, Rumbold to FO, 9 Jan. 1917.

[34] PRO, FO 371/53387/169554, Kilmarnock to FO, 9 Oct. 1918.

just how far Attachés had departed from their pre-war behaviour can be gleaned by the work of the Naval Attaché in Copenhagen. In January 1918 he co-operated with his American counterpart and the Danish Secret Service to burgle papers from the bank strongbox belonging to an Austrian agent.[35] Heads of legation did not normally engage in military espionage themselves, but they were prepared to transmit the results which their attachés gathered to London. Sir Horace Rumbold in Berne regularly sent naval and military intelligence to the Foreign Office supplied 'by an agent of a person in confidence of this Legation'.[36] The Director of Military Intelligence thought so highly of such sources that he promptly complained when the Foreign Office was slow in forwarding them to the War Office.[37]

Britain's allies also engaged in similar activities and the British benefited, to some extent, by co-operating with them. Since the start of the war the War Office had supplemented the work of their existing Military Attachés by maintaining Military Missions with the Allied General Staffs. In addition to exchanging information about operational matters, they also assisted each other by exchanging intelligence material.[38] But efforts to achieve closer co-operation were to some extent vitiated by the fear lest an ally compromise their own sources. Thus, for example, Rear-Admiral 'Blinker' Hall, the Director of Naval Intelligence, who controlled the operations of the Admiralty's code-breaking organisation, Room 40, was adamantly opposed to any attempts by the Allies to work together to decrypt enemy wireless messages, for fear of compromising security. But he did pass on some decrypts to the Allies and in the spring of 1917 a team of Room 40 cryptanalysts were sent to Italy to co-operate with their Italian counterparts. There was also some interchange of information with the French. The officer at General Headquarters (GHQ) in France responsible for compiling the German order of battle was in almost daily contact with his French counterpart at *Grand Quartier-Général*,[39] while the DMI at the War Office received regular bulletins, supplemented by telegrams containing urgent information, from both GQG and Petrograd, detailing the whereabouts of German divisions.[40]

As the war progressed, one of the most fruitful sources of information

[35] PRO, FO 371/3133/29588, Paget to Hardinge, 30 Jan. 1918.

[36] PRO, FO 371/3078/11943, Rumbold to FO, 15 Jan. 1917.

[37] PRO, FO 371/3086/222430, DMI 3 to Hardinge, 21 Nov. 1917.

[38] PRO, WO 106/5130. Buckley to Lassiter, 5 April 1917; Cox to Spears, 3 July 1917, LHCMA, Spears Papers, 1/15. For an analysis of the work of the missions with the French and Russian armies see D. French 'Watching the Allies: British Intelligence and the French Mutinies of 1917', *Intelligence and National Seacurity*, 6 (1991), pp. 575, 583–84; and K. Neilson, '"Joy Rides"? British Intelligence and Propaganda in Russia, 1914–1917', *Historical Journal*, 24 (1981), pp. 885–906.

[39] J. Marshall-Cornwall, *Wars and Rumours of Wars* (London, 1984), p. 23.

[40] Cox to Spears, 3 July 1917, LHCMA, Spears Papers, 1/15.

about German capabilities and intentions proved to be information derived from intercepting German wireless messages. The British developed no less than six signals intelligence services during the war, the Admiralty's Room 40, a section under the Postal Censor, a branch of the intelligence department of the Indian Army, two organisations at the War Office (MI1b and MI1e) and agencies at the GHQs of armies in the field. In 1917–18 the Army deployed eight Wireless Observation Groups in France and one each in Palestine, Mesopotamia, Italy and Salonika.[41] Their tasks included not only deciphering intercepted messages but also deducing by traffic analysis 'from field wireless stations as to changes in organization and location of the German troops'.[42] They also liaised with their French and American counterparts. They broke into the German traffic by means of deductions and inference and through the use of captured German codebooks.[43] The information they gathered was often of tactical or operational significance, including 'identifications of units and information of much tactical value (times of counter-attacks, warning of gas shoots, times of sending out patrols, times of relief, reports on information obtained by patrols, company strengths, etc'.[44]

It is therefore apparent that in 1917 the British possessed a highly-developed intelligence gathering organisation. The task of analysing the information it collected was the business of two organisations. At the War Office the Directorate of Military Intelligence was led by the taciturn but able Director of Military Intelligence, Sir George Macdonogh. In France Haig maintained his own intelligence organisation at GHQ led by the much less able Brigadier John Charteris. By June 1917 Macdonogh had concluded that, because of his overoptimistic estimates of German manpower losses, Charteris was a 'dangerous fool'. By late 1917 relations between the two men were strained.[45] Relations between the two departments improved significantly on the eve of the German Spring Offensive only because in January 1918, Charteris was replaced by one of Macdonogh's own subordinates, Brigadier Edgar Cox.

The root cause why these two organisations failed to predict correctly the German's operational intentions in the spring of 1917 and of 1918 lay in the inability of their intelligence analysts to draw the correct conclusions from the information they had at their disposal. In an attempt to overcome the problem of discovering a common and easily applicable calculus

---

41 Ferris, 'The British Army and Signals Intelligence', pp. 23–31; Ferris, *The British Army and Signals Intelligence during the First World War*, passim.

42 PRO, WO 158/898, Charteris to MacDonogh, 25 June 1917.

43 PRO, WO 158/898, MacDonogh to Charteris, 16 June 1917 and Charteris to MacDonogh, 18 June 1917.

44 PRO, WO 158/962, Cox to Major-General, Organization, 26 Feb. 1918.

45 Sir H. Wilson, diary 8 June 1917, I[mperial] W[ar] M[useum], Wilson Papers, microfilm reel 7.

to predict their opponents' future actions, British military intelligence officers during the First World War usually based their forecasts upon the German order of battle. They reasoned that if they could plot the geographical location of the main units of the German Army they would have a useful analytical tool which would point to their future intentions and capabilities. 'As everyone knows', wrote a senior intelligence officer who served at GHQ in France, 'the basis [of intelligence work] is the building up of the enemy's order of battle, for when this has been done the identification of one unit is prima facie evidence of the presence of the division to which it belongs and possibly also of the corps or even army.'[46] They were often successful. In May 1917 the BEF captured a copy of the German army's order of battle in France which showed that the Directorate of Military Intelligence had been able to discover the order of battle of the entire German army in the west with the exception of a single Landwehr regiment.[47] But such information was by no means always trustworthy. Reliance on such an apparently simple yardstick might leave British intelligence analysts the victim of deliberate deception by the Germans. If the Germans could successfully feed them with false intelligence about their order of battle, whilst at the same time hiding the actual whereabout of a significant portion of their army beneath a security blanket, they could conjure up in the minds of the British a completely false picture of their intentions. This was exactly what they did succeed in doing in the spring of 1917 and of 1918.

By the autumn of 1916 the German High Command, *Oberste Heeresleitung* (OHL) had become deeply disturbed by the great weight of men and munitions which the British and French had thrown at them during their summer offensive astride the Somme. General Ludendorff, the First Quartermaster General, feared that the German Army in the west would not be able to withstand similar attacks in 1917 if they were prolonged, especially if the French and British attacked early in the new year before his own troops had the opportunity for a proper period of rest and refitting. Ludendorff discounted the possibility that he might mount a spoiling attack to upset the Entente's own plans because the German Army had insufficient manpower reserves.

Consequently, on 5 September 1916, OHL ordered work to begin on the planning of five strong rearward defensive systems in the west. The northernmost, the Flandern Line, was to run from the Belgium coast via the Passchendaele ridge, the Messines salient to Lille. The second, the Wotan Line, was to extend from Lille to the rear of the Loos-Arras-Vimy

[46] Kirke to Major-General F.S. Pigott, and enc., 29 July 1947, I[mperial] W[ar] M[useum], Kirke Papers, WMK 13.
[47] PRO, CAB 23/2/WC145, War Cabinet 25 May 1917.

and Somme battlefields of 1915 and 1916. The third, the Siegfried Line, was to begin at Arras and proceeded west of St-Quentin and Laon to the River Aisne east of Soissons. The fourth, the Hunding Line, began near Peronne on the Somme and ran to Etain on the Meuse and then north east of Verdun. Finally, the Michel Line was to run from Etain to Pont-à-Mousson on the River Moselle. When it was completed the *Siegfried* line was approximately ninety miles long and, by pinching-out the Noyon salient, would shorten the German line by twenty-five miles. But the decision to construct these new defences was not synonymous with the decision to retire to them. As late as 13 November Ludendorff still regarded them as merely a precautionary measure which would enable him to economise manpower if it proved to be necessary. It was not until 4 February 1917 that he was reluctantly persuaded to sanction a voluntary withdrawal to the position that the Allies came to call the Hindenburg Line.[48] This operation – codenamed 'Alberich' brought the Germans two advantages. It released thirteen divisions and fifty batteries of heavy artillery, forces which he hoped to employ in an offensive in co-operation with the Austrians which he was planning to mount against the Italian army. And by disrupting the Entente's preparations it also promised to give the Germans two months' respite before the Anglo-French Armies in the west would be ready to launch their own spring offensive. Such a breathing space was extremely important because, by the beginning of February, it was apparent that German industry had failed to meet the ambitious targets for the production of guns and munitions which it had been set under the Hindenburg programme in November 1916.[49]

The Germans were thus creating for themselves the *capability* to withdraw from the Noyon salient as early as November 1916 but they did not decide to employ that capability until the beginning of February, less than three weeks before their retreat actually began. British intelligence was successful in detecting some indications of the new German capability but they failed to understand their intentions. In late October and early November 1916, RFC reconnaissance flights and reports from escaped Russian prisoners did point to isolated attempts by the Germans to construct defensive positions some fourteen miles behind their present line near St-Quentin. But it was to be some months before they gleaned anything definite about the remainder of its course. As late as the end

[48] General Erich Ludendorff, *My War Memoirs, 1914–1918* (London, 1919), i, pp. 305–8; G.C. Wynne, *If German Attacks: The Battle in Depth in the West* (London, 1940), pp. 133–34; R.B. Aspery, *The German High Command at War: Hindenburg and Ludendorff Conduct the First World War* (New York, 1991), pp. 273, 304.

[49] Wynne, *If Germany Attacks*, pp. 137–38; M. Kitchen, *The Silent Dictatorship: The Politics of the German High Command under Hindenburg and Ludendorff, 1916–1918* (London, 1976), pp. 67–84.

of January 1917, information gleaned from prisoner interrogations and refugees that the Germans were constructing reward defences were still treated as unconfirmed rumours at GHQ.[50] On 26 January a refugee from occupied France reported that the Germans were building a new defensive position from Arras to Laon. 'The Cojeul switch, which has been reported by aviators as far east as the Bois de Bourlon, appears to be continued in a southerly direction west of Cambrai, and to follow the St-Quentin canal as far as St-Quentin. Thence it is said to run by La Fère to Laon.'[51] On 30 January GHQ (Intelligence) reported that

> According to a prisoner's statement the enemy does not intend to offer determined resistance in his present front line between Serre and the Ancre.
>
> According to the prisoner, a very strong line of defence is being made by civilians from Croisilles through Ecoust St Menin, Noreuil, Lagnicourt, Doignes and Hermies.[52]

Both reports ended with the same phrase, 'Confirmation is required.' By mounting an elaborate operation to deceive the British and French about their intentions, the Germans made it difficult for the British to gain that confirmation. Ludendorff's order to begin the retreat was accompanied by another telling his troops 'to mislead the enemy by furnishing them with special news'.[53]

The German deception plan fell into two parts. The first was designed to deprive the British of information about OHL's real capabilities and intentions; the second was intended to persuade them that, far from retreating, the Germans actually planned to mount an offensive in the west. OHL achieved its first objective by partially blinding some of the most important British collection agencies. Falls was right to highlight the fact that poor weather and the superiority of the German air force did hamper aerial reconnaissance. What he did not mention was that in late September 1916 the German Navy intercepted a packet-boat sailing between Holland and Britain. On board was a British diplomatic courier carrying a Foreign Office bag which contained intelligence material gathered by agents working for the British in occupied France and Belgium. The courier threw the bag overboard but, because it was not fitted with enough lead weights, it did not sink and the Germans were able to retrieve it. From the information in the bag they were able to arrest a number of agents

---

[50] PRO, WO 157/17, Intelligence Section GHQ, summary of information, 30 Jan. 1917.

[51] PRO, WO 157/17, GHQ, summary of information, Intelligence Section, GHQ, 26 Jan. 1917.

[52] PRO, WO 157/17, GHQ, summary of information, Intelligence Section, GHQ, 30 Jan. 1917.

[53] Ludendorff, *My War Memoirs*, ii, p. 407.

working for the British and to smash a large part of the train-watching networks behind their lines.[54] Thus the British Secret Service in Belgium was temporarily blinded. Meanwhile on the ground the troops of Crown Prince Rupprecht's Army Group mounted a wireless deception campaign to blind the BEF signals intelligence service. It was so successful that it was not until 21 February that the British detected any indications that the Germans had begun to dismantle some of their wireless stations. Even then Haig had to confess that his intelligence staff did not understand their reasons for doing so.[55]

These steps gave the Germans some measure of security against the preying eyes of British intelligence. But the Germans went one pace further and tried to plant in the minds of British intelligence a deliberately misleading idea of their intentions. Ever since the reign of Elizabeth I, British policy-makers had been determined to ensure that no great power was allowed to occupy the coast of the Low Countries for, as Elizabeth had remarked 'If the nation of Spain should make a conquest of these [Low] countries . . . in that danger ourself, our countries and people might shortly be.'[56] By the early twentieth century fear of the Germans had taken the place of fear of the Spanish. In August 1914 the British government entered the war because of its fears that if Germany succeeded in fastening her hegemony over western Europe, and more especially if she occupied the Channel ports, Britain would become dangerously vulnerable to an invasion from across the Channel. 'We cannot', Asquith informed his confidant Venetia Stanley on 2 August 1914, 'allow the Germans to use the Channel as a hostile base.'[57] But from November 1914 that is exactly what the Germans were able to do. They occupied nearly thirty miles of the Belgian coast, including the ports of Ostend, Zeebrugge and Blankenberghe. From these ports their submarines and destroyers were able to menace the BEF's communications between Folkestone and Dover and the French Channel ports of Dunkirk, Calais and Boulogne. In November 1915 the Admiralty warned that German naval forces based on the Belgian ports constituted a 'growing danger to the transport of troops and supplies to France'. If Haig had not been constrained by the Anglo-French alliance to attack along the Somme in the summer of 1916, he would probably have preferred to mount an offensive to free

[54] Kirke diary, 24 Sept. and 14 Nov. 1916, IWM, Kirke Papers; Colonel W. Nicolai, *The German Secret Service* (London, 1924), p. 172.

[55] Occleshaw, *Armour against Fate*, pp. 114–15; PRO, WO 256/15, Haig diary, 21 Feb. 1917.

[56] Quoted in P.M. Kennedy, *The Rise and Fall of British Naval Mastery* (London, 1976), pp. 28–29.

[57] M. and E. Brock, *H.H. Asquith: Letters to Venetia Stanley* (London, 1982), p. 146.

the Belgium coast.[58] On 22 November 1916, less than two weeks before his fall from power, Asquith told the Secretary of the War Committee, Sir Maurice Hankey, to write to the Chief of the Imperial General Staff, Sir William Robertson, urging an attack on the Belgian ports and insisting that 'there is no operation of war to which the War Committee would attach greater importance than the successful occupation, or at least the deprivation to the enemy, of Ostend and especially Zeebrugge'.[59]

The German deception plan was designed to persuade the British that they intended to mount an offensive against the Channel ports. They had not set themselves an easy task, for at the end of 1916 both Charteris and Macdonogh were agreed that the Germans would remain on the defensive in the west at least for the next few months. On 3 December 1916 Robertson sent Lloyd George a memorandum by Macdonogh on Germany's likely plans during the coming winter, which suggested that as Bucharest would probably fall very soon the Germans would either use the Rumanian collapse as an opportunity to make a separate peace with Russia or, if her offer was refused, remain on the defensive in the east until the spring of 1917. Meanwhile in the west it was likely that she would rely upon her U-boats to strangle the allied economies. Like Charteris, Macdonogh believed that it was unlikely that the Germans would mount their own offensive in the west and would probably use the winter months to strengthen their defences.[60]

This was not the first occasion on which the Germans had tried to plant disinformation on the British. After their unsuccessful efforts to destroy the BEF during the first Battle of Ypres in October and November 1914, OHL had decided to switch reinforcements to the eastern front. They chose to conceal their intentions by spreading rumours through neutral embassies that they were in fact planning to concentrate troops on the Western Front prior to mounting yet another offensive.[61] In late 1916 and early 1917 they did much the same, using several channels through which to pass a variety of stories. Some, particularly those pointing towards a German raid or invasion of Britain or a turning movement through Switzerland, were considered and dismissed by British analysts. These failed to achieve their purpose of concentrating British attention

---

[58] Sir J.E. Edmonds, *History of the Great War. Military Operations France and Belgium, 1917* (London, 1948), ii, p. 2. The fullest analysis of the concern of British policy-makers with Belgium and the Channel coast is W.J. Philpott, 'British Military Strategy on the Western Front: Independence or Alliance, 1904–1918', (unpublished D.Phil. thesis, Oxford University, 1991). I am most grateful to Dr Philpott for allowing me to read his thesis.

[59] PRO, CAB 42/24/10, [Hankey] to Robertson, 22 Nov. 1916.

[60] PRO, WO 106/1511, Memo by M.I., German plans for the winter of 1916/17 (nd but *c.* 1 Dec. 1916); Brigadier-General John Charteris, *At GHQ* (London, 1931), p. 181.

[61] Kirke to Major-General F.S. Pigott and enc., 29 July 1947, IWM Kirke Papers, WMK 13.

elsewhere or of causing them to withhold forces from France. Thus on 2 and 3 January 1917 the British Ministers in Norway and Denmark both reported that the Germans intended to despatch their whole fleet, plus up to fifteen Zeppelins, to raid the English coast.[62] The date predicted for the offensive, 10 January, came and went without anything happening. But the possibility of such an operation, accompanied perhaps by a force of troops in transports, caused the War Cabinet to spend some time considering the possibility of a German invasion and whether the 500,000 men tied up in home defence might be better used elsewhere. However, on 22 January, without entirely dismissing the possibility that the Germans might indeed try to strike directly against the British Isles, they decided it would be safe to reduce the mobile forces available for home defence from ten to eight divisions and to send the two thus freed to France.[63] Other reports current a few days later in Paris, which indicated that the Germans were massing troops to turn the southern end of the French line by invading Switzerland, were also dismissed. Both the chief of the Swiss General Staff and Macdonogh believed that such reports referred to newly-raised units which the Germans had sent to southern Germany for training.[64]

Those reports which indicated a German offensive against the Channel ports were believed precisely because they struck the rawest of British strategic nerves. At the beginning of January Charteris noted that the Germans 'still have a formidable number of troops opposite the Ypres salient and in the Somme area, and if we weaken our line unduly the possibility of an attack would certainly arise'.[65] Further substance was given to his fears by entirely accurate reports that the Germans were engaged in raising as many as twelve new divisions which might enable them to gather a strategic reserve with which to strike against the Allied line in the west.[66] On 28 December Lord Bertie, the British Ambassador in Paris, heard 'from a good source that the Bosche are concentrating a large force in the Province of Antwerp, the object being, it is said, Walcheren with Flushing'.[67] Lloyd George was so alarmed at this possibility that he raised it the next day at the War Cabinet and was not entirely mollified when the Director of Military Operations, Sir Frederick Maurice, reassured him that the General Staff had no intelligence that the Germans had

---

[62] PRO, FO 371/3078/1971, Paget to FO, 2 Jan. 1917; PRO, FO 371/3078/2726, Findlay to FO, 3 Jan. 1917.

[63] PRO, CAB 23/1/WC40, War Cabinet, 22 Jan. 1917.

[64] PRO, FO 371/3039/7148, Rumbold to FO, 9 Jan. 1917; PRO, WO 106/5130, Buckley to Wyndham, 11 Jan. 1917.

[65] Charteris, *At GHQ*, p. 189.

[66] PRO, CAB 23/1/WC32, War Cabinet, 11 Jan. 1917.

[67] Lady A.G. Lennox (ed.), *The Diary of Lord Bertie of Thame, 1914–1918* (London, 1924), ii, p. 96.

concentrated troops for this operation. Nor was he satisfied when Maurice promised to watch carefully the extreme left flank of the Allies after Sir John Jellicoe, the First Sea Lord, had mentioned reports that the Germans were concentrating troops on the coast at Nieuport, hoping to land them by sea behind the Allied line.[68] Maurice only temporarily put these fears to rest the next day when he reported that there were no special German troop concentrations near Antwerp and that German troop movements on the Belgium coast merely consisted of the substitution of one tired division for one which had previously been sent there to rest.[69]

The possibility that the Germans might be about to strike in Flanders proved to be the most persistent and successful part of the German deception campaign. This was probably because it was accompanied by actual movements by real German troops. It was significant that reports of a German offensive planned against Loos or Arras for mid February were discounted by GHQ's Intelligence staff precisely because they could acquire no physical corroboration of troop concentrations in those areas.[70] By contrast, in December 1916 and January 1917, OHL's fear that the announcement that Germany was about to make, declaring unrestricted U-boat warfare, might provoke neutral or Entente retaliation led them to reorganise and reinforce their own forces along the Dutch–Belgian and Dutch–German frontiers. On the Dutch border, frontier troops were grouped into divisional formations and placed under an army corps staff based at Munster, whilst units released from the fighting in Rumania were moved to Belgium in case they were needed along the frontier.[71]

By the middle of January 1917 British analysts were taking seriously the possibility that the Germans might be about to launch an offensive in Flanders. On 13 January the Belgian consul at Maastricht in neutral Holland reported that the Germans had concentrated 350,000 troops for an offensive due to begin on 25 January, with the apparent purpose of cutting-off the Ypres salient and advancing on Calais.[72] The Belgium General Staff discounted the report but Charteris himself visited Second Army, who were holding the Ypres salient, and came away convinced that, although the report grossly exaggerated the size of the German concentration, there were indications that they were planning an offensive with some five or six divisions.[73] The consul's report was soon followed by another delivered to the British legation in Berne which had been 'brought out of Germany in [the] last few days by an agent of a person

---

[68] PRO, CAB 23/1/WC22, War Cabinet, 29 Dec. 1916.

[69] PRO, CAB 23/1/WC23, War Cabinet, 30 Dec. 1916.

[70] PRO, WO 256/15, Haig diary, 30 Jan. 1917.

[71] Ludendorff, *My War Memoirs*, i, p. 319.

[72] PRO, FO 371/3078/10449, Sir F. Villiers to FO, 13 Jan. 1917.

[73] Charteris, *At GHQ*, p. 190.

in the confidence of this Legation'. This indicated that the Germans were planning to forestall the forthcoming Allied offensive in the west by moving troops and heavy artillery to the Western Front in order to mount their own offensive. 'Information points to offensive rather than defensive measures in anticipation of the Allies advance. Germans evidently seeking to obtain final decision on this front.'[74]

Robertson was sceptical about reports suggesting a major German offensive. He told the War Cabinet on 22 January that, beyond some slight increase in the numbers of divisions and heavy artillery in the Ghent region, there were no signs that the Germans were massing troops in the west because the bulk of their reserves were concentrated on the Eastern Front.[75] But over the next two days he did confess that he was baffled by the fact that in the preceding three weeks they had moved five divisions from the eastern to the western front. Whilst two had been located in Alsace, the other three, together with some heavy artillery from the Somme had been located opposite the Ypres salient.[76] By 26 January the War Cabinet was so alarmed that they asked GHQ for a report on the state of the defences in the Ypres salient.[77] Reports of German troop movements westwards in preparation for a major offensive multiplied in early February. The acting military attaché in Copenhagen forwarded a report from a neutral traveller that the Germans had withdrawn eight divisions from the Balkans and sent them to the west. An agent told the British minister in Berne on 'best authority' that 'All available troops are being sent to Western front as Germans feel they can safely neglect Russian front for the moment' and would be used against the Ypres salient. Only the date of the offensive, variously estimated as likely to be between mid February and mid March, remained uncertain.[78] In February Haig still discounted the possibility of a major German offensive on the grounds that they lacked sufficient troops but he did take seriously the possibility of a smaller operation at the junction of the British and Belgium armies just to the north of the salient.[79]

The success of the German deception campaign can be measured in two ways. On 28 January so convinced were GHQ that the Germans would mount an offensive against Ypres and the Channel ports that they despatched an extra division and twenty batteries of heavy artillery to reinforce Second Army.[80] And on 23 February Robertson told the War

[74] PRO, FO 371/3078/11943 and 16412, Rumbold to FO, 15 and 20 Jan. 1917.

[75] PRO, CAB 23/1/WC40, War Cabinet, 22 Jan. 1917.

[76] PRO, CAB 23/1/WC41 and WC43, War Cabinet, 23 and 24 Jan. 1917.

[77] Robertson to Kiggell, 26 Jan. 1917, LHCMA, Kiggell Papers, IV/6.

[78] PRO, FO 371/3078/27817, Paget to FO, 4 Feb. 1917; PRO, FO 371/3078/28677 and 28801, Rumbold to FO, 5 Feb. 1917.

[79] PRO, WO 256/15, Haig diary, 8 Feb. and 20 Feb. 1917.

[80] PRO, WO 256/15, Haig diary, 28 Jan. 1917; Kiggell to Robertson, 28 Jan. 1917, LHCMA, Kiggell Papers, V/79.

Cabinet that recent German troops movements between the eastern and western fronts gave no clear indication of their intentions but that they would not voluntarily shorten their line in the west unless the Allies attacked and compelled them to do so. He was wrong, for two days later the first indications that the Germans were indeed making a voluntary withdrawal reached GHQ.[81]

The commencement of the retreat did not mean that the Germans had abandoned their attempts to deceive the allies as to their real intentions on the western front, for they continued with their deception campaign.[82] On 8 March Robertson told the War Cabinet that the Germans were making preparations to increase their troops concentrations in eastern Belgium.[83] Eleven days later, having consulted Jellicoe, he also raised the possibility that the Germans might be planning to land 20–30,000 troops behind the Allied line near Nieuport.[84] Charteris calculated that the withdrawal to a shorter line would enable the Germans to take as many as twelve divisions out of the line. Robertson raised the figure to between fifteen and twenty. Haig and his staff feared that, once the BEF had been committed to the forthcoming Anglo-French offensive, the Germans would be able to use the reserve of divisions they had amassed for an offensive at Ypres designed to cut the BEF's communications with the Channel coast. It was this danger, at least as much as the genuine irritation which he felt at the 'very *commanding* tone' which Nivelle now adopted to him, which caused Haig to complain to the War Cabinet about the implementation of the Calais agreement which had placed him under the command of the French Commander-in-Chief.[85]

The German deception campaign which preceded their retreat to the Hindenburg Line was an excellent example of what Professor Ferris has described as 'the higher and more successful form of the art [of deception] . . . misleading the enemy in a precise fashion'. One year later, in the spring of 1918, the Germans were less successful. But although they failed to mislead their enemies about their precise intentions, they did succeed in 'engendering confusion' in the minds of British analysts to

[81] Charteris, *At GHQ*, p. 197; PRO, CAB 24/6/GT49, Robertson, Germany's intentions, 23 Feb. 1917.

[82] PRO, FO 371/3078/44142, Findlay to FO, 27 Feb. 1917; PRO, FO 371/3078/493, Paget to FO, 7 Mar. 1917.

[83] PRO, CAB 23/2/WC91, War Cabinet, 8 Mar. 1917.

[84] PRO, CAB 23/2/WC99, War Cabinet, 19 Mar. 1917.

[85] Charteris, *At GHQ*, p. 197; PRO, CAB 24/8/GT229, Robertson, A general review of the situation in all theatres of war, 20 Mar. 1917; PRO, WO 256/15, Haig diary, 28 Feb. 1917; D.R. Woodward, *Lloyd George and the Generals* (Newark, NJ, 1983), p. 149; PRO, CAB 24/1/GT98, Haig to CIGS, 3 Mar. 1917; Haig to Kiggell, 6 Mar. 1917, LHCMA, Kiggell Papers, 11/10.

such an extent that their preparations to meet the German offensive were dangerously flawed.[86]

Between July and November 1917 Haig tried and failed to capture the Channel ports and liberate Belgium. But his failure did not diminish his anxiety to achieve this objective. In October 1917, faced with the possibility that the Germans might soon reinforce their forces in the west, following the Russian collapse, he continued to insist that there was little to fear from a German attack because their divisions were all of poor quality and that the best way to counter any increase in German strength in France was to follow his preferred policy of resuming the Flanders' offensive in the spring of 1918.[87] Haig's undiminished concern for the security of the Channel coast once again left the British vulnerable to a German deception plan which promised to threaten the northernmost part of the BEF's line. By the autumn of 1917 unrestricted U-boat warfare had obviously failed to win the war for Germany. The USA represented an enormous accretion of *potential* strength to the Entente alliance and, despite the Russian collapse, Ludendorff realised that Germany's ability to continue fighting was finite. In April 1917 he had decided that Germany would eventually have to abandon the defensive in the west in favour of an offensive.[88] At a conference at Mons on 11 November he decided that, as the Central Powers were only held together by the hopes the Turks, Bulgarians and Austrians invested in a German victory, it was vital for him to provide it in 1918. To do so Germany would have to switch its armies from the Eastern to the Western Front and strike a major blow in the west before the Americans had mobilised their enormous military potential and could deploy it against his armies in France.[89]

Ludendorff considered three possible locations for the offensive: in Flanders where a penetration of Haig's line would threaten the Channel ports; on the Somme where the British and French lines met; or in the south against the French. The German High Command finally decided to mount their spring offensive against the BEF because they believed that its commanders were less tactically adept than the French; because they had too few divisions to destroy the French army; and because the BEF was so situated that it might be possible to outflank all or part of it and turn a tactical breakthrough into an operational victory by destroying a large part of Haig's army. By contrast it would be much more difficult to

[86] Ferris (ed.), *The British Army and Signals Intelligence*, p. 171.

[87] PRO, CAB 24/28/GT2243, Haig to Robertson, 8 Oct. 1917; PRO, WO 256/23, Haig diary, 18 Oct. 1917; PRO, WO 106/407, Haig to Robertson, 19 Oct. 1917.

[88] H.H. Herwig, 'The Dynamics of Necessity: German Military Policy during the First World War', in A.R. Millett and W. Murray (eds), *Military Effectiveness*, i, *The First World War* (Boston, 1988), p. 100.

[89] Ludendorff, *My War Memoirs, 1914–1918*, ii, pp. 538–43; Aspery, *The German High Command at War*, pp. 364–67.

defeat the French army because part of the line it held, along the Vosges mountains, was excellent defensive country; and because it could more easily retreat, exchanging space for time, than could the British.[90] On 8 February OHL fixed the provisional date for the assault for 21 March. Ludendorff did not believe that his offensive would immediately result in a complete and final success and he contemplated fighting a series of attritional battles which would be mounted consecutively throughout the spring and summer.[91] The first would be in the centre where forty-seven divisions would attack on a sixty-three-mile front between Arras and La Fère, the point at which the BEF made contact with the French Army. General Otto von Below's Seventeenth Army on the right was to advance between Arras and Cambrai, General von Marwitz Second Army in the centre would advance south of Cambrai towards Péronne and Amiens and, on the left, General von Hutier's Eighteenth Army would advance north and south of St-Quentin.[92] These attacks would fall upon Sir Julian Byng's Third Army and Sir Hubert Gough's Fifth Army. A successful offensive here would divide the British and French armies, open the road to Paris and, Ludendorff hoped, ignite the kind of revolution in France and Britain which had already brought down Russia. Ludendorff expected that Haig would react by withdrawing troops from Flanders to reinforce the threat to his right. When he did so the Germans would switch their efforts northwards, and he ordered that simultaneous preparations were to be made to mount an offensive in Flanders with the objective of reaching the coast. In case the opportunity should arise of attacking the French, he also told his staff to prepare an offensive against Pétain's forces on the Aisne.[93]

Because the German's numerical superiority on the Western Front in the spring of 1918 was quite small, Ludendorff went to great efforts to multiply the effectiveness of his forces by misleading the British and French as to his precise intentions. The German deception plan took three forms. At the strategic level they attempted to suggest that, despite the fact they were massing large numbers of troops in the west, their real effort would be in another theatre, perhaps Italy or the Balkans. This was done in an effort to persuade the Entente to deploy troops in secondary theatres and so reduce the forces which would face the Germans when

---

[90] B.I. Gudmundsson, *Stormtroop Tactics: Innovation in the German Army, 1914–1918* (New York, 1989), pp. 155–56.

[91] G. Ritter, *The Sword and the Sceptre: The Problem of Militarism in Germany*, iv, *The Reign of German Militarism and the Disaster of 1918* (London, 1968/73), p. 230.

[92] R. Parkinson, *Tormented Warrior: Ludendorff and the Supreme Command* (London, 1978), pp. 143, 149.

[93] R. Paschall, *The Defeat of Imperial Germany, 1917–18* (North Carolina, 1989), pp. 131–33; Ludendorff, *War Memoirs*, ii, pp. 589–591.

they did strike in the west. This was the most ambitious part of their deception campaign and it failed.

The British had few doubts that the enemy were trying deliberately to deceive them for, as Robertson remarked to the War Cabinet on 6 December 1917 when he 'called attention to the prevailing rumours regarding projected attacks by the enemy on many fronts. It was not possible that they could all be true, and some were demonstrably false.'[94] The Germans spread a plethora of rumours pointing to a variety of operations. In November 1917, for example, a British agent in Switzerland reported that the Germans planned to mount an offensive in Macedonia in the spring of 1918. A month later the French premier, Georges Clemenceau, told the British Ambassador, Lord Bertie, that the Papacy had been informed by its Nuncios in Vienna and Munich that the next major effort by the Central Powers would be against Italy.[95] Abdul Kerim, a diplomat close to the Turkish leader Enver Pasha, told the arms dealer and part-time British agent Sir Basil Zaharoff that, at a War Council held in the first week of December, the Central Powers had agreed to mount two offensives, one in the west and another at Salonika.[96] Lloyd George treated his report with the utmost seriousness, describing it as emanating from 'a secret source which has hitherto proved reliable . . .'[97] A Secret Service report which found its way into the Prime Minister's hands from an agent codenamed 'Bright', who was rated by his masters as being 80 per cent reliable, suggested in late January that in addition to planning an offensive in the west the Germans were also considering attacking the Italians once again.[98] Only two days before the commencement of the actual offensive the intelligence branch at GHQ noted a plethora of rumours pointing to imminent German and Austrian offensives in northern Italy, Macedonia and even against Egypt.[99]

Some members of the War Cabinet, particularly Lloyd George who had little confidence in the predictions of military intelligence, never entirely discounted the possibility that rather than do the obvious and use their build-up of forces to attack in the west, the Germans might do the unexpected and strike against Italy or Salonika. On 5 November Lord Milner suggested that the Germans would emulate Frederick the Great, who 'when not sufficiently strong to follow up a blow, [had been apt] to strike now here, now there, first at one country, then at another, not with the object of giving a knock-out blow, but always with that of great

94 PRO, CAB 23/4/WC293, War Cabinet, 6 Dec. 1917.

95 PRO, CAB 24/32/GT2665, information regarding enemy plans from an agent in Switzerland, 8 Nov. 1917; PRO, FO 800/173/It/17/10, Bertie to Balfour, 9 Dec. 1917.

96 Zaharoff to Calliard, 15 Dec. 1917, HLRO, Lloyd George Papers, F/6/1/5.

97 PRO, CAB 63/23, Lloyd George to Wilson, 18 Dec. 1917.

98 From agent 'Bright', late January 1918, HLRO, Lloyd George Papers, F/199/8/1.

99 PRO, WO 157/29, daily intelligence summary, GHQ I. Branch, 19 Mar. 1918.

political effect'.[100] But the Germans could not conceal the movement of large numbers of divisions from the eastern to the western fronts. On 19 October the British Military Attaché in Petrograd, Colonel Alfred Knox, reported that he believed that the Germans had moved five divisions from the Riga front to France since the beginning of October.[101] On 9 November Maurice told ministers that there were 149 German divisions in the west, eighty-three in Russia and six in Italy.[102] Beginning on 24 December the War Cabinet received a regular series of briefings detailing the build-up of German divisions in the west from information supplied by British and Allied intelligence services.[103] By mid January these showed that the Germans now had 163 divisions in the west.[104] A month later, Robertson estimated that the figure stood at 177 divisions compared to an Allied strength of 162.[105] Other evidence also pointed to the fact that the Germans were concentrating large numbers of troops in the west. In January the British detected the establishment of a new corp and army headquarters in the west, developments which, according to Robertson 'had now given it [the German army in the west] the character of an offensive force'.[106] Cox had discovered that the Germans had created four large artillery practice camps near Antwerp, Namur and Tournai. By the beginning of February Macdonogh had discovered that either sixty-two or sixty-three German divisions were undergoing intensive training for an offensive behind the German line in the west.[107] By mid February GHQ knew that the Germans had re-established their General Head Quarters in the west at Spa, near Liège.[108] By the end of February French signals intelligence had informed GHQ that von Below, who had led the successful German assault at Caporetto, and whom Haig's intelligence staff rated as the best German commander for an offensive, now commanded an army north of Cambrai.[109] The British also discovered for themselves that the Germans were building small numbers of tanks, weapons they could only use in an offensive.[110]

This all pointed to a concentration of forces in preparation for a major

---

[100] PRO, CAB 23/4/WC265, War Cabinet, 5 Nov. 1917.

[101] PRO, CAB 24/29/GT2373, Military Attaché, Petrograd, to DMI, 19 Oct. 1917.

[102] PRO, CAB 23/4/WC269, War Cabinet, 9 Nov. 1917.

[103] PRO, CAB 23/4/WC305, War Cabinet, 24 Dec. 1917.

[104] PRO, CAB 23/5/WC320, War Cabinet, 11 Jan. 1918.

[105] PRO, CAB 23/5/WC345, War Cabinet, 13 Feb. 1918.

[106] PRO, CAB 23/5/WC316, War Cabinet, 8 Jan. 1918.

[107] PRO, CAB 23/5/WC336, War Cabinet, 1 Feb. 1918; PRO, WO 256/27, Haig diary, 25 Jan. 1918; PRO, WO 157/28, GHQ intelligence summary, A. Branch, 27 Feb. 1918.

[108] PRO, WO 157/28, GHQ intelligence summary, A. Branch, 15 Feb. 1918.

[109] PRO, WO 157/28, GHQ intelligence summary, A. Branch, 27 Feb. 1918; PRO, WO 157/29, GHQ intelligence summary, A. Branch, 2 Mar. 1918.

[110] PRO, CAB 23/5/WC347, War Cabinet, 15 Feb. 1918; PRO, FO 371/3435/21098, Findlay to FO, 2 Feb. 1918.

offensive and convinced most policy-makers that the Germans did indeed intend to strike in the west.[111] In mid December Maurice had no doubt that 'the enemy really did mean to attack on the western front'.[112] By early January 1918 Brigadier Cox, then still head of the German section of the Directorate of Military Intelligence in London, looked forward to a German offensive in the west. The only doubt that both men entertained was that the Germans might also mount a subsidiary offensive in Italy.[113]

The Germans were much more successful at the operational level in misleading their enemies as to the exact time and place they would strike on the western front, so ensuring that reinforcements which might have been used to block their advance were tied down elsewhere waiting for an imaginary offensive. Ludendorff's preference for a series of offensives at different locations, taken in conjunction with 'dummy works on fronts remote from the attack', was intended to make it difficult for Allied intelligence to predict exactly where and when the initial German blow would fall.[114] British intelligence analysts were not always misled by German deception measures. In January 1918 the Military Attaché at Copenhagen described the reports about the timing of the German offensive he was sending to London as 'plainly mendacious'.[115] In mid January Rumbold telegraphed from Switzerland that 'persons coming out of Germany and Austria mostly mention Calais as real objective of Germans who are evidently anxious to put this report about. Reims and Nancy are also mentioned.'[116] Similarly Maurice recognised that German troop concentrations in Holstein did not represent preparations for an invasion of Britain but that the troops concerned were being trained for operations in France.[117]

Although they recognised that there was an element of disinformation in the intelligence they were gathering, British analysts experienced considerable difficulty to sorting the wheat from the chaff. In late November 1917 the Belgium government informed the British Minister that they had detected large-scale German preparations for an attack in

[111] PRO, CAB 23/5/WC316, War Cabinet, 8 Jan. 1918; PRO, CAB 23/5/WC336, War Cabinet, 1 Feb. 1918; PRO, WO 256/27, Haig diary, 25 Jan. 1918; PRO, WO 157/28, GHQ intelligence summary, A. Branch, 27 Feb. 1918; PRO, WO 157/28, GHQ intelligence summary, A. Branch, 15 Feb. 1928; PRO, WO 157/28, GHQ intelligence summary, A. Branch, 27 Feb. 1918; PRO, WO 157/29, GHQ intelligence summary, A. Branch, 2 Mar. 1918; PRO, CAB 23/5/WC347, War Cabinet, 15 Feb. 1918; PRO, FO 371/3435/21098, Findlay to FO, 2 Feb. 1918.

[112] PRO, CAB 23/4/WC296, War Cabinet, 12 Dec. 1917.

[113] Cox to Spears, 2 Jan. 1918, LHCMA, Spears Papers, 1/15; PRO, CAB 23/5/WC356 and WC365, War Cabinet, 28 Feb. and 13 Mar. 1918.

[114] Ludendorff, *War Memoirs*, ii, p. 589.

[115] PRO, FO 371/3435/16660, Paget to FO, 25 Jan. 1918.

[116] PRO, FO 371/3435/7734, Rumbold to FO, 13 Jan. 1918.

[117] PRO, CAB 23/5/WC318, War Cabinet, 8 Jan. 1918.

Flanders.[118] In December agents, working for the British Naval Attaché in Copenhagen, reported that the Germans planned to attack the British between Cambrai and the North Sea.[119] The French Military Attaché in Madrid learnt from the King of Spain that the Germans intended to mount two major offensives, in the Champagne and Upper Alsace.[120] The Portuguese Minister of Foreign Affairs told the British Minister in Lisbon that his own minister in Berne had learnt that the Germans would strike against Maubeuge.[121] In January 1918 the British began to receive reports from Russia suggesting that the Germans would mount a major offensive in Flanders in a few months time, accompanied by a demonstration further south.[122] In February, exactly a month before the offensive began, Clemenceau told the British Ambassador that the offensive would be directed against the British Army with the objective of seizing Calais.[123] In early March the French Military Attaché in Copenhagen learnt from the Danish General Staff that the main point of impact by the Germans would be between St-Quentin and Cambrai.[124] The way in which both good and bad reports could emanate from the same source was shown by two reports from the Military Attaché in Copenhagen. On 5 January he was correctly informed by his Russian counterpart that his agents believed that the objective of the German offensive would be the point at which the French and British armies joined. Three days later one of the British attaché's own agents, who had recently left Germany, had learnt from German staff officers that they were planning two major offensives in the west, one in Flanders and the other against Verdun.[125]

The possibility that the main German attack might fall on the French army rather than upon the BEF was seriously entertained by French intelligence, who were convinced that the Germans would strike against their own armies. This was precisely what the Germans wished them to believe, for they had gone to the trouble of using dummy radio traffic to create a phantom army opposite the French front.[126] At the end of October Pétain confided to a British liaison officer that he feared a German attack against his line in Lorraine in the spring of 1918.[127] In

[118] PRO, FO 371/3086/224695, Villiers to FO, 24 Nov. 1917.

[119] PRO, CAB 371/3079/233332, Paget to FO, 8 Dec. 1917.

[120] PRO, CAB 24/36/GT3051, Spears to WO, 17 Dec. 1917.

[121] PRO, FO 371/3079/244240, Carnegie to FO, 27 Dec. 1917.

[122] PRO, CAB 23/5/WC322, War Cabinet, 15 Jan. 1918.

[123] PRO, FO 800/171/Ge/18/2, Bertie to Lloyd George, 21 Feb. 1918.

[124] PRO, WO 157/29, daily intelligence summary, GHQ Intelligence Branch, 10 Mar. 1918.

[125] PRO, FO 371/3435/3381, Paget to FO, 5 Jan. 1918; (4974), Paget to FO, 8 Jan. 1918.

[126] Ferris (ed.), *The British Army and Signals Intelligence during the First World War*, pp. 81–82.

[127] PRO, WO 158/43, Clive, conversation with General Pétain, 25 Oct. 1917.

early January French intelligence was worried that the movement of a high quality division from opposite the British front to their own front at Reims pointed to an impending German attack there.[128] By February the Deuxième Bureau at the War Office in Paris expected a series of diversionary assaults followed by two major thrusts, one around Arras against the British and another around Reims against the French, whilst GQG told Haig that they expected the German attack to come at Reims in early March.[129]

The Germans were equally diligent in trying to conceal the exact timing of their offensive. At the beginning of December, American sources in Switzerland suggested that the Germans would mount an offensive in the west within two weeks.[130] The Naval Attaché at Copenhagen also forwarded agents reports of a German offensive before Christmas.[131] These reports were supported by Abdul Kerim who informed Zaharoff in mid December that an offensive in the west would begin almost at once 'as the troops coming from the Russian front were accustomed to the cold'.[132] At the end of December Portuguese and Swedish sources suggested the Germans would begin their offensive in mid January.[133] On 25 January the Military Attaché at Copenhagen reported that 'sources of all kinds' were insisting that the offensive would begin within two days. When it did not the Norwegian General Staff told the British Minister in Norway on 27 January that the attack would begin on 28 January.[134] At the beginning of March the British Minister in Berne explained the continuing delay by reference to a conversation during which the German Minister in Switzerland had told his Dutch colleague that the Germans would not attack until after they had made peace with Russia and Rumania.[135]

The result was that British intelligence received so many reports of German preparations for an offensive in the west at so many different locations and times that it was not until mid February that they were finally convinced that the Germans did indeed intend to launch a major blow between Arras and St-Quentin within about three to four weeks.[136]

128 PRO, CAB 23/5/WC311. War Cabinet, 2 Jan. 1918.

129 C. à Court Repington, *The First World War, 1914–1918* (London, 1920), ii, p. 224; Blake (ed.), *The Private Papers of Douglas Haig*, p. 285.

130 PRO, WO 256/25, Charteris to Haig, 2 Dec. 1917.

131 PRO, FO 371/3079/233332, Paget to FO, 8 Dec. 1917.

132 Zaharoff to Calliard, 15 Dec. 1917, HLRO, Lloyd George Papers, F/6/1/5.

133 PRO, FO 371/3079/244240, Carnegie to FO, 27 Dec. 1917; PRO, FO 371/3432/3381, Howard to FO, 31 Dec. 1917.

134 PRO, FO 371/3435/16660, Paget to FO, 25 Jan. 1918; PRO, FO 371/3435/16935, Findlay to FO, 27 Jan. 1918.

135 PRO, FO 471/3435/39643, Rumbold to FO, 2 Mar. 1918.

136 R. Blake (ed.), *The Private Papers of Douglas Haig 1914–1918* (London, 1952), p. 291; PRO, WO 157/29, daily intelligence summary, GHQ I. Branch, 5 Mar. 1918.

At the same time, however, they also gave equal credence to reports which indicated that this would only be one of a series of German offensives and that the enemy was also planning to strike a major blow in Flanders to capture the Channel ports at some stage in the spring or summer.[137]

The basic reason for their confusion was a simple failure of intelligence. The Germans had again tried to conceal their real intentions behind a thick security blanket, although they were not quite as successful as they had been a year previously. In the weeks before the commencement of the offensive they tried to blind the BEF's signals intelligence service by regularly changing their wireless codes and call signs. Just before the start of the attack they introduced an entirely new code system. The sheer quantity of wireless traffic also swamped the capacity of the British Wireless Observation Groups to make sense of all of it: at the end of February Cox had to write to the War Office requesting an increase of personnel.[138] British aerial reconnaissance was hampered by the fact that German troops advancing to the front were only allowed to move at night and were kept well to the rear until the eve of the attack. Once again poor weather also hampered aerial reconnaissance: for four days immediately before the attack early morning reconnaissance flights were impossible due to thick cloud and rain. Yet the weather was never so bad as to prevent the RFC from photographing some aspects of German preparations for the offensive.[139] Nor, in contrast to their success in the winter and spring of 1916/17, was German counter-intelligence able seriously to disrupt the work of British agents watching the flow of German troops trains in occupied Belgium.[140]

Even so the German deception and security measures sufficed to confuse the British and French. By late January the Allies had lost track of the German order of battle. In late December the Directorate of Military Intelligence was alarmed when their French counterparts informed them that they suspected the existence of an extra twenty German divisions on the Western Front whose whereabouts they could not determine.[141] By the end of January GHQ had still not located them either. Although Cox believed they had travelled south through Liège into France, the French still could not pin-point them.[142]

The result was to engender in the minds of British intelligence analysts

---

[137] PRO, CAB 23/5/WC322, War Cabinet, 15 Jan. 1918; PRO, FO 371/3086/224695, Villiers to FO, 24 Nov. 1917; PRO, CAB 371/3079/233332, Paget to FO, 8 Dec. 1917; PRO, FO 800/171/Ge/18/2, Bertie to Lloyd George, 21 Feb. 1918.

[138] PRO, WO 158/962, Cox to Major-General Organization, War Office, 26 Feb. 1918; Ferris, *The British Army and Signals Intelligence*, p. 40.

[139] Jones, *The War in the Air*, pp. 264–65, 269.

[140] Andrew, *Secret Service*, pp. 168–70.

[141] Cox to Spears, 1 Jan. 1918, LHCMA Spears Papers, 1/15.

[142] PRO, WO 256/27. Haig diary, 23 Jan. 1918.

and policy-makers a dangerous degree of confusion concerning the precise whereabout of the German offensive: on 5 March Derby wrote to Haig that 'It now looks as if an attack might come within a very short time on your front, and on that part of the front of which Gough is in command',[143] at a time when other intelligence was encouraging Haig to fix his attention further north. In February Haig predicted that the German offensive would fall upon his First and Third Armies. Only their extreme left would engage Gough's Fifth Army for the main German effort would be against the French.[144] In mid March Cox had located the German Fourteenth Army at Vimy – he believed that it indicated 'the possibility of the front of the German attack being extended more to the North'.[145] What neither GHQ nor the Directorate of Military Intelligence at the War Office detected was that the Germans would also attack south of St-Quentin between St-Quentin and La Fère.[146]

The British – or at least GHQ and the War Cabinet – therefore looked towards the German offensive with a considerable degree of equanimity. On 2 March Haig told his army commanders that the defences along the fronts of the three armies he had recently inspected were so strong that his only fear was that the Germans would hesitate to attack for fear of the losses they might sustain.[147] Haig's opinion about the strength of his defences was also shared by Sir Maurice Hankey, the Secretary to the War Cabinet and by General Smuts, a member of the War Cabinet. They visited the front in late January and told the Prime Minister that 'The design of the defences is good and sound'. They were already strong and in six weeks they would be very strong.[148] On 16 March Cox presented Haig with a thoroughly confusing report about the timing of the German attack, suggesting that the German's preparations were not yet complete but that they might, or might not, attack in the near future.[149] On 21 March, the very morning of the attack and when the Germans were bombarding the British line on an eighty-kilometre front between the rivers Scarpe and Oise, the new CIGS, Sir Henry Wilson, could tell the War Cabinet that it might not presage a major offensive; that 'there was the possibility that it might only develop into a big raid or demonstration'; and that the real German attack might come further north.[150] The force of the German

[143] Occleshaw, *Armour against Fate*, p. 246.

[144] Sir H. Gough, *The March Retreat* (London, 1934), pp. 31–32.

[145] PRO, WO 157/29, daily intelligence summary, GHQ, Intelligence Branch, 10 Mar. 1918.

[146] PRO, CAB 23/5/WC354, War Cabinet, 26 Feb. 1918; PRO, WO 157/29, daily intelligence summary, GHQ I. Branch, 3 Mar. 1918.

[147] Blake (ed.), *The Private Papers of Douglas Haig*, p. 291.

[148] Hankey to Lloyd George, 22 Jan. 1918, HLRO, Lloyd George Papers, F/23/2/11.

[149] PRO, WO 256/28, Haig diary, 17 Mar. 1918.

[150] PRO, CAB 23/5/WC369, War Cabinet, 21 Mar. 1918; N. Maurice (ed.), *The Maurice Case: From the Papers of Major-General Sir Frederick Maurice* (London, 1972), p. 76.

thrust against Gough's army therefore came as a most unpleasant surprise to both GHQ and the War Office, both of whom more than half expected the initial offensive to be but a preliminary to a more dangerous German thrust towards the Channel ports.

The Germans owed their initial success in March 1918 to several factors. The British had first encountered German stormtroops at Cambrai in December 1917 but had failed to recognise their significance. Their defensive doctrine was faulty, some of their defences were poorly prepared and they failed to anticipate the fog which so assisted the stormtroops' infiltration tactics at the start of the battle.[151] Even more important was the fact that Haig's reserves were in the wrong place to seal off a penetration on the front of the Fifth Army. Although the first German offensive was directed against the southernmost part of the BEF's line held by Gough's army, Haig had allocated only two of the eight divisions he held in GHQ reserve to support Gough. He did so despite the fact that Gough was in more need of reserves than any of his army commanders. Gough's army had only twelve infantry and three cavalry divisions to hold a front of forty-two miles. By contrast the Third Army had fourteen divisions to hold a front of twenty-eight miles and the First Army had fourteen divisions to hold a front of thirty-three miles. Significantly, the Second Army holding the Ypres salient and the road to the Channel ports had twelve divisions to hold a front of only twenty-three miles.[152]

By the end of March 1917 it was apparent that the burden of defeating the German army in the spring of 1917 would fall upon the French and British armies. But it was equally apparent that, by hardly firing a shot, the German High Command had seriously disrupted Nivelle's plan to do so and, as the subsequent inter-allied disagreement over the Calais agreement demonstrated, sown a major seed of discord between the British and French. Falls's suggestion that even had the British been able to discern the German intention to retire to the Hindenburg Line in February 1917, they would still not have been able to exploit the situation to achieve more than a local advantage is probably correct.[153] The Hindenburg Line was a formidable defensive position. As the Cambrai offensive of November 1917 and the eventual crumbling of the line in September and October 1918 demonstrated, the BEF did not yet have the quantities of tanks and artillery, and the understanding of how to combine them with their other arms, to achieve a breakthrough. Looking back to the spring of 1917 in his

---

[151] R.K. Hanks, 'How the First World War was Almost Lost: Anglo-French Relations and the March Crisis of 1918' (unpublished MA thesis, University of Calgary, 1992), pp. 55–68.

[152] M. Middlebrook, *The Kaiser's Battle, 21 March 1918: The First Day of the German Spring Offensive* (London, 1978), p. 78.

[153] Falls, *History of the Great War. Military Operations France and Belgium, 1917*, p. 94.

memoirs, Ludendorff had every right to congratulate himself that, thanks to OHL's deception planning and due 'to the false intelligence we had circulated, they [the British] had not even interfered with our work of demolition and clearance'.[154]

In the spring of 1918 the German efforts to deceive the allies as to the place and timing of their offensive scored an even greater success. In London Sir Henry Wilson and the War Cabinet harboured real doubts as to the reality of a major German offensive in France up until the moment it was actually launched. In France by mid March GHQ knew that a major attack was imminent but, because of Haig's preoccupation with the Channel ports – a preoccupation upon which the German deception planners seemed to have played with some skill – GHQ focused too much attention and too many of its reserves too far to the north. It was only in the days before the offensive that GHQ's estimation of the area to be attacked finally shifted to the Arras to St-Quentin sector. That was correct as far as it went, but they did not expect the attack to extend as far south as it did to Barisis and the junction of the Fifth Army and the French Sixth Army. Even after the attack began, Haig still expected a major attack towards Arras and kept reserves in the north and thickened the centre rather than right of his line to support Gough.[155] Ludendorff's post-war judgement was correct: had the German deception campaign not succeeded to the extent which it did Haig's 'defensive measures would have been more effective, and his reserves would have arrived more quickly'.[156] In his official history Edmonds skirted over the fact. While he avoided perpetrating a deliberate untruth by never arguing explicitly that the British were agreed that they knew precisely when and where the German offensive would begin, that was the misleading impression he probably hoped that all but the most assiduous of his readers would gain.

---

[154] Ludendorff, *My War Memoirs*, ii, p. 408.
[155] PRO, CAB 45/192, Dill to Edmonds, 5 Dec. 1932.
[156] Ludendorff, *My War Memoirs*, ii, p. 596.

4

Managing the War: Britain, Russia and Ad Hoc Government

Keith Neilson

During the First World War what has been called the 'transformation of British government' occurred.[1] The relatively clear-cut administrative boundaries that existed prior to 1914 between departments of state were blurred by the exigencies of war and the new ministries that were created to cope with the changed circumstances the war brought to government. Such changes have been reasonably well served by historians, attracting both official histories and recent historical works.[2] Still, a gap remains. The *ad hoc* committees set up to deal with particular aspects of the war largely remain unstudied, despite the fact that much of the actual day-to-day functioning of wartime government in practice devolved on such bodies.[3] While these committees were prolific, only the growth of the cabinet secretariat (itself a somewhat different, although related, case) has attracted much study.[4]

In some ways, this is understandable. None of the *ad hoc* bodies lasted much beyond the end of the war. Once the reason for their coming into being ended, they were disbanded. However, this fact does not mean that the wartime committees should not be studied; without some knowledge of them, a distorted view of how government worked during the period from 1914 to 1918 results. A number of questions about such committees that need to be answered. How and why did committees come into existence?

[1] Kathleen Burk, ed., *War and the State: The Transformation of British Government, 1914–1919* (London, 1982).

[2] In addition to ibid., HMSO, *History of the Ministry of Munitions* (12 vols; London, 1920–24); R.J.Q. Adams, *Arms and the Wizard: Lloyd George and the Ministry of Munitions, 1915–1916* (London, 1978); E.M. Lloyd, *Experiments in State Control at the War Office and the Ministry of Food* (London, 1924); R. Henry Rew, *Food Supplies in Peace and War* (London, 1920); W.H. Beveridge, *British Food Control* (London, 1928); P.E. Dewey, *British Agriculture in the First World War* (London, 1989); L. Margaret Barnett, *British Food Policy during the First World War* (London, 1985); Keith Grieves, *The Politics of Manpower, 1914–18* (Manchester, 1988).

[3] For a brief consideration of some of them, see John Turner, 'Cabinet, Committees and Secretariats: The Higher Direction of War', in Burk (ed.), *War and the State*, pp. 67–69.

[4] John Turner, *Lloyd George's Secretariat* (Cambridge, 1980); John F. Naylor, *A Man and an Institution: Sir Maurice Hankey, the Cabinet Secretariat and the Custody of Cabinet Secrecy* (Cambridge, 1984).

Who served on them, and how and from where were their members recruited? In what way did such committees change in structure and function over the course of the war? How were they incorporated into the existing structures of government? And, finally, how important were they to the prosecution of the war and what was the extent of their influence on decision-making? Some tentative answers to such questions can be found by looking at a particular case study: the various committees created to manage Britain's relations with Russia during the period from 1914 to 1918.

The study of these committees dealing with Russia also serves another purpose: it provides an insight into the practical difficulties of coalition warfare. Debates over military strategy, war aims and the issue of compromise peace figure large in alliance politics, and are commonplace in writing about alliances. But the intertwined issues of finance and supply are less often considered. As economic and financial co-operation between Britain and Russia was largely effected through *ad hoc* committees, an analysis of them permits an understanding of the wider aspects of the Anglo-Russian alliance.

The fact that bodies existed at all was entirely a product of the war. Prior to 1914, there were no plans for Anglo-Russian co-operation. In the days when the British 'believed in the Russian steam-roller', the war was thought certain to be short with the Russians and French assuring victory on land and the British providing the necessary financial and naval support.[5] Such optimism proved to be false. The war lasted more than four years and the British contribution stretched far beyond the narrow bounds imagined before the war. Britain's relations with Russia became complex, involving the provision of extensive amounts of money and munitions of war in an attempt to help the steam-roller get underway. This relationship was administered through a series of *ad hoc* committees, whose growth, scope of activity and relationship to the more established institutions of British government provide some insights into the general questions outlined above.

Anglo-Russian matters were dealt with by at least five bodies. The first of these to be formed was the *Commission Internationale de Ravitaillement* (CIR). This was supplemented in the summer of 1915 by the creation of the War Office's Russian Purchasing Commission (RPC). The RPC existed for almost exactly one year and was subsumed in August 1916 into the Russian Supplies Committee (RSC) of the Ministry of Munitions. The RSC continued on into 1917 when, in turn, it was absorbed into a new body, the so-called Milner Committee. Finally, at the end of 1917, the Russia

[5] Lord Beveridge, *Power and Influence* (London, 1953), p. 119; Keith Neilson, *Strategy and Supply: The Anglo-Russian Alliance, 1914–1917* (London, 1984), p. 43; David French, *British Strategy and War Aims, 1914–1916* (London, 1986), pp. 1–19.

Committee was created. These five committees dealt with a wide range of issues between Britain and Russia and form the centre of this study.

The CIR was set up in August 1914 at the behest of the French government.[6] The purpose of this body was

> to co-ordinate the purchase of food supplies, munitions of war, and field equipment by the two Allied governments; to prevent harmful competition in the same markets and a consequent inflation of prices; to place the French government in communication with firms known to be capable of carrying out orders satisfactorily and at a reasonable price; and to spread the orders in such a way as to distribute employment and thus accelerate delivery.[7]

The functions of the CIR were exactly similar with respect to Russia. After the CIR had been officially created on 18 August 1914, questions arose as to whether its membership should be expanded to include all the Allies. Parallel Russian inquiries about inter-Allied economic co-operation led to a British suggestion that Russia join the CIR, a suggestion to which the Russian government formally agreed on 22 September.[8]

The British departmental representation on the CIR reflected its role. The Admiralty, the War Office, the Board of Agriculture and Fisheries, the Foreign Office, the Treasury and the Board of Trade were the original members of the CIR.[9] After the Ministry of Munitions was created in 1915, it put a member on the CIR, and there were other additions as the war progressed. Originally, the CIR met at the Board of Trade, but as it grew larger and more complex, it took further offices in India House, Canada House and Empire House. By April of 1917, the CIR consisted of about 350 British members and approximately 2000 members drawn from the Allies.[10] Its initial location reflected the fact that the nucleus of the CIR was provided by the Board of Trade. Ulick Wintour, the CIR's first Director, came to the position from the Board of Trade, where he had served with distinction after leaving the Chinese Customs Service in 1904. While Wintour was the CIR's Director for only a few months, he deserves some attention, for he remained intimately connected with

---

[6] 'Commission Internationale de Ravitaillement: Constitution and Function', ns, nd; 'CIR Establishment and Function', R.F.H. Duke (secretary, CIR), n.d., both PRO, MUN, 5/7/170/25; 'Note on the Constitution and Functions of the Commission Internationale de Ravitaillement', not signed, Dec. 1916, MUN 4/1293, and see also Kathleen Burk, *Britain, America and the Sinews of War, 1914–1918* (London, 1985), pp. 44–45.

[7] Untitled memo, Sir Edmund Wyldbore-Smith (head, CIR), 12 February 1915, PRO, MUN 4/5262.

[8] See the correspondence in Buchanan (British Ambassador, Petrograd) to Grey (British Foreign Secretary), telegram 65, 28 Aug. 1914, PRO, FO 368/1077/44234; FO to Buchanan, telegram 84, 11 Sept. 1914, FO 368/1077/47816 and Benckendorff (Russian Ambassador, London) to Grey, note, n.d., FO 368/1077/52115.

[9] 'List of Committees Appointed to Consider Questions Arising during the Present War', not signed, 1 March 1915, PRO, CAB 42/2/2.

[10] Untitled memorandum, Wyldbore-Smith, n.d. (but April 1917), PRO, CAB 27/189.

Russian munitions as Director of Army Contracts (DAC) at the War Office before leaving that post in 1917 to become Permanent Secretary to the Ministry of Food.[11] Wintour was a man of refined taste and a capable administrator, described as 'a brilliant mediator of other men's ideas', but imperious by nature.[12] This latter trait led to a series of quarrels with other administrators and his eventual sidetracking in the Civil Service.[13] However, during his time as Director of the CIR and as DAC, Wintour's very real abilities as an administrator were to the fore, and he was a key individual in Anglo-Russian dealings concerning munitions.

Sir Edmund Wyldbore-Smith served as Director of the CIR from the time of Wintour's transfer to the War Office in October 1914 until the CIR was disbanded in 1919. Like Wintour, Wyldbore-Smith was a pre-war member of the Board of Trade and, again like Wintour, had spent the years immediately prior to 1914 as part of that body's Exhibitions Branch. While the men had similarities in their careers, they had important differences in their personalities. While Wintour often did not get along well with others, Wyldbore-Smith, according to a man who worked closely with him, 'could charm the most unruly member of his flock to eat out of his hand by dint of tact and kindness'.[14] Such qualities provide an explanation of why Wyldbore-Smith had his long, unbroken tenure as the head of the CIR. Tact and suasion were essential qualities for heading a body where sharply differing national priorities were sorted out.

Under Wyldbore-Smith, the CIR became a key body in Anglo-Russian relations. Its membership expanded rapidly. By 1915 Belgium, Serbia and Portugal had all joined. The Allied representation on the CIR varied, but the initial Russian members were its commercial attaché, its service attachés and their assistants, and a technical expert from the Ministry of War. The CIR not only acted as the clearing house for the orders of the various Allies, but also did the preliminary work involved with blockade, obtaining permission to export goods on the prohibited list.

By the spring of 1915, for a variety of reasons that will be discussed below, it was clear that the co-operation effected between the British and Russian governments through the CIR was inadequate to provide the Russians with the munitions they needed. The collapse of the Russian front, in the aftermath of the German offensive at Gorlice-Tarnow, gave rise to fears that Russia would be driven out of the war unless she were provided with supplies from abroad. Lord Kitchener, the British Secretary

[11] See José Harris, 'Bureaucrats and Businessmen in British Food Control, 1916–19', in Burk, ed., *War and the State*, pp. 135–56; and Barnett, *British Food Policy during the First World War*, pp. 125–26 for the context and Wintour's role at the Ministry of Food.

[12] José Harris, *William Beveridge: A Biography* (New York, 1977), p. 239.

[13] Barnett, *British Food Policy*, pp. 145, 185–86; Harris, 'Bureaucrats and Businessmen', p. 145.

[14] C.E. Callwell, *Experiences of a Dug-Out, 1914–1918* (London, 1920), p. 306, but cf. Neilson, *Strategy and Supply*, p. 216.

of State for War, sent a personal representative, Colonel W.E. Ellershaw, to Russia in an effort to improve matters. On 19 May, Ellershaw and the Russian Commander-in-Chief, the Grand Duke Nicholas Nikolaevich, signed an agreement giving Ellershaw the right to purchase goods for the Russian government abroad.[15] When Ellershaw returned to Britain in June, Kitchener set up the RPC. In some ways, this was an anomaly. For, as a result of growing concerns in Britain about the supply of munitions generally, in May a new Department of State, the Ministry of Munitions had come into existence with David Lloyd George, previously the Chancellor of the Exchequer, as its head.[16] Logically, the Ministry of Munitions should have dealt with Russian munitioning, but the RPC was left with the War Office.[17] This reflected two things: the fact that the Ellershaw agreement had been in the nature of a personal bond between Kitchener and the Grand Duke Nicholas; and the fact that Kitchener deeply resented the criticism of his handling of munitions production implicit in the creation of the Ministry of Munitions. Leaving the RPC in the Field-Marshal's hands was a sop to wounded *amour propre*.

The composition of the RPC was both functional and an attempt to prevent any demarcation problems between the War Office and the Ministry of Munitions. Wintour, the chairman, represented the interests of the War Office, while Ellershaw reflected Kitchener's personal involvement with the Committee. Other British members included Wyldbore-Smith, for the CIR, and George Booth, for the Ministry of Munitions.[18] Booth was a key figure. The son of Charles Booth, the prominent social scientist and businessman, the younger Booth had become involved in munitions work through a web of family connections.[19] Particularly significant was his friendship with Sir Hubert Llewellyn Smith, the Permanent Secretary at the Board of Trade, and the man who had been instrumental in setting up the CIR.[20] A chance encounter with Llewellyn Smith in August 1914 led to Booth's services being unofficially utilised by Kitchener at the War Office. When the Ministry of Munitions was created, Llewellyn Smith became its Permanent Secretary, and Booth became one

[15] Hanbury Williams (British military representative) to Kitchener, 19 May 1915, Kitchener Papers, PRO, 30/57/67.

[16] See Adams, *Arms and the Wizard*, for a laudatory account of Lloyd George's time at the Ministry; for a more analytical view, Chris Wrigley, 'The Ministry of Munitions: An Innovatory Department', in Burk (ed.), *War and the State*, pp. 32–56.

[17] See WO to Ministry of Munitions, 14 June 1915, PRO, MUN 4/524 for the official reasoning behind the division.

[18] *History of the Ministry of Munitions*, ii, pt 8, pp. 10–12.

[19] Duncan Crow, *A Man of Push and Go: The Life of George Macaulay Booth* (London, 1965), pp. 66–115.

[20] On Llewellyn Smith's early career, see Roger Davidson, 'Llewellyn Smith, the Labour Department and Government Growth, 1886–1909', in Sutherland, G. (ed.), *Studies in the Growth of Nineteenth-Century Government* (London, 1972), pp. 227–62.

of the Deputy Director Generals of the Munitions Supply Department of the new ministry.

The provision of supplies for Russia was thus divided between the RPC and the CIR until June 1916, when HMS *Hampshire* sank en route to Russia, killing Kitchener. After some delay, in mid August 1916, the RSC was created at the Ministry of Munitions.[21] Booth was the chairman of the RSC, but its membership was wide-ranging. The War Office was represented by Major-General Sir Charles Callwell. Callwell had retired from the Army in 1909 but, on the outbreak of war had been re-activated as the Director of Military Operations (DMO). Early in 1916, after having been replaced as DMO, Callwell was sent on a special mission to Russia, in an attempt to bring about closer co-operation between Britain and the Tsarist regime.[22] At the same time as the RSC was created, Callwell joined the Ministry of Munitions as the head of a 'special "Military and Political" Department'.[23] As Ellershaw had died along with Kitchener, this new department was in fact the reconstituted RPC, and Callwell's brief was to

> deal with questions affected by strategical and political considerations and be in touch with the Secretary of State for War, the CIGS etc. All cases requiring decisions in general Russian policy, and in particular any refusals of important applications, can be immediately referred to General Callwell.

Other members included Wintour, Philip Hanson (the Director of Munitions Contracts at the Ministry of Munitions); W.J. Benson, the head of the Russian Supplies Section at the Ministry of Munitions; Captain Montfries, the Treasury's representative, and E.N.R. Trentham (Secretary). Wyldbore-Smith, as Director of the CIR, was an *ex officio* member of the RSC. This membership was not constant. In December 1916, B.H. Dobson was appointed Assistant Director of the CIR, 'so far as Russian matters are concerned', and in this role became a member of the RSC.[24] At the same time, Montfries was replaced as the Treasury's representative by G.L. Barstow, who in turn was succeeded by J.M. Keynes in early 1917. The way in which Keynes was recruited for Anglo-Russian matters paralleled Booth's involvement. Keynes had been co-opted for war-time work from Cambridge by Basil Blackett, the senior clerk in the Treasury's 1D (finance) Department.[25] Until 1917, Keynes' work had been largely concerned with Allied loans. Contemporaneously with joining the RSC, Keynes had been

[21] For the formation, see 'Russian Government Supplies', confidential, not signed, 27 June 1916, PRO, MUN 4/6254.

[22] Callwell, *Experiences of a Dug-Out*, pp. 237–52.

[23] This and the following quotation are from 'Procedure in Regard to Russian Government Applications', R.F. Duke (secretary, CIR), 15 Aug. 1916, PRO, MUN 4/5504. For Callwell, see Cubitt (WO) to Foreign Office, 3 Aug. 1916, FO 368/1617/152499.

[24] 'Procedure relating to Russian Purchases', ns, 8 Dec. 1916, PRO, MUN 4/5504.

[25] Neilson, *Strategy and Supply*, pp. 23–24.

appointed the head of a new Department (the 'A' division) created to deal with such matters exclusively.

In March 1917, as a result of the inter-allied conference at Petrograd, a thorough restructuring of the British committees dealing with Russia occurred.[26] On 14 March, the Minister of Munitions, Christopher Addison, called for the formation of a special Cabinet committee to deal with all Russian munitions matters, a suggestion strongly supported by Lord Milner, Minister without Portfolio and a member of Lloyd George's inner cabinet.[27] Milner's championing of the idea ensured that, later in the month, the Committee on Russian Supplies (generally referred to as the Milner Committee after its chairman) was set up.[28] Officially sanctioned by the War Cabinet on 4 April, the Milner Committee was charged with ensuring that the supply agreements reached at the Petrograd conference were carried out.[29] In practice, as will be seen below, the Milner Committee dealt with a wide sweep of Russian-related subjects throughout 1917. Upon the formation of the Milner Committee, the RSC was dissolved, with the Russian Supply Section of the Ministry of Munitions (renamed the Russo-American Supply Section) reporting directly to and represented on the new Committee.[30]

In composition, the Milner Committee was similar to the RSC. Despite the fact that Milner was its titular head, the committee's meetings were generally handled by the Vice-Chairman, Sir Laming Worthington-Evans, the Parliamentary Secretary to the Ministry of Munitions. The War Office was represented by Callwell and Wintour, the CIR by Dobson and the Treasury by Keynes. In addition to Worthington-Evans, the Ministry of Munitions sent two other representatives: Walter Layton, the Director of Munitions Requirements and Statistics (DMRS); and George Booth (for the Russo-American Supplies section, although Benson often attended in Booth's stead). Reflecting the fact that the Milner Committee's primary role was to ensure that Russia received supplies efficaciously in 1917, there were two maritime representatives: Captain Grant, R.N.; and Kemball Cook of the Ministry of Shipping. These were just the core of the Milner Committee, for often experts were invited to speak to particular topics and occasionally representatives of the other departments concerned with Russian matters attended the meetings. The Milner Committee outlived the Russia it had been created to serve and lasted into early 1918. After a

[26] Neilson, *Strategy and Supply*, pp. 225–48.

[27] 'Minutes of Meeting Held to Discuss the Russian Munitions Programme for the Year 1917, at 4, Whitehall Gardens, on Wednesday March 14th', not signed, 14 March 1917, PRO, MUN 4/367.

[28] 'Minutes of the 2nd Interdepartmental Conference on the Russian Munitions Programme', n.d., W. Ormsby-Gore (MP and private secretary to Milner), PRO, MUN 4/367.

[29] 113th meeting of the War Cabinet, 4 April 1917, PRO, CAB 23/2.

[30] 'Russian Supplies Section of the Ministry: Suggestions for Co-ordination with the Lord Milner Committee', W.J. Benson, 2 April 1917, PRO, MUN 4/367 and minutes.

meeting at the Foreign Office on 16 January, the Milner Committee was officially dissolved on 8 February 1918.[31] Its nucleus was transferred to the Foreign Office, where it was placed under the Restriction of Enemy Supplies Department (RESD) of the Ministry of Blockade.

The dissolution and dispersal of the Milner Committee reflected two things: first, Russia was no longer considered an ally and it was important that supplies intended for her did not fall into German hands; secondly, many of the wider functions of the Milner Committee had been taken over by the Russia Committee of the Foreign Office. This latter came into being in mid December 1917 as an inter-departmental (Foreign Office, Treasury and War Office) body to deal with affairs in South Russia.[32] However, after the meeting of 16 January, the Russia Committee became a more powerful body, and its ambit grew wider to encompass all Russia. This resulted from several things. First, there was the dissolution of the Milner Committee and the transfer of matters dealing with supply to the RESD. Secondly, there was a reorganisation at the Foreign Office in which a special Russian Section was hived off from the War Department to ensure co-operation between the RESD and the Russia Committee.[33] Finally, Lord Robert Cecil, the Minister of Blockade, took an active interest in the Russia Committee, and served as its chairman. Its composition reflected its power. In addition to Cecil, the Foreign Office was represented, until the beginning of February 1918, by Sir George Clerk, the head of the War Department and the man who had travelled to the Petrograd Conference as the Foreign Office's representative. Clerk was then replaced by Sir Ronald Graham, the Assistant Undersecretary in charge of the War Department. The War Office was represented by Major-General Sir George Macdonogh, the Director of Military Intelligence (DMI), while Dudley Ward often attended for the Treasury (which was also represented on occasion by Keynes). The CIR had no direct representation on the Russia Committee; coordination with it was effected through the RESD, various members of which frequently attended the Russia Committee. The Russia Committee lasted until the end of the end of the war, although it gave up the responsibility for Russian matters as they pertained to Persia to another body, the Eastern Committee, early in April 1918.[34] But the shutting down of the Russia Committee did not quite bring an end to the bodies dealing with Russia. Fittingly, given that it was the first *ad hoc* body to be created to deal with Russia, it was the CIR that was the last of them

[31] 'Record of a Meeting Held at the Foreign Office on Wednesday, January 16th at 4 pm', ns, 16 Jan. 1918, PRO, CAB 27/189/20; 'Memorandum of Conference on Russian Supplies', Lord Robert Cecil (Minister of Blockade), 16 Jan. 1918, PRO, FO 95/802.

[32] See the recognition of it in 308th meeting of the War Cabinet, 31 December 1917, CAB 23/4; Roberta M. Warman, *The Foreign Office, 1916–18: A Study of its Role and Function* (New York, 1986), pp. 175–99.

[33] On the War Department, see Neilson, *Strategy and Supply*, pp. 15–22.

[34] 41st meeting of the Russia Committee, 4 April 1918, PRO FO 95/802.

to disband. In the post-war, the CIR was transferred to the Department of Overseas Trade of the Board of Trade, and was slowly wound down, ending its activities in October 1919.[35]

The functioning of these *ad hoc* bodies was a complicated matter, and needs to be considered in the larger context of British financial and economic assistance to the Allies, and particularly to Russia, in the First World War. Prior to 1914, the British had no plans for providing supplies or money to her Allies.[36] Indeed, Britain had no Allies in any formal sense and only limited plans for becoming involved in any European war. By the middle of August 1914 all this had changed: Britain was a fully-fledged member of the Entente and was becoming the keystone of a complicated system of inter-allied finance and supply. This lasted throughout the war, with Britain's acting as both the armourer and banker to the Entente, particularly with regard to the large amount of supplies that were purchased in the United States.[37] That this was so is not surprising. Prior to the First World War, Britain was the financial centre of Europe and the world. British capital amounted to 44 per cent of all the capital invested overseas by the Great Powers.[38] Further, Great Britain and her Empire controlled some 47.9 per cent of the world's steam-powered merchant shipping, giving her an unparalleled ability to tap the world's resources in a long war.[39] With naval supremacy ensured by the Royal Navy, Britain was ideally situated to serve a central economic and financial role in the Entente.

This was the context for the formation of the CIR. The need for some such body was quickly manifest. Early in October 1914, the British Ambassador to Washington, Sir Cecil Spring-Rice, reported that 'from various sources I hear that British, French and Russian are competing in United States markets against each other'.[40] In Britain, it was widely believed that the Russian delegates to the CIR 'were not quite "playing the game" . . . [and] apt . . . to take advantage of their positions in order

[35] This can be followed in PRO, BT 61/3/2.

[36] Pre-war planning is best followed in David French, *British Economic and Strategic Planning, 1905–1915* (London, 1982); John Gooch, *The Plans of War: The General Staff and British Military Strategy, c. 1900–1915* (London, 1974).

[37] In addition to Burk, *Sinews of War*, see her two articles, 'The Diplomacy of Finance: British Financial Missions to the United States, 1914–1918', *Historical Journal*, 22, (1979), pp. 351–72; and 'The Mobilisation of Anglo-American Finance during World War One', in Dreisziger, N.F., ed., *Mobilisation for Total War: The Canadian, American and British Experience, 1894–1918, 1939–1945* (Waterloo, Ontario, 1981), pp. 23–43.

[38] Sidney Pollard, 'Capital Exports, 1870–1914: Harmful or Beneficial?', *Economic History Review*, 2nd series, 38 (1985), p. 492.

[39] C.E. Fayle, *History of the Great War Based on Official Documents: Seaborne Trade*, i, *The Cruiser Period* (London, 1920), pp. 18–19; Avner Offer, *The First World War: An Agrarian Interpretation* (Oxford, 1989).

[40] Spring Rice to FO, telegram 73, urgent, PRO, FO 371/2224/57870.

to put commissions into their own pockets!'.[41] Just as worrying was the fact that the Russian government did not feel limited in its right to purchase as a result of its membership in the CIR. On 30 October Wintour complained that the Russians had placed orders with Vickers, the British armaments firm, for 'very large quantities of war material of which neither we [the War Office] nor Wyldbore-Smith have any knowledge'.[42] Equally disconcerting was the report that the Russian government in Petrograd was placing orders 'through merchants, agents, etc., instead of through their Delegates on the Commission [CIR]'.[43] It was not just the British who were kept in the dark about such orders, for the head of the Russian deputation to the CIR told Llewellyn Smith that he was 'entirely ignorant' of 'large orders' placed by his own government in the United States.[44] On 2 February 1915, Wyldbore-Smith reported that 'the Central Authorities at Petrograd are showering orders on this country without informing any of their Delegates [to the CIR] what they are doing'.[45] By the beginning of 1915, and despite the work of the CIR, there was no satisfactory solution to the problem of the control of Russian purchasing.

Nor was there any control of inter-allied finance. One of the general beliefs before the First World War had been that any European war would be short. This was founded both on military assumptions and on the belief that the European economic and financial system was so interdependent that the dislocation caused by war would necessarily force the belligerents to seek peace rapidly.[46] By the beginning of 1915 this assumption had proven false, as all the belligerents showed a surprising economic and financial resilience. None the less, there were distinct problems for the Allies in the money markets. Russia was particularly hard hit. Before 1914, the ruble was a much 'softer' currency than was either the pound sterling or the French franc. Much of Russia's foreign exchange before the war had been provided by the export of grain, and, with the closing of the Straits when the Ottoman Empire declared its belligerency, Russia faced exchange-rate problems.[47] In the autumn of 1914, the Russians had

[41] The minute (11 October 1914) on Grey to Benckendorff (Russian Ambassador, London), PRO, FO 368/1077/58712; see also, Spring-Rice to Foreign Office, despatch 89 (commercial), 26 Oct. 1914, FO 371/2224/63616.

[42] Wintour to A. Law (Controller, Commercial and Consular Affairs, FO), 30 Oct. 1914, PRO, FO 368/1087/66260.

[43] H. Fountain (Board of Trade) to Foreign Office, 3 Nov. 1914, PRO, FO 368/1087/66974.

[44] Llewellyn Smith to FO, 20 Oct. 1914, PRO, FO 371/2224/69615.

[45] Wyldbore Smith to J.A.C. Tilley (FO), 2 Feb. 1915, PRO, FO 371/2447/13198.

[46] L.L. Farrar, Jr, *The Short War Illusion* (Santa Barbara, CA, 1974); the literature is introduced in Jon Lawrence, Martin Dean and Jean-Louis Robert, 'The Outbreak of War and the Urban Economy: Paris, Berlin, and London in 1914', *Economic History Review*, 45 (1992), pp. 564–65.

[47] 'Russian War Finance', Hugh O'Beirne (British Councillor, Petrograd), 26 November 1914, PRO, FO 371/2096/81744; A.L. Sidorov, *Finansovoe polozhenie Rossii v gody pervoi mirovoi voiny* (Moscow, 1960), ch. 1; Norman Stone, *The Eastern Front, 1914–1917* (London, 1975), pp. 153–56.

attempted to solve this difficulty by negotiating loans in both Britain and the United States.[48] The latter attempt was a failure, but the British provided the Russians with a loan of £20,000,000 in mid October and a further loan for £40,000,000 was being negotiated between the two countries at the end of 1914.

At the beginning of 1915, the British took further steps to ensure that the Entente's purchasing in the United States was done in a concerted fashion. On 15 February the British signed an agreement with J.P. Morgan & Co., making the banking firm the sole purchasing agents in the United States for the British government, which, through the CIR, made Morgans the representatives for the Entente as a whole.[49] Morgans, which was part of an interlocking series of firms (Morgan Grenfell in London and Morgan Harjes et Cie in Paris), was ideally situated to attempt to bring some order to the complicated matter of Allied purchasing in the United States. However, while this improved matters, it was not a complete solution. The Russian government had its own representatives in the United States, and they continued to purchase war *matériel* outside the structure provided by Morgans.[50] Only when Russian purchases were funnelled through the CIR could the British be certain of their nature and extent.

Meanwhile, further steps were taken in an attempt to regularise Russia's purchasing of supplies. In mid January 1915, the Russian government sent General Timchenko-Ruban to London to head a new body, the Russian Government Committee (RGC).[51] Its brief was to arrange all Russian purchasing in Britain and to ensure better co-operation with the British about purchases made overseas. This latter was fortunate, for Wyldbore-Smith noted on 26 January that he had been 'very much in the dark as to how arrangements for the placing of future Russian orders in the United States and Canada' would be carried out until he was informed of Timchenko-Ruban's arrival.[52] The RGC included many of the Russian members of the CIR, but remained independent of it. All seemed promising for better co-ordination. But there still remained the delicate matter of how to pay for these supplies. With the Russian loan for £40,000,000 still not agreed upon by the beginning of February 1915, money for Russia was a key note at the inter-allied financial conference held at Paris on 4–5 February.

At the conference, the Russian government received the backing of the British and French governments for a loan of £100,000,000 to be raised

[48] Neilson, *Strategy and Supply*, pp. 54–57,.

[49] Burk, *Sinews of War*, pp. 15–22.

[50] See, for example, Wyldbore-Smith to Tilley (FO), 2 Feb. 1915, PRO, FO 371/2447/13198; Burk, *Sinews of War*, p. 47; Neilson, *Strategy and Supply*, pp. 190–91, 205–7.

[51] Buchanan to FO, private and secret, 23 January 1915, PRO, FO 371/2447/9016 and attached correspondence; on Russian representation generally, A.L. Sidorov, 'Missiia v Angliiu i Frantsiiu po voprosu snabzheniia Rossii predmetami vooruzheniia', *Istoricheskii arkhiv*, 4 (1949), pp. 351–86.

[52] Wyldbore Smith to Tilley, 26 Jan. 1915, PRO, FO 371/2447/9932.

in London and Paris.[53] The two western Allies each agreed to lend Russia £25,000,000, with that amount to be deducted from the loan when the latter was fully subscribed. In order to maintain British credit in the United States, France and Russia each conceded to lend the Bank of England £12,000,000 in gold. The conference was a signal success; the issue of gold and Russia's credit was, however, to dog Anglo-Russian financial relations for the rest of the war. Since the autumn of 1914, the Russian government had opposed the idea that any British loans to Russia would involve the transfer of gold.[54] The issues were clear. Britain refused to weaken her own credit by granting Russia unsecured credits and loans. Russia refused to surrender her financial independence and viewed the British attitude as grasping, given both that Russia would have to repay the money and that Russia was paying a price in blood on the battlefield far surpassing any sanguinary outlay by the British.[55]

These, along with the desperate Russian need for munitions during the German offensive, were the circumstances that led to the creation of Kitchener's RPC in the spring of 1915. But the RPC, even working with the CIR and the RGC, found it difficult to bring order to Russian purchasing. This resulted from two facts. The first was that the provision of munitions for the Russian army was enmeshed in Russian domestic politics. On one level, there was bureaucratic ineptitude in Russia.[56] The original Russian delegates to the CIR had not represented the two most powerful departments – Engineering and Artillery – of the Russian War Ministry, and these two refused to stop ordering independently of the CIR.[57] This problem was partially solved by the addition of personnel: Timchenko-Ruban was sent as a representative of the Engineering Department and, in May 1915, two more men – Colonel N. Beliaev and Major-General E. Hermonious, both of the Artillery Department – went to Britain to join the RPC. On another level, Russia's purchasing of munitions abroad was a political issue, for many in Russia used the fact of the shell shortages as a stick to beat the Tsarist government for its incompetence.[58] Thus,

[53] For the Paris Conference, see Neilson, *Strategy and Supply*, pp. 66–68.

[54] Ibid., pp. 54–57; 65–66.

[55] Stone, *Eastern Front*, pp. 153–6.

[56] See Buchanan to Foreign Office, telegram 33, private and secret, 24 Feb. 1915, PRO, FO 371/2447/22147.

[57] For an example of confusion and cross-purpose, see Keith Neilson, 'Russian Foreign Purchasing in the Great War: A Test Case', *Slavonic and East European Review*, 60 (1982), pp. 572–90. There was also a division between front and rear: see D.W. Graf, 'Military Rule behind the Russian Front, 1914–1917: The Political Ramifications', *Jahrbücher für Geschichte Osteuropas*, 22 (1974), pp. 390–411.

[58] D.S. Babichev, 'Deiatelnost Russkogo pravitelstvennogo komiteta v Londone v gody pervoi mirovoi voiny, 1914–1917', *Istoricheskie zapiski*, 57 (1956), pp. 276–92; T.D. Krupina, 'Politicheskii krizis 1915 g. i sozdanie osobogo sobeshchaniia po oborone', ibid., 83 (1969), pp. 58–75; and Lewis H. Siegelbaum, *The Politics of Industrial Mobilization in Russia, 1914–17* (London, 1983), pp. 24–84.

British efforts to attempt to get the Russians to improve the co-ordination of their purchasing had to be done very carefully lest these efforts appear to intrude into Russian politics.[59]

Another problem for Anglo-Russian purchase and supply was the situation in the United States. Although the agreement with Morgans was supposed to ensure that all Russian purchasing was vetted by the CIR, this was not the case. At the same time as Hermonious and Beliaev had gone to Britain, Major-General A.V. Sapozhnikov had been sent to the United States to create the Russian Purchasing Committee in New York, the equivalent of the RGC in London.[60] Sapozhnikov and the New York office gained a reputation for irritating methods and independent orders. In an attempt to end such (and other, related) problems, Hermonious and Ellershaw travelled to New York in July 1915. While their mission managed to patch up some matters, it was a temporary fix. More permanent measures were required. The catalyst for them was an increased demand for money to cover Allied purchases in the United States. During July and August 1915, there was a temporary exchange-rate crisis caused, in part, by large orders placed in the United States by Hermonious and Ellershaw without informing the RGC and Morgans.[61] This became a matter for the Treasury. On 20 August, British and French financial representatives met at Boulogne and agreed each to hold £200,000,000 in gold ready for shipment to the United States in order to protect Allied credit there. A similar step was urged on the Russian government. While the Russians twisted and turned, not wanting to tie the shipment of Russian gold to the creation of Allied credit generally, the Treasury was unwilling to compromise. The Joint Permanent Secretary to the Treasury, Sir John Bradbury, outlined why the British were reluctant to create credit for the Allies:

> That we must provide for the allies the *things* which are essential to them for carrying on the war to the utmost limit of our capacity, goes without saying, but it will be much better for us, and in the long run for them, that we should provide them with the *things* as and when we produce or obtain them instead of providing them with power to bid in our markets for things which we cannot produce or obtain and to dislocate both our markets and our production in the process.[62]

The result was the Anglo-Russian financial agreement of 30 September 1915 (the so-called Treasury Agreement).[63]

[59] See, for example, the minutes on Buchanan to Foreign Office, despatch 111, 11 Aug. 1915, PRO, FO 368/1399/121793.

[60] Knox (British Military Attaché, Russia), to MO3 (War Office), despatch T, 22 April 1915, PRO, WO 106/1057.

[61] Burk, *Sinews of War*, pp. 62–67; Neilson, *Strategy and Supply*, pp. 105–7.

[62] 'Creation of Credits for Allies', Bradbury, 16 Sept. 1915, Bradbury Papers, PRO, T 170/73.

[63] The text of the agreement is found in PRO, T 172/255.

The Treasury Agreement provided a framework to ensure that the worst aspects of independent purchasing by the Russians were curbed. The British extended Russia a monthly credit of £25,000,000 for the ensuing twelve months, but the Russians had to commit themselves to providing £40,000,000 worth of gold to the Bank of England. Restrictions were placed on the uses to which this credit could be put. The money could be spent for existing contracts placed in Britain, the Empire, the United States and (to a limited extent) Japan. New credit, to a maximum of £4,500,000 millions per month, was provided for orders placed according to the conditions outlined in the annexe to the Agreement. None of the credit could be used in France or for propping up the ruble on the exchange markets. Instead, the British provided some £200,000,000 of 'equivalent obligations' to Russia, upon the security of which the Russians could increase their fiduciary issue.

It was the annexe to the agreement that aided the British most in their attempt to regularise the purchase of munitions and that aspect was of most immediate interest to the *ad hoc* committees. The annexe provided that all Russian purchasing in Britain, the Empire and the United States that was paid for by British funds would have to be placed by a group of Russian experts sitting in London. With respect to war *matériel*, the Russians would consult with the RPC; with respect to all other goods, the Russians would work through the CIR. While in theory the annexe should have provided a comprehensive solution to the matter of munitions purchasing, in practice it did not.

The reason for this was simple: despite the provisions of the annexe, the RGC and the Russian Purchasing Committee in New York continued to place orders without consultation. A long discussion of this problem in British munitions circles in November 1915 illustrated nicely the delicate nature of Allied co-operation.[64] Booth pointed out that the annexe had no teeth; that Britain was only consulted about Russian purchasing and had no right of veto short of denying Russia funds. Looking ahead to an impending inter-allied conference on munitions, Booth advocated that the annexe be revised in order to give Britain more direct power over Russia's ordering of goods. He also noted some organisational weaknesses. When the office of Director of Army Contracts had been split in half in the autumn of 1914, Wintour had retained the Quarter-Master General aspect of affairs, while the Master-General of the Ordnance aspect had been placed under Hanson. When the Ministry of Munitions was formed, Hanson's section had become part of the new ministry (with Hanson's becoming the Director of Munitions Contracts).

[64] 'War Office Russian Buying Commission', confidential memorandum, Booth, 9 Nov. 1915, Black Papers, PRO, MUN 5/533; the earlier 'Memorandum of Conference Held in Director of Army Contracts' Room on the 14th October, 1915, to Consider the Interpretation of the British-Russian Financial Agreement', ns, 14 Oct. 1915, MUN 7/149, and 'Memorandum', not signed, 2 Nov. 1915, Llewellyn Smith Papers, MUN 4/7054.

But Kitchener's retention of Russian purchasing through the RPC at the War Office meant that Wintour and Hanson often operated in direct competition with one another over supplies for Russia. Perhaps more significant, Booth opined, was the fact that, when the same munitions were required by both the Russian government and the British government, the Ministry of Munitions was forced to choose between their competing demands. Booth felt that all these problems could be resolved only if the Ministry were given complete control over Russian purchasing.

Hanson's reply to Booth's remarks drove home the realities of the Anglo-Russian alliance.[65] The Director of Munitions Contracts pointed out that the Treasury Agreement and annexe had been negotiated with great difficulty, and that the Russian government was unlikely to be willing to surrender any further powers to the British. With the present military difficulties in the Balkans, it was imperative to maintain her close co-operation, given the importance of her influence on events in that region: the withdrawal of British financial support under the terms of the Treasury Agreement would affect Anglo-Russian relations adversely. Even if Britain did decide to take this serious step, Hanson was not certain that it would result in Britain's obtaining complete control over Russian purchasing. While, through the Ministry of Munitions, such control might be possible to gain in Britain and the Empire, in the United States the Ministry of Munitions had no authority, and Russia would still be free to place such orders as she could. Though the Treasury Agreement was an imperfect instrument, in Hanson's opinion it was the best means that the British were likely to get for co-ordinating Russian purchasing with British requirements and capabilities.

Hanson's remarks were prescient. At the inter-Allied conference on munitions, held on 23–25 November in London, all attempts to circumscribe Russia's power to purchase independently were rejected.[66] The Russian delegate, Admiral A.I. Rusin, put his government's position clearly, albeit obliquely. In response to a proposal made by the French Minister of Munitions, Albert Thomas, for the creation of a centralised inter-Allied body to co-ordinate purchasing, Rusin accepted Thomas' idea 'in principle', 'provided that while the details were being arranged existing arrangements were not interfered with'.[67] His agreement was so vague as to constitute a refusal, and the inter-allied body never became more than a pious aspiration.

Another major problem in Anglo-Russian relations concerning munitions arose early in 1916. This centred on shipping.[68] By that date

65 'Note on Memorandum on Munitions Contracts for the Allies', not signed (but Hanson), nd (but *c.* 20 Nov. 1915), PRO, MUN 7/149.

66 The proceedings of the conference are in MUN 4/5068.

67 'Conference between Representatives of the Allied Governments' second day, not signed, 24 Nov. 1915, PRO, MUN 4/5068.

68 The following is based on Neilson, *Strategy and Supply*, pp. 176–81.

there was a severe Allied shortage of tonnage as a result of dramatically increased demand for ships to move munitions and foodstuffs across the Atlantic and from Australasia. Since the Russians did not have sufficient merchant shipping to move their own orders, they were dependent on the British to provide such tonnage. Sending goods to Russia was a difficult matter, for the only available routes were via Vladivostok (and the length of this route meant a further strain on shipping), by trans-shipment through neutral Sweden (and this entailed other difficulties),[69] and through Archangel on the White Sea. Despite its being ice-bound for part of the year, Archangel was the port of choice for shipping munitions; however, its restricted port facilities and inadequate rail links meant that there was substantial congestion at the port.[70]

Given this restriction and the shortage of tonnage, the British had two concerns. First, they opposed the Russians' placing large orders overseas for *matériel* that could not be shipped to Russia. Secondly, they did not see any point in allocating more tonnage to the Russians when much of the goods already shipped to Russia remained at Archangel and Murmansk. The Russian response was the same one that they had made with respect to credit and supplies: if Russia were not granted sufficient shipping to move her purchases, then the Russian war effort would be reduced to the detriment of the Allied cause. At the same time, the Russians tended to resist any British attempts to take complete control of shipping, regarding this an infringement on Russian sovereignty. The realities of war forced both sides to compromise. After long, tedious and often acrimonious negotiations, on 5 May 1916 the British Admiralty agreed to provide Russia with 2,000,000 tons of shipping in the twenty-five week period commencing 15 May and to organise the on- and off-loading at Archangel.[71] In exchange, the Admiralty was given control of all shipping in the White Sea. The Russian government agreed to close the White Sea to all shipping except that approved by the CIR and to provide adequate manpower and transport for all of the above to be effected.

Despite this success, by June 1916 it was clear that the functioning of the Anglo-Russian alliance with respect to finance and supply was in need of an overhaul. Any request by the Russian government for supplies or for money for purposes that were not immediately obvious triggered voluminous correspondence and caused long delays. In addition, Russian expenditure in the United States and the ill-will generated by their business methods threatened to undermine the ability of the Entente to

[69] Keith Neilson and B.J.C. McKercher "'The Triumph of Unarmed Force": Sweden and the Allied Blockade of Germany, 1914–1917', *Journal of Strategic Studies*, 7 (1984), pp. 178–99.

[70] Stone, *Eastern Front*, pp. 157–58.

[71] The best Russian-language account is M.A. Stoliarenko, 'Anglo-Russkie soglasheniia o severnykh portakh Rossii v gody pervoi mirovoi voiny', *Vestnik Leningradskogo Universiteta*, 16 (1961), pp. 46–58.

purchase in America. An attempt to seek a solution to this problem was one of the motives for Kitchener's ill-fated voyage, but his death delayed any inter-allied consideration of matters until July. Negotiations in that month reinforced the arguments that had characterised the Anglo-Russian relationship since the beginning of the war. On 13–15 July all the Allies met in London to discuss matters of supply and finance.[72] As usual, the Russians tied their military effort to the provision of large amounts of munitions, money and tonnage. As usual, the British countered with arguments based on scarcity, priorities and control. Neither party could agree on figures. Lord Curzon, the head of the British Shipping Control Committee, wondered aloud whether the Russian estimates of the capacity of their ports were 'sometimes moving perhaps in the region of hope rather than in the region of recognizable fact'.[73] With respect to finance, the Russians rejected the British suggestion that they should both limit their purchases to the amounts that could be transported and make clear exactly what were the concrete needs of the Russian war effort. As an interim measure, the Treasury offered the Russians a credit of £25,000,000 per month for the next six months, with £4,000,000 of this amount to be unencumbered by restrictions. Further, Russia was granted an immediate credit of £63,000,000 to place military orders with a further £63,000,000 to be paid in two equal instalments in October and November. In exchange, Russia was to agree to ship £40,000,000 in gold to British should it be required.

The conference also reached two significant administrative arrangements. On 14 July, an agreement was signed creating a joint Anglo-Russian sub-committee in New York to consider all Russian purchases in the United States.[74] Under the provisions governing the function of the sub-committee, its British members had the power of veto over any purchases for which financing had not been arranged. Further to such concerns, the Allies had signed a general 'protocol' on 15 July that bound them to consult with one another before placing orders in or obtaining loans from neutral countries.[75] More observed in the breach than in the observance, the 'protocol' was a nod to the long-held French ideas of pooling Allied resources for the common good.

These issues emerged again at the inter-Allied conference on supply held in London on 8–10 November 1916.[76] The focus of the conference

---

[72] The proceedings of the conference are in PRO, MUN 4/5068.

[73] 'Minutes of Proceedings at a Conference on Russian Requirements', not signed, 13 July 1916, Black Papers, PRO, MUN 5/533.

[74] The sub-committee is outlined in the agreement signed by Bark (Russian Finance Minister) and Grey (British Foreign Secretary), 14 July, PRO, MUN 4/4866.

[75] 'Protocol', signed by Bark, Ribot (French Minister of Finance), McKenna (British Chancellor of the Exchequer), 15 July 1916, PRO T 172/385.

[76] The conference may be followed in 'Summary of the Proceedings of the Inter-Ally Munitions Conference Held in London November 8th, 9th and 10th 1916', PRO, MUN 4/5068.

was the determination of the needs of each of the Allies for the 1917 campaign. Here, for the first time, Russian and French requirements were clearly at odds. As they had at previous conferences, the Russians produced a shopping list that was in no way related to the ability of the Allies to transport supplies to Russia. The French, on the other hand, insisted that their needs were so great that Russia must reduce her demands. It was a measure of the increase in Allied, especially British, production capacity that Lloyd George was optimistic that the British could go some way towards fulfilling the extravagant Russian demands. The limiting factor remained the availability of shipping, but again Russia was given priority, mainly on the grounds that a strong Russian military effort in 1917 promised the best likelihood of a victory in that year.

The November conference did not address the matter of organisation. By the beginning of 1917, both British and Russian officials were very unhappy with the cumbersome way in which supplies for Russia were procured. Hermonious wrote two long letters complaining about the lengthy procedures involved in ordering and approving supplies.[77] According to him, at least six weeks were required for an individual order to be processed; he felt that the RGC should be allowed to place orders first and get British approval second. This approach ran counter to the thrust of all British thinking since the outbreak of the war and was unlikely to find much favour in British circles. However, there was some sympathy for his complaints. Wyldbore-Smith felt that much of the congestion could be relieved by the abolition of the RSC.[78] He argued that the RSC acted as a barrier between the CIR and the Ministry of Munitions, to the detriment of Russian supply.

Clearly, despite the progress that had occurred since the outbreak of war, there were still matters unresolved in Anglo-Russian finance and supply at the beginning of 1917. The Petrograd Conference, held from 30 January to 20 February 1917, was a belated attempt to resolve such matters in the context of the Anglo-Russian war effort generally.[79] But, while the conference represented a laudable intention, its results reflected the near impossibility of finding solutions that suited all concerned. The sessions on *ravitaillement* echoed the problems that had confounded earlier conferences. The Russians, no doubt tired of having their requests denied on the grounds that Russian ports were incapable of off-loading the goods already delivered to them, began the discussions by asserting that the capacity of their ports for the period until mid 1918 was 9,500,000 tons and demanded that the Allies provide them with goods totalling

[77] Hermonious to Ministry of Munitions, 8 and 10 Jan. 1917, Black Papers, PRO, MUN 4/533.

[78] 'Memorandum on Commission Internationale de Ravitaillement. Ministry of Munitions Procedure', Wyldbore-Smith, 20 Jan. 1917, PRO, MUN 5/137/1010.

[79] See Neilson, *Strategy and Supply*, pp. 225–48, for the Petrograd Conference.

this amount.[80] The British rejected this figure as profoundly optimistic and offered instead to ship some 4,000,000 tons. As usual, the Russian response was that Britain did not appreciate the magnitude of the Russian military effort with the implicit threat that a failure to provide as much as they demanded would lead to a decreased Russian military presence in 1917. When the British insisted that the Russians put their needs in order of priority, the Russian response was anger and a certain hauteur. While arguments over finance at the conference lacked this bitterness, all that was achieved was a continuance of the status quo.[81]

But the aftermath of the Petrograd Conference did achieve at least one thing. In late March and early April 1917, the formation of the Milner Committee brought about a complete reorganisation of the machinery dealing with Anglo-Russian supply. While the Milner Committee represented the penultimate rationalisation of the British side of the administrative relationship with Russia, the committee's linkage to Russia's administration was, if anything, more complicated than before. This was the result of the fact that, during the Petrograd Conference, the Russian government had agreed to the creation of two British bodies in Russia to deal with munitions. The first of these, the British Military Equipment Section, under Brigadier-General F.C. Poole, was intended to ensure that British supplies sent to Russia were utilised fully.[82] The second, an arm of the Ministry of Munitions and headed by Colonel F. Byrne, was set up to ensure a close liaison between the various departments of the Russian government and the Ministry of Munitions.[83] These two bodies infringed upon many of the roles of the RGC. The willingness of the Russian government to sanction their creation reflected the dissatisfaction, noted above, of many departments in the Russian government with the RGC and their belief that the RGC either did not represent their interests or else usurped their powers. In fact, there were several attempts to abolish the RGC, but it outlived both the Tsarist and Provisional Governments, coming to an end only in 1918.[84]

For the remainder of 1917, with Russian participation in the war and the efficiency of that participation a matter of contention, Anglo-Russian supply and finance became tied closely to evaluation of the political

[80] 'Conférence des Allies à Petrograd: Commission de Ravitaillement', 1st session, 30 Jan. 1917, PRO, CAB 28/2 IC 16(B).

[81] 'Financial Questions Raised at the Conference', not signed, 7 February 1917, PRO, CAB 21/42; 'Procès verbal of the Allied Financial Conference at Petrograd, Feb. 7 1917', not signed, 7 Feb. 1917, CAB 28/2 IC 16(a).

[82] 'Report of the Work of the British Military Equipment Section in Russia', Poole, 17 Jan. 1918, PRO, WO 106/1145.

[83] Neilson, *Strategy and Supply*, pp. 240–41; 3rd meeting of the Milner Committee, 11 April 1917, Worthington Evans Papers, PRO, MUN 4/396.

[84] See Byrne's diary entries, 13 Feb. and 13 March 1918, PRO, CAB 27/189/21.

stability of the Russian government.[85] When Russia showed signs of being militarily effective, or when she threatened collapse if not supported, supplies and money (or, at least the promise of them) were forthcoming. Since, however, the British discounted the possibility of Russia's acting as an effective partner in the alliance from as early as March 1917, as little as possible was earmarked for Russia; as the resources were felt better given to British and other Allied forces. By the beginning of 1918, with the Bolsheviks in power and the armistice of Brest-Litovsk shutting down the Eastern Front, much of the machinery for Anglo-Russian economic cooperation was no longer needed.

Instead, the Russia Committee centred its activities on ensuring that the blockade of the Central Powers was maintained as efficaciously as possible despite Brest-Litovsk, on dealing with the detritus (the RGC and Russian monies) left over from the pre-Bolshevik regimes and on evaluating how best to support those elements in Russia (and elsewhere, as in the case with Japan) that promised to maintain an active Eastern front. These activities, particularly the latter, were overtly political, and the Russia Committee served as the body that both provided the Foreign Secretary, Arthur Balfour, with advice and made day-to-day decisions about the carrying out of policy.[86]

The *ad hoc* bodies dealing with Russia were clearly an important aspect of the British government during the First World War. The very fact that they were created makes this conclusion inescapable, for they were not brought into existence as the result of some comprehensive plan for managing the alliance but rather as the result of need. The existing structures of the War Office, the Board of Trade, the Admiralty, the Treasury and the Foreign Office were designed with British affairs of state, not the joint needs of a coalition. Just as command structures had to be established to co-ordinate the Allied armies and navies, so, too, did organisations to co-ordinate the Entente's economic and financial collaboration. For the most part, the *ad hoc* bodies served as co-ordinating and executive bodies, for neither the British nor the Russian governments were willing to give them decision-making power at the highest level. However, with regard to some of the issues that the *ad hoc* bodies dealt with, it was difficult to separate executive and decision-making functions. The cumulative effect of many small decisions taken in by the various *ad hoc* bodies with respect, say, to shipping and purchasing was to circumscribe what could be decided at higher levels. Clearly, the *ad hoc* bodies were a significant part of the machinery for the war's direction.

The nature and timing of their creation was largely a matter of chance.

---

[85] Keith Neilson, 'The Breakup of the Anglo-Russian Alliance: The Question of Supply in 1917', *International History Review*, 3 (1981), pp. 62–75.

[86] Warman, *The Foreign Office*, pp. 181–95. For the background, see Richard H. Ullman, *Anglo-Soviet Relations, 1917–1921*, i, *Intervention and the War* (Princeton, 1916), pp. 58ff.

Each of the *ad hoc* bodies discussed above had a different genesis. Despite the fact that 'from the beginning of the war the British Executive Staff of the CIR have concentrated special attention on Russian requirements', the establishment of the CIR had little to do with Russia and that body remained firmly inter-Allied in nature.[87] The fact that its leadership was largely recruited from the Board of Trade's Exhibitions Department reflected the fact that these men had experience both with trade and foreigners, the natural ambit of the CIR. The RPC's creation was quite different and stemmed from Kitchener's concern about Russia's military role in the Entente.[88] Concerned that bureaucratic inefficiency and red-tape were hamstringing the Russian war effort, Kitchener decided to cut the Gordian knot by means of a personal emissary and the subsequent creation of a body directly responsible to himself. This highly-personalised approach was typical of Kitchener, who was secretive and autocratic by nature and whose own military experience had been with much smaller campaigns.[89] Indeed, the creation of RPC can be seen as a small example of Kitchener's attempts to run the war by himself, best exemplified by his efforts to keep recruiting and munitions within his own purview. Just as these two latter attempts were unsuccessful and led to the establishment of the Ministry of Munitions and the Ministry of National Service, the RPC gave way to the RSC.

The RSC, even working closely with the CIR, was not, however, capable of dealing with all the complexities of the Anglo-Russian alliance. In particular, the need both to control spending by the Russian government and to provide shipping for the Russian purchases meant that matters needed to be considered at a level higher than that of inter-departmental committees. The creation of the Milner Committee, with its official status as a committee of the War Cabinet and its being headed by one of Lloyd George's inner Cabinet, meant two things: first, much squabbling over jurisdiction between the CIR and the Ministry of Munitions could be settled definitively; secondly, Milner's implicit presence and authority gave the Committee's decisions more clout, since it could be presumed that they carried the weight of the War Cabinet behind them. Milner's own link to Russia – he had headed the British delegation to Petrograd – meant that he could, if necessary, bypass the Russian representatives in London and speak directly to the requisite Russian authorities in Petrograd. The Milner Committee represented, in its organisation and authority, the culmination of all the efforts of the British to co-ordinate their war effort with Russia during the First World War.

The Russia Committee was an anomaly in that respect, for it came into

[87] Wyldbore Smith's untitled memorandum for Lord Milner, n.d. (but April 1917), PRO, CAB 27/189.

[88] On this, see Keith Neilson, 'Kitchener: A Reputation Refurbished?', *Canadian Journal of History*, 15 (1980), pp. 207–27.

[89] On Kitchener, see George Cassar, *Kitchener: Architect of Victory* (London, 1977).

being when Russia had effectively left the war. While it took over many of the personnel who had served in its predecessors, their functions became analogous to those of a company acting as a receiver for a bankrupt firm: they ensured that the assets of the defunct Tsarist state were both protected from hostile predators and preserved for Russia's creditors. The rest of the Russia Committee had a completely new function: to endeavour to resuscitate the Eastern front and to advise on the formulation of a British policy to meet the new circumstances in Russia.

The functioning of the *ad hoc* bodies illustrate a number of important points about the functioning of alliances. A major point is the paramount need for a proper organisational framework to ensure the smooth functioning of joint endeavours. Since Britain and Russia had no pre-war alliance, they had no plans afoot for wartime collaboration. In Britain, despite the early creation of the CIR, dealings with and responsibility for Russia were fragmented. The War Office, the Admiralty, the Treasury, the Board of Trade, the Foreign Office and, later, the Ministry of Munitions each had interests in various facets of the economic and financial aspects of the Anglo-Russian alliance. As each department had its own priorities, the possibility of divergent and competing policies was strong. At the very least, such fragmentation meant that there were untimely delays and a needless duplication of administration.

To some extent, the administrative problems of the alliance were overcome by the simple expedient of overlapping memberships. A number of key people were not only members of the CIR but also of the RPC and RSC. To a greater extent, though, there was a gradual improvement in the functioning of the alliance through bureaucratic innovation. The creation of the Milner Committee reflected the growing organisational sophistication of the government generally with respect to the prosecution of the war. By centralising all matters dealing with Russia in one committee (although anomalies still existed), a co-ordination of policy was forced upon the competing departments that dealt with Russia. Although the execution of the Milner Committee's decisions was still the realm of a variety of bodies, at least all of them (at least in theory) were aware of the actions of the other departments.

The economic and financial aspects of the Anglo-Russian alliance were complicated further by the fact that many of them functioned outside the direct control of either the British or the Russian governments. The fact that both Allies had extensive dealings in the United States meant that there was greater scope for misunderstanding and conflict than would have been the case had the alliance functioned exclusively in Britain and Russia. Whereas the British government had means of controlling its own firms, they had no way either to coerce American firms to report Russian orders or to ensure that such firms were able to carry out their obligations. The fact that the Russians believed that the British had such means, and blamed them for any and all delays, tended to inject an extra element of acrimony into the alliance.

The principal point that the functioning of the economic and financial aspects of the Anglo-Russian alliance illustrates is the problem of conflicting expectations. Initially, the British believed that the Russian Army would be the element that would, in the end, defeat the Germans and that Britain's role in the war would be a limited one: essentially, naval, economic and financial. The Russians saw Britain in a similar way, although they believed that British economic and financial resources were virtually unlimited. Any British refusal to grant Russian requests reflected, in Russian eyes, a British failure to appreciate the magnitude of her ally's effort. This was not so. When the war dictated that Britain create a massive army, the British were faced with a dilemma. If they were to remain the financier and armourer of Russia to the extent expected by the Russians then they would be unable to equip and finance their own armies without risking financial and economic ruin. This ruin might either prevent an Allied victory or make such a victory a Pyrrhic one for Britain. From the British perspective, the economic and financial aspects of the alliance became a delicate balancing act. Much of this act was played out in the venue provided by the *ad hoc* committees.

Did the *ad hoc* committees dealing with Russia have a long-term impact and represent a 'transformation of British government'? To this, the answer is no. Their ephemeral nature makes it evident that the *ad hoc* bodies were almost entirely a war-time phenomenon. The 'transformation of British government' that took place occurred at other levels, in the strengthening of the Treasury's powers and in the creation of the Cabinet secretariat.[90] While the *ad hoc* organisations dealing with Russia had some impact on the first of these, that role was not great. The precedent set by such bodies was not, however, lost: the prosecution of the Second World War owed much to the First in just such organisational matters.[91]

[90] Kathleen Burk, 'Editor's Introduction', in Burk (ed.), *War and the State*, p. 6.
[91] See the administrative procedures discussed in Joan Beaumont, *Comrades in Arms: British Aid to Russia, 1941–1945* (London, 1980).

5

Wheat and the State during the First World War

Kathleen Burk

There are those who are interested in the First World War not because of the romance of the Somme but because of the romance of the state. That is, the First World War was a dry run for the Second in the sense that the British Government, trying not to lose the war, experimented with the role of the state in organising and mobilising for war. Beginning with 'business as usual', continuing with halfway – or half-hearted – arrangements for industrial and commercial mobilisation, finally developing full-blooded British organisations and culminating in inter-allied organisations, the adventure ended with the state in most respects rejecting its interventionist role after the end of the war – but leaving memoranda whose purpose was to instruct the Civil Service on how to do it if it had to be done again. The experience of the wheat trade is a case in point. Beginning with no plans for state interference with the trade, the government rapidly moved first into secret purchasing, then open purchasing and transporting for itself, and then for itself and its allies. At the end of the war the government's primary organisation, the Royal Commission on Wheat Supplies, was wound up, leaving only a history behind. It is notable, however, that in both the written and the philosophical senses, it is an international rather than a domestic history. Political forces prevented the expansion of wheat production to any significant extent in Britain: wheat therefore had to come from abroad.

The British government never planned to control the purchase and distribution of wheat. Indeed, it went further and planned not to do so. This decision arose from the response of the Balfour government in 1903 to public agitation about the dependability of food supplies in time of war. This in turn arose from the concerns in the late 1890s of certain naval officers, insurance underwriters, grain merchants, millers, landowners and farmers, concern which was built on by a captain in the Gordon Highlanders, S.L. Murphy, who in 1900 'began a self-imposed mission to alert the country to the dangers of famine in wartime'. Retiring in 1902 to devote all of his time to such a campaign, he began it in February 1903 'with a burst of orchestrated activity'. The Duke of Sutherland held a meeting of the newly-founded 'Association to promote an Official Enquiry into our Food Supply in Time of War', which was soon followed by a published manifesto, meetings of Trades Councils, and a meeting of representatives of finance, shipping, insurance and commerce at Mansion House, all of which culminated in a deputation to the Prime Minister on 5 March. Balfour was unenthusiastic, but the line of least resistance was clearly to grant a Royal Commission.[1] He was not too inert, however, to ensure that its membership would be balanced in his favour.

The Royal Commission on the Supply of Food and Raw Material in Time of War began its hearings in May 1903 and issued its report in 1905. The Commission's figures revealed that, in the period before a harvest, national reserves could fall to just over six weeks' stocks; furthermore, opinion was split in the Admiralty over how far the Royal Navy would be able to safeguard supply lines in wartime, and, indeed, over just what priority should be given to defending the merchant marine. However, none of this worried the commissioners: as they wrote in their report, 'A blockade of the United Kingdom is said to be virtually impossible, so that this topic need not further detain us.'[2] They therefore turned down a proposal to set up national granaries, in which supplies of wheat could be accumulated in peacetime for distribution during time of war. Furthermore, because modern warships were not equipped to take prizes, food would not be treated as contraband (and presumably food ships would sail on by enemy warships). In addition, the commissioners decided, food traders would find it impossible to profiteer, the interests of consumers being protected by international law. In short, profiteering would not take place. And if it did, there was little the government would be able to do about it, since 'any attempt by the government to build up emergency supplies would be excessively expensive and ultimately self-defeating, since it would seriously disrupt normal channels of trade'. In the end the Report of the Commission merely recommended that the Board of Agriculture improve its gathering of food statistics, and that during war the government should indemnify shipowners whose ships fell victim to the enemy, thereby ensuring that they would continue to try to ship food.[3]

When war came, therefore, Britain – alone amongst those who went to war in 1914 – had no arrangement for safeguarding food supplies.[4] Yet Britain was very dependent on imported wheat, a legacy of the decline in wheat-growing in Great Britain since the competition of the prairies began taking its toll in the last third of the nineteenth century.[5] Nevertheless, it is worth emphasising that, for the first two years of the war, the supplying

---

[1] Avner Offer, *The First World War: An Agrarian Interpretation* (Oxford, 1989), pp. 222–24.

[2] *Royal Commission on Supply of Food and Raw Material in Time of War: First Report* i, Parliamentary Papers, 1905 (Cd. 2643), pp. 30–1, quoted in José Harris, 'Bureaucrats and Businessmen in British Food Control, 1916–19', in Kathleen Burk, ed., *War and the State: The Transformation of British Government, 1914–1919* (London, 1982), p. 136.

[3] Ibid.

[4] Frank H. Coller, *A State Trading Adventure* (London, 1925), p. 10.

[5] In 1872 the UK had 24,000,000 acres under crops, in 1913 only 19,500,000, a drop from 51.3 per cent to 41.6 of the cultivated area. See L. Margaret Barnett, *British Food*

of grain was left to private enterprise, with the government confining itself to building up an emergency supply of wheat.[6] One reason for this was that the war was only expected to last for a few months and it was therefore felt to be unwise to disarrange the usual trading channels. Indeed, the production of grain was never the problem: all that the British Government had to do was to agree to pay world prices for the wheat and the farmers would grow it. What eventually forced increasing government controls over the supply of grain was the increasing pressure of lack of finance to pay for it and the increasing shortage of the shipping required to move it from producer countries to Britain and the Continent.

Wheat was not the only foodstuff likely to be in short supply, and within the first week of war a Cabinet Committee on Food Supplies was set up.[7] The Committee immediately instructed the Royal Navy to divert British grain-carrying ships from enemy to British ports and to take over the cargoes. The reaction, however, demonstrated the danger inherent in such activity: American grain-dealers were outraged and they threatened to suspend all shipments to Britain unless the Royal Navy stopped seizing their property. Dependence on American grain – and on American goodwill in general – meant that Britain had little choice but to give in: on 20 August 1914 the Admiralty was instructed to stop diverting the grain-carrying ships.[8]

An obvious question in the circumstances is, why did the government not take steps to encourage increased production of wheat in Britain itself? First of all, there was the overarching perception that the war would not last for very long, and that therefore keeping the normal channels and methods going was the best approach. There were also political problems involved, in that some of those suggesting that the government should do more were tariff reformers, and as such members of the Conservative Party. A Liberal government, virtually by definition a free trade government, was hardly likely to support proposals which

---

Continued

Policy during the First World War (London, 1985), p. 3. 'The most alarming aspect of these figures was the shift away from grain production, especially wheat. Some grainlands were used for other crops, particularly vegetables and market garden produce, but much was transformed into pasture. The collapse of world grain prices in the 1870s led British farmers, unprotected as they were by tariffs, to turn to livestock raising. Grazing proved much more remunerative.'

[6] 'The History of Commodities Control', p. 168, PRO, MAF 60/7, Ministry of Agriculture, Fisheries and Food Papers, PRO.

[7] The Cabinet Committee included Reginald McKenna (Home Secretary and Chairman of the Committee), Walter Runciman (President of the Board of Trade), Lord Lucas (President of the Board of Agriculture) and Edwin Montagu (Financial Secretary to the Treasury). CID Historical Section, 'Report on the Opening of the War', 1 Nov. 1914, CAB. 17/102B.

[8] David French, *British Economic and Strategic Planning, 1905–1915* (London, 1982), pp. 101–2. For the general context of Anglo-American trading and financial relations, see Kathleen Burk, *Britain, America and the Sinews of War, 1914–1918* (London, 1985), passim.

would foster this. Pragmatically, increasing the production of wheat would require more than retooling a factory production line: it would require changing farming methods, a much more problematic venture. As Margaret Barnett has pointed out, there would have been strong resistence in the farming community itself to increasing grain production by reducing grassland on which herds grazed, since farmers had a lot of money tied up in livestock. Furthermore, 'subsidiary problems also hindered the adoption of new farming techniques. Wheat drains the soil of nutrients more thoroughly than most other crops. Besides extra men and horses for ploughing, farmers would therefore need larger supplies of fertilizers than usual [and] these were not available.' There were also legal problems involved, in that most farmers were tenant farmers and their leases typically contained clauses governing the usage of the land. There were penalties for breach of contract. Most farmers would not consider changing the land use until the legal problems had been resolved; the government, however, refused to give any assurances.[9] In short, very little was done to improve domestic grain production, the blame for which fell mostly on Lord Lucas, the President of the Board of Agriculture, who remarked reassuringly, with regard to wheat, 'why trouble growing it when you could import any amount you wanted?'[10]

Lucas therefore supported the accumulation of a strategic reserve of wheat, primarily by purchasing it abroad, a suggestion which appealed to the Cabinet Committee on Food Supplies. It would solve more than one problem. First and most importantly, it would build up supplies of grain. Secondly, it would address an urgent problem of the grain supply trade: some North American exporters had demanded special arrangements for payment or even threatened to break contracts, and the trade were calling for government help. Accumulating such a reserve would do both without involving the government in more than limited intervention in the market. Therefore, the Committee decided that the government would establish a reserve large enough to see the armed forces through to the following summer. To carry this out, they established in October 1914 a Grain Supplies Committee, chaired by Sir Henry Rew, Assistant Secretary at the Board of Agriculture, and consisting of civil servants from the Board of Trade, the Treasury, the Admiralty and the War Office.[11]

The goal of the Grain Supplies Committee was to purchase 1,500,000 tons of wheat and 500,000 tons of flour, with the intention of releasing these supplies slowly onto the market during 1915 to prevent too great a rise in prices. The questions were, by what means and from where? It would have to be done in secret, since if it were known that the British Government was buying the price would streak upwards. The Committee therefore worked through the normal trading channels, utilising as agent

[9] Barnett, *Food Policy*, pp. 25–6.
[10] Milner to Selborne, 4 April 1915, as cited in ibid., p. 27.
[11] Ibid., p. 27.

Messrs Ross T. Smyth & Co. of Liverpool and London, to both buy and sell. Where would they buy? Supplies from Russia and the Balkans had been lost when enemy action closed the Dardanelles; the Australian crop had failed; the Government of India requisitioned the Indian surplus and took it off the market to try and curb price rises there; and there were rumours that the US might embargo the crop there to ensure supplies for themselves. This left Canada and the Argentine.

Smyth's were instructed to buy heavily in Argentina, 'the most expensive market of the time, and . . . acted clumsily, buying at higher prices than other merchants and then selling at less than the normal price'. Operations began in December but were temporarily suspended in January, the Treasury objecting greatly to the agent's buying and selling at a loss; the Cabinet agreed, ordering operations to cease in Argentina and the US (where prices were also high). Acute competition was provided by the Allied governments, all of whom were buying for their own populations; the irony was that much of this was being financed by British loans.[12]

Purchasing resumed, in February 1915, but the whole question was soon at the centre of a political row. The Dardanelles campaign, which was *inter alia* intended to open up the route to and from the Black Sea, would have as one consequence the recovery of Allied access to the Russian bread basket. Naturally grain prices fell as traders stopped trading until they could see more clearly the outcome. One company, however, continued trading in the Argentine market. This was Ross T. Smyth. As Barnett notes, 'questions were asked and the truth came out'.[13] This was especially embarrassing for the government because they had misled the House of Commons: Walter Runciman, the President of the Board of Trade, told the House on 17 February 1915 that the Government had rejected the idea of buying wheat on its own account, adding, in response to a suggestion by Andrew Bonar Law, the Leader of the Opposition, that reserves be built up by government purchase, that such a move would not be consistent with the government's policy of depending on the private sector.[14] 'The government now had to mollify angry deputations from the grain trade with promises that its forays into the market would cease. There was no intention of keeping this promise. The Cabinet Committee had already decided to buy the Indian surplus and were soon making arrangements to ship some 2,500,000 quarters of wheat. This time six firms acted on the government's behalf and, as the purchasing committee negotiated a price well below current market rates, no charges of wastefulness were forthcoming.'[15]

Assessment of the government-sponsored purchasing very much dep-

[12] Ibid., pp. 28–29. For details of allied competition and the result, both institutionally and financially, see Burk, *Sinews of War*, ch. 3, 'Purchasing and the Allies, 1914–1917'.

[13] Barnett, *Food Policy*, p. 29.

[14] Hansard, *House of Commons Debates*, 5th series, 69, cols 1178, 1179.

[15] Barnett, *Food Policy*, p. 29.

ends on the point of view. On the one hand, grain was acquired. On the other, it was probably acquired at a higher price than necessary and dislocated the grain trade itself. By early April 1915 the importing of wheat had 'practically come to a standstill'. The wheat trade remained sluggish until the end of 1916, when a new government organisation, the Wheat Committee, began operations. 'Far from improving matters, the Grain Supplies Committee contributed to the fall of wheat stocks to eight weeks at the beginning of April instead of the end of May as originally calculated. In the opinion of the next President of the Board of Agriculture, Lord Selborne, it was only the purchases of Indian wheat that averted a crisis in 1915. Moreover, the experience cost the country £5,250,000.'[16]

Wheat prices continued to rise – they rose by 80 per cent in the first twelve months of the war – and the activities of international speculators continued to be encouraged by competitive purchasing by the Allies.[17] The Cabinet Committee on Food Supplies therefore decided in early 1916 to establish an International Joint Committee at the Board of Agriculture, to be chaired by Rew, which was to co-ordinate all purchases for the British reserves, for the Italian Government and for the War Department of the French Government. Messrs Smyth acted as purchasing agent for the committee. Portugal and Belgium subsequently appointed representatives. Yet the French Government's Department of Commerce, which purchased wheat for civilian requirements, refused to work through the joint committee and continued to compete actively in the world's markets.[18]

By midsummer of 1916 objections to government intervention were fading away, and official circles certainly supported a more forthright governmental policy. The poor harvest of autumn 1916 brought matters to a head, but there was a concatenation of causes which led to a reversal of policy. In the first place, there was a likelihood of crop failure in both North and South America, which would ensure a world deficit of wheat; secondly, even if the wheat were available on the world market, the German submarine campaign was steadily depleting the amount of tonnage available to carry the wheat; and thirdly, Britain's growing financial straits made it more and more difficult for the private trader in wheat to purchase foreign currency (to pay for foreign wheat) at reasonable rates. In these circumstances, the grain trade became unable to maintain the normal system.[19] Finally, a change in policy was encouraged by the growing political crisis, in which 'the demand for a more positive

[16] Ibid., pp. 29–30.

[17] R Henry Rew, *Food Supplies in Peace and War* (London, 1920), p. 45.

[18] 'Memorandum in Answer to the Circular of the CID of 25 July 1916', nd, PRO 30/68/2, Sir Alan Anderson Papers, the Royal Commission on Wheat Supplies, PRO.

[19] 'History of Commodities Control', 168, PRO, MAF 60/7.

food policy became one of the main spearheads of attack on the Asquith coalition'.[20]

The Board of Trade and the Board of Agriculture therefore made representations to the Cabinet Committee on Food Supplies in September 1916, when it was decided that the government must now assume the responsibility for importing wheat. On 10 October 1916 the Royal Commission on Wheat Supplies was appointed, with Lord Crawford, now President of the Board of Agriculture and Fisheries, as the chairman.[21] It was soon found that control could not be confined to wheat and flour. On 27 October the powers of the Commission were extended to 'other grains', and on 25 April 1917 to 'all pulses and all substitutes for wheat, pulses and their products'.[22]

The Commission on Wheat Supplies was presumably modelled on the Royal Commission on Sugar Supplies, which had been set up in August 1914 (with full control over the trade), in that its conduct, in view of the technical nature of the business, was left as much as possible in the hands of those with the necessary commercial experience. In the case of sugar, purchases were negotiated by members of the commission in daily touch with the market, brokers representing every export market laying their offers before the commission; if business resulted, they were paid by the producers.[23] There was always a sufficient supply of sugar to be bought, however, which was not the case with wheat, so that it was vital in the latter case to eliminate competition as much as possible. Rather than use the usual procedure of sending cables to American shipping houses – which of course stimulated competition – it was decided to appoint representatives in the United States 'to purchase as near to the farmer as possible'.[24] A new firm, the Wheat Export Company, was set up in New York to represent the commission, under the direction of the only two British grain firms which were already operating and resident both in London and New York. These were Messrs Ross T. Smyth, which had, as noted, been acting as a purchasing agent for the British Government on and off since 1914, and Samuel Sanday & Company. They provided the Commission with a fully equipped agency as well as with a channel of communication.[25] The Wheat Export Company of New York was only one of several which the commission set up (there was another in

[20] Harris, 'Bureaucrats and Businessmen', in Burk, ed., *War and the State*, p. 138.

[21] 'Memorandum in Answer to the Circular of the CID of 25 July 1916', PRO 30/68/2.

[22] 'History of Commodities Control', 168, PRO, MAF 60/7. Later in 1979 the Wheat Commission was also put in charge of the mills in the UK and 'generally delegated to act as the [Ministry of Food's] agent with respect to domestic food supplies'. Barnett, *Food Policy*, p. 126.

[23] 'History of Commodities Control', PRO, MAF 60/1. 'Control of Sugar', MAF 60/6. Barnett, *Food Policy*, p. 30.

[24] 'Memorandum in Reply to the Circular of the CID of 25 July 1916', PRO 30/68/2.

[25] Barnett calls Sanday & Co. 'the largest of the British exporters'. *Food Policy*, p. 85.

Canada, for example).[26] Since the circumstances governing the purchase
and shipment of supplies varied so greatly between the different countries,
no uniform method could be adopted. Therefore each commissioner in
the various countries held considerable powers both of negotiation and of
local organisation.[27]

In New York the President of the Wheat Export Company was G.F.
Earle, an Englishman who had spent his entire career exporting grain
from the US with Sanday & Co., who headed the grain-purchasing
department of the new company. Serving as chairman and first vice-
president of the new company was H.T. Robson, also English, a partner
in the Smyth firm and a member of the Wheat Commission. He had been
in charge of grain purchases for the British Government in the Argentine
in 1914–15, and in charge of purchasing grain in the US and Canada for
the International Joint Committee on behalf of Britain, France and Italy in
1916.[28] As the scope of purchases grew, so did the organisation, although
by April–May 1917 it was clearly not developed enough. H.D. Vigor, the
Secretary of the Wheat Commission, visited the company during his visit to
the US as a member of the Balfour Mission (see below), and reported back
that he had had to devote over a month in New York to reorganising it.

'The Company had been run mostly on the lines of a small private firm, and its
staff and organisation were inadequate to the huge business which was passing
through its offices. This was partly attributable to a pressure of business larger
than the Directors had anticipated, but London had failed to keep closely in
communication with New York by letter, and therefore, the Directors could
not really know the magnitude of the organisation being built up in London,
and that their own office should be developing to respond. The two constituent
firms . . . still retained their separate organisations with regard to staff and
office arrangements. Grain accounting arrangements were quite satisfactory,
but understaffed, the arrangements for following up contracts, for loading
ships, for dealing with flour and London grain purchases, and the general
stock records were both understaffed and insufficiently organised . . . Even so,
the Company had carried through its large purchasing, shipping and financial
business remarkably well.'

The directors accepted Vigor's suggestions for changes. By the time
he returned to Britain, having meanwhile 'endeavoured to promote a

[26] The Commission secured the services of K.B. Stoddart Ltd, and as the Commission
noted: 'The action of the Commission conferred a virtual monopoly of purchase in North
America on behalf of the UK and Allies upon Wheat Exports, and considerable resentment
was felt in Canada by the firms whose business was disturbed and who regarded themselves
as being supplanted by their rival Stoddart in his position as purchaser for Wheat Exports
. . .' 'Memorandum in Answer to the Circular of the CID., 25 July 1916', PRO 30/68/2.

[27] 'History of Commodities Control', 169, PRO, MAF 60/7. 'Memorandum in Answer to
the Circular of the CID of 25 July 1916', PRO 30/68/2.

[28] *Who's Who in the British War Mission to the United States of America 1917* (New York,
1917), pp. 15, 41.

complete fusion of the two constituent firms', he was able to report happily that 'this was successfully accomplished.'[29]

The primary reason for the growth in the Wheat Export Company in New York was that by the end of 1916 it was empowered to purchase for France and Italy as well as for Britain. Before the establishment of the commission, an international joint committee representing Britain, France and Italy had purchased a limited amount of wheat, as noted above, but the growing difficulties of supply and finance led, at the instigation of France, to the formation of the Wheat Executive, which was to meet the requirements of the Allies by purchasing, allocating and *transporting* all cereals.

The reason for the setting up of the Executive was that by this time the most serious shortage was that of ships. It was therefore crucial that it took three times as much tonnage to ship the same amount of wheat from Australia as from North America (the main reason the bulk of purchasing fell on the Wheat Export Company of New York). As Sir Arthur Salter, the Director of Ship Requisitioning, later explained matters,

'North America was the nearest source of wheat supplies to Italy, France and Great Britain alike. Each of the three countries, so long as it made its own arrangements, tried to buy from this source so as to economize on sea transport, which was already becoming the weakest link in the whole chain of the Allied war effort. But North America had not enough wheat for all. Much had to come from Australia. And though Italy is nearer to North America than to Australia it is nearer to Australia than Great Britain is. To exchange an Italian cargo in North America for a British cargo in Australia meant a saving of two thousand miles of steaming. This the Wheat Executive now made possible. No longer did empty Italian ships going west for American wheat and empty British ships going east for Australian wheat pass each other in the Mediterranean.'[30]

At the same time as the Wheat Executive was set up, the new Ministry of Food was also established, the latter intended by the new Prime Minister, David Lloyd George, to control the production and importation of all foodstuffs. This was, of course, a recipe for bureaucratic infighting of the first order. As the internal history of the Ministry of Food put it, the new ministry

confronted existing bodies [the Wheat and Sugar Commissions] occupying positions of some independence. Their relations to the Ministry were not

[29] H.D. Vigor, 'Report on Visit to North America, April–August 1917', 4 Sept. 1917, PRO 30/68/11.

[30] Sir Arthur Salter, *Slave of the Lamp: A Public Servant's Notebook* (London, 1967), p. 77. 'History of Commodities Control', 171, PRO, MAF 60/7. 'Memorandum in Answer to the Circular of the CID of 25 July 1916' and Thomson to Wheat Commission, 28 Dec. 1916, both PRO 30/68/2.

clearly defined for some time and they regarded control by the Ministry with some suspicion. Friction of a rather indeterminate character occurred from time to time, and though the right of the Ministry to control was not denied, the exercise of this right was, to say the least, not welcomed.[31]

It was decided to keep the Wheat Commission separate from the ministry, although all coercive power and administrative finance came from the ministry. The official history, in fact, considerably understates the case when it refers to conflict, and – to look ahead – the semi-detached position of the commission relative to the Ministry of Food set the stage for a battle in 1917–18. Sir John Beale became chairman of the commission in August 1917. Beale was a director of the Midland Bank who numbered politicians such as Reginald McKenna and Bonar Law amongst his personal friends; he had wide connections in manufacturing industry and in the City of London. In short, he was a 'powerful and dynamic business representative' who was used to making top-level decisions in business organisations and who wanted state control to be as minimal and simple as possible.[32] Not surprisingly, he immediately, and continually, objected to his position's being interpreted as one of administrative subordination to the Permanent Secretary to the Ministry of Food, Ulick Wintour, a position which was confirmed by Lord Rhondda, the Minister of Food, in May 1917. The conflict was only resolved in September 1918 by Wintour's forced resignation and Beale's assumption of Wintour's former position as Permanent Secretary.[33] In the event, the Wheat Export Company in New York remained relatively untouched by the infighting in London.

By the time the United States joined the war in April 1917, the organisation to supply Britain (and some of the Allies) with wheat and other grains was as follows: the Ministry of Food was in overall charge of food production and importation; semi-detached from it was the Royal Commission for Wheat Supplies, who had the direct responsibility for providing grains; these were purchased on its behalf by private trading firms which had been taken over for the duration by the government, but which continued to purchase in the same manner and through the same channels as before the war. These firms constituted, most importantly, the Wheat Export Company of New York, which was soon to purchase the bulk of supplies for the Allies. At the same time, by early 1917, there was in place the Wheat Executive, which organised the supply and, critically, the transport of wheat for Britain and her major allies.

Once the US joined the war in April 1917, these arrangements were not so much cancelled as modified and extended. There were obvious, immediate problems. First of all, what would happen to the supply of

[31] 'History: General Memorandum', PRO, MAF 60/1.
[32] Harris, 'Bureaucrats and Businessmen', in Burk, ed., *War and the State*, p. 145.
[33] Ibid., pp. 145–46.

grains for Britain and the Allies if the US now had to supply newly-formed armed forces? Strictly speaking, not much, since numbers should be the same whether they were soldiers or civilians, but in fact the grain would of course have to be taken off the market by the government for the use of the armed forces. Secondly, the US had a distinct lack of ships; if they had to ship their own supplies, for example, they might have to use Allied vessels which might otherwise be used for grain. This, however, was not an immediate problem; once it became one the following year as US troops moved to France it was coped with by organisations which were by then in place. On the other hand, the fact that the US, source of supply as it was, was now an ally meant that other problems could be solved: the US Government might control prices so that wheat would not be so expensive – in April 1917 it was still a subject for speculators; furthermore, it might now be possible to establish controls over the railways in order to organise them efficiently, so that empty freight cars did not clutter up the ports and goods did not languish in the country awaiting transport. What actually happened over the subsequent year was that gradually the US established its own control over the production and supply of food, while becoming part, with Britain, of various inter-allied organisations which controlled allocation and transport.

The British Government *in toto*, not just the Royal Commission on Wheat Supplies and the Ministry of Food, were eager to grab the opportunity of American accession to the war to try and resolve a whole slew of problems. It was decided, therefore, on the day the US declared war, that a major political mission would go out to the US and that it would be headed by the Secretary of State for Foreign Affairs, A.J. Balfour, a former Prime Minister. Lord Crawford, Chairman of the Wheat Commission, and Lord Devonport, the newly appointed Food Controller, seized the chance to send out representatives. Therefore two members of the Balfour Mission were representatives of the Wheat Commission: one was Alan Anderson, a director of P & O Shipping and vice-chairman of the commission, and H.D. Vigor, the secretary of the commission. Their brief included emphasising the prime importance of food as a war need- not to let it be shut out by the need for munitions, for example; examining the commission's local machinery, the Wheat Export Company (as described above); and establishing relations with any Food Controller who might be appointed in the United States. The mission left Liverpool on 13 April 1917, after being held up for some hours by reports of German submarines sighted in the Irish Sea. They arrived at Halifax, Nova Scotia, on 20 April, reaching the Maine border the following day.[34]

Before leaving, Anderson and Sir John Beale had talked to the Shipping Controller, Sir Joseph Maclay, about a possible wheat shortage: in Feb-

[34] War Cabinet Office to Oliphant, 12 April 1917, pp. 239–42, PRO, FO 800/208, and Alan G. Anderson, 'Memorandum', 22 June, no. 158680, FO 371/3073, Charles Hanson Towne, *The Balfour Visit* (New York, 1917), pp. 15–22.

ruary, North American shipments of wheat had fallen without warning from a promised 260,000 tons to an actual 120,000 tons. Consequently, if the wheat was available it was needed – but would there be the ships to transport it? While sailing to North America Anderson brought to Balfour's attention the question of establishing priority, at least for the time being, of wheat shipments over those of munitions. W.T. Layton of the Ministry of Munitions, who was also on board ship, demurred at this suggestion, so Balfour finally cabled the Cabinet for a decision. Upon arrival at New York, however, Anderson learned that France, Italy and Britain had all taken alarm about possible food shortages. Consequently the Shipping Controller had offered a substantial increase in tonnage for wheat, achieved by decreasing the amount for munitions. One further task of Anderson's was therefore to find enough wheat to fill all the ships now available.[35]

On arrival in New York Anderson met Layton and George Booth of the Ministry of Munitions, Connop Guthrie, the head of the Ministry of Munitions mission in the US, and H.T. Robson, of the Wheat Export Company of New York, to discuss ways of finding the necessary extra wheat. The problem was apparently not so much finding and buying the extra wheat to fill the newly-provided ships: rather, it was actually getting enough wheat to port. The problem was the organisation of Allied internal traffic in the US: Guthrie routed Allied wheat shipments, an official of the Ministry of Munitions mission routed British munitions, and Russian, French and Italian missions all routed their own munitions – and the American railway system was in a state of chaos. Consequently, the group agreed that Guthrie's organisation should be responsible for organising the rail transport of all American goods purchased by the Allies. This was a beginning, although it took some time before all of the British departments, let alone all of the Allies, agreed to this proposal.

Anderson decided that the real problem was obviously the independence of the Allies, but that if he could get the Ministry of Munitions to give responsibility to Guthrie for routing munitions, the Allies would have less excuse to demur. The Wheat Commission accepted the suggestion with alacrity and, when questioned, so did the Railway Executive, the committee of American railway heads who were attempting to organise the system for war purposes. Layton changed his mind several times, since he knew that the Ministry of Munitions preferred to keep its own transport organisation, but finally on 3 May Anderson got him to send a message to the Minister of Munitions, Christopher Addison, recommending the concentration of all traffic under Guthrie. Addison refused to approve this proposal for some time, probably because of personal antipathy towards Guthrie, but upon his return to London Anderson learned that a scheme for

[35] Anderson 'Memorandum', 22 June 1917, no. 158680, PRO, FO 371/3073. Balfour to Lloyd George, ? April 1917, p. 167, FO 800/208. Wheat Commission to Anderson, 23 April 1917, PRO 30/68/10.

a Traffic Executive controlled by Guthrie had been approved and was being implemented. Thereafter all routing of grain, and munitions, for the Allies was under the control of one organisation from the producer to the Allied countries.[36]

Anderson's other main task was to establish contact with Herbert Hoover, the future President of the US, who was soon to be in charge of the United States Food Administration. (Hoover, who had been in charge of the Belgian Relief Commission, arrived back in Washington on 6 May, and within a week President Wilson had asked him to take charge of food matters.) Because of Congressional opposition, the Food Administration did not formally come into being for three months. The British nevertheless assumed that Hoover would be in charge of food matters and acted accordingly. There was some fear that Hoover and David Houston, the Secretary of Agriculture, would clash, but although they did not agree on policy – Hoover favoured much more national control than Houston – Houston supported Hoover.[37] They were 'both keen to help' the Allies.[38] Hoover proposed to set up a Wheat Executive (Anderson tactfully convinced him to call it the Grain Executive) which would purchase all wheat in the US at the grain elevators. It would sell all the wheat available for the Allies to the Wheat Export Company at cost plus charges. For its part the Wheat Export Company would agree to purchase all wheat offered. The Wheat Commission strongly approved the scheme – although the Treasury was probably less than pleased – but its implementation had to wait until Hoover received his powers from Congress in July 1917.[39]

Anderson and Robson visited Chicago from 9 to 13 May at the invitation of the Chicago Board of Trade, during which visit a lucky coincidence enabled them to achieve another desire: lower wheat prices. As Anderson later wrote:

> Our great demand upon North American wheat had skied the price up from 155 cents a bushel in October 1916, to 297 cents a bushel in May 1917, and

[36] Anderson to Wheat Commission, 23 April 1917, PRO 30/68/10. Duncan Crow, *A Man of Push and Go: The Life of George Macaulay Booth* (London, 1965), pp. 143–50. Anderson, 'Memorandum', 22 June 1917, no. 158680, PRO, FO, 371/3073. 'No. 1. Wheat Exports: Food Supply and Transport', 24 April 1917, pp. 333–38, FO 800/208. Anderson to Wheat Commission, 26 April 1917, PRO 30/68/10. 'Minutes of Meeting with the Railway Executive Committee', 26 April 1917, pp. 286–87, FO 800/208. Layton to Anderson, 9 May 1917, no. 94575, FO 371/3118. Anderson, 'Wheat Export Company Progress Report No. 10', 7 May 1917, PRO 30/68/11. The Chairman was M. Sevel in deference to French pressure, but Guthrie as Director-General had executive control. Ministry of Munitions, *Official History of the Ministry of Munitions*, 12 vols (London, 1921–22), iii, p. 73.

[37] Herbert Hoover, *An American Epic, ii, Famine in Forty-Five Nations: Organization behind the Front, 1914–1923* (Chicago, 1960), pp. 29–37.

[38] Anderson to Wheat Commission, 11 May 1917, PRO 30/68/10.

[39] Anderson to Wheat Commission, 21 May and 27 May 1917, Wheat Commission to Anderson, 26 May 1917, all PRO 30/68/10.

if traders were allowed to gamble in futures there seemed no reason why the top should ever be reached. On the other hand, we did not want to check production, or to hamper even for a time the flow of wheat to the seaboard. Supply was the first consideration, taking precedence even of price. The situation was critical and the fact that our insistent demand and its reaction on price caused severe discomfort to the American consumer of bread, made it certain that the Food Administrator would be forced to take charge of the problem for us in a drastic way if we did not suggest a remedy to him. Our remedy was to stop trade in futures and by a lucky chance it so happened that when Robson . . . and I were visiting Chicago . . .the bubble burst and we had our chance. The wheat traders of Chicago had sold in several consecutive months much more wheat than existed and during our visit they discovered that someone had definitely cornered the market on a scale which had never before been achieved. Our hosts of the Board of Trade, after some hours of suspicion of one another, reached the true conclusion that we were the culprits, but it was easy to convince them that the blame should be put, not upon us, but upon the War. They were feeling, for the first time, the full weight of three nations insisting on being fed by them, and when we pointed out to them that the last thing in the world we wanted was to spread ruin over the traders of the great nation which had just joined in the War on our side, and that the first thing we wanted was to get the wheat moving fast and steadily to feed the armies and nations of the Allies, they accepted the position in the best possible spirit, and after a few days consideration, on our return call at Chicago, they agreed to send out missionaries round the wheat exchanges of the US to stop trading in futures.[40]

The arrangement decided upon was that traders who had sold short would be allowed to purchase actual wheat as it came to the elevators in order to liquidate their commitments, while the exchanges would be closed to trading in futures for the duration of the war. This brought the price down. Within a few months the Allies bought at fixed prices from only one source in the US, the Grain Executive.[41]

The other problem related to the supply of wheat was that of paying for it. The idea of supply taking precedence even of price was not a view which the Treasury would accept lightly, certainly not for very long. The accession of the US to belligerent status gave the Treasury the opportunity of sloughing off some of the financial responsibility for the war, in particular the responsibility for financing its own, plus Allied, purchases in the US.[42] In the case of wheat, Britain had the advantage that Hoover, with the interests of American farmers and middlemen as well as Allied soldiers and civilians in mind, supported the British in their

---

[40] Anderson, 'Report', 5 January 1922, PRO 30/68/11.

[41] Ibid. Anderson, 'Agenda and Report of Visit to Chicago and Minneapolis, 9–13 May', nd, pp. 317–26, FO 800/208.

[42] See Burk, *Sinews of War*, chs 4, 5, 9; Kathleen Burk 'The Diplomacy of Finance: British Financial Missions to the United States, 1914–1918', *Historical Journal*, 22 (June 1979), pp. 351–72.

attempts, which were largely successful, to gain financial help from the American Treasury towards the Allied purchase of wheat.

The main hitch was Canadian wheat – vital to feed Allied Europe, but not American wheat and therefore not on the face of it eligible for American financial aid to enable the British to purchase it. This particular problem in fact symbolised a larger problem: whether or not American financial aid could be spent outside of the US. Consequently, although negotiations began at the level of head of financial mission, they were eventually taken over and resolved by the head of all of the British War Missions in the US, Lord Reading.

The head of the British financial mission to the US was Sir Hardman Lever. Although British, before the war he had been a partner in a firm of chartered accountants in New York; once the war broke out he returned to Britain and joined the Ministry of Munitions in 1915 as Assistant Financial Secretary, moving to the Treasury as Financial Secretary.[43] In mid February 1917 he went out to the US and took over responsibility for British financial relations with the US. Lever opened the question of the use of American credits abroad when he wrote to Oscar T. Crosby, the Under Secretary of the US Treasury, on 23 August 1917: the Canadian wheat crop was shortly coming on to the market and the Wheat Commission wished to buy the surplus for the Allies, which would reduce the Allied need for American wheat. Crosby replied on 28 August and, while not flatly refusing, emphasised that if at all possible Canadian wheat purchases should be settled without reference to the American Government, a position which he restated a week later.[44]

The British Government found this an alarming position for the US Treasury to have taken. The Chancellor of the Exchequer, Andrew Bonar Law, sent an urgent cable to Lever warning what the result would be if the Americans held to their position: 'Position as regards Canadian wheat in particular is causing anxiety. Unless Wheat Commission are authorised to make purchases within few days result will be dangerous shortage in UK food supplies by end of year, a condition of affairs which submarine situation makes it imperative to avoid'.[45] Yet a cable from Lever to Sir Robert Chalmers, a Permanent Secretary to the Treasury (there were three at that time), makes it clear that the British were already using American funds to purchase Canadian wheat: 'In spite of risk of objection being raised later I agree that in all circumstances we may continue to make payments from New York funds.'[46] Possibly the Treasury wished

[43] Treasury to Balfour to Spring Rice, 1 Feb. 1917, no. 25944, PRO, FO 371/3070.

[44] File 30, box 221, US Treasury Papers, National Archives, Washington, DC. Lever to Chancellor of the Exchequer, 6 Sept. 1917, p. 94, T. 172/435.

[45] 7 Sept. 1917, pp. 80–81, PRO, T 172/435.

[46] 11 Sept. 1917, p. 59, PRO, T 172/435. Britain had no more funds to spare for Canada, and Canadian liquidity problems precluded their increasing aid to Britain. Both countries therefore saw American funds for wheat (and for anything else) as vital. By 1918, in fact,

to make such purchases on a much larger scale – or possibly they hoped that the Americans would fail to notice.

This was how the position stood when Lord Reading, the Lord Chief Justice and former financier, and future British Ambassador to the US, arrived in Washington in mid September 1917 on a special financial mission. Lever immediately told him about the problem of paying for Canadian wheat, emphasising that it 'ranked as a most pressing matter'.[47] The problem for Britain in Canada, as in the US, was the need to purchase exchange: the need to buy Canadian dollars was threatening the pound to such an extent that British purchase of Canadian products was becoming problematical – in fact, the purchase of cheese had ceased in June 1917, thereby throwing the Canadian cheese industry into turmoil.[48] Reading met the US Secretary of the Treasury, William Gibbs McAdoo, a former Wall Street financier and President Woodrow Wilson's son-in-law, twice during his first week in Washington to discuss the matter. At the latter meeting Reading proposed that since it was imperative that the Canadian Government knew by the following day whether the Wheat Commission could purchase the Canadian wheat (because of the need to arrange for shipping), and since the American government was reluctant to commit itself to a large expenditure of money without a detailed examination of the position, the US Government should place $50,000,000 at the disposal of the British Government for the purchase of Canadian wheat without prejudice to its future policy (that is, the British Government would not cite this action as a precedent). McAdoo telephoned his acquiescence. Crosby finally confirmed that the USA would supply the $50,000,000, although he registered his disapproval of the transaction.[49]

Reading was quick to use the British need for Canadian wheat to gain further financial concessions from the US Treasury. As he reported to the Chancellor of the Exchequer:

> I have explained to Crosby our intention subject to his acquiescence to employ $15,000,000 monthly of credits he gives us for various Canadian purchases. He is not prepared to agree in principle to use of US credits for Canadian purchases. But I gather that he is prepared to overlook payments within above total provided we are able to make out that our Canadian contracts involve directly or indirectly expenditure in US to this amount.[50]

Continued

Canada absolutely required British or American funds to cover its trade deficit with the US. See Michael Bliss, *A Canadian Millionaire: The Life and Times of Sir Joseph Flavelle, Bart 1858–1938* (Toronto, 1978), pp. 363–72.

[47] Lever to the Chancellor, 13 Sept. 1917, p. 47, PRO, T 172/435.

[48] Gerald Rufus Isaacs, Marquess of Reading, *Rufus Isaacs, First Marquess of Reading 1914–1935* (London, 1945), p. 63.

[49] Reading to McAdoo, 18 Sept. 1917, file 30, box 221; Crosby to Reading, 27 Sept. 1917 and Crosby to the President, 24 Oct. 1917, both file GB 132.1, box 117, all US Treasury.

[50] 28 Sept. 1917, p. 25, PRO, T 172/433.

Crosby in fact considered that it was improper to use American credits voted by the Congress to purchase goods outside of the US, basing his conclusion on his interpretation of the Bill authorising the Liberty Loans (the American War Loans) and on McAdoo's assurances to the House of Representatives' Ways and Means Committee in open committee hearings that the proceeds of the loans to the Allies would not be used outside the US.[51] (R.G. Leffingwell, soon to become Assistant Secretary of the Treasury and a future partner in the New York investment bank J.P. Morgan & Co., later called his reasoning 'an exposition of the law by a civil engineer' and asserted that Crosby was absolutely wrong.)[52] By the end of October the US Treasury was assuming that about $60,000,000 a month from its advances to the British Government were being used for outside purchases.[53]

Reading travelled to Canada for three days to persuade a group of Canadian bankers to float a loan to help finance the wheat crop, since the American Treasury had insisted that Canada must do more to help itself. After talking to the Canadian Cabinet and the principal Canadian bankers, he reported to the Chancellor on 6 October:

> Estimate of exportable wheat and oats is about $350 mil. US Treasury have already agreed to advance $50 mil. for October ... [Sir Thomas] White [the Canadian Finance Minister] and bankers have already agreed to lend to HMG, half this year and half next spring, for two years .... This proposition to be contingent upon US Treasury finding the balance of $200 mil..[54]

Reading returned to Washington and discussed the situation on 8 October:

> Crosby is disinclined to give promise beyond immediate necessity. I have pressed for decision and explained Canada's promise conditional only ... He is consulting President ... This case challenges policy of US Treasury as to payments abroad and is for us good ground of attack.[55]

It seems quite clear that by this time, the need for the wheat itself rather than the need to use it as a vehicle had receded rather into the background, at least as far as Reading was concerned.

On 12 October Reading and Crosby went over the proposal. Reading finally extracted a promise from Crosby that the US would advance the $200,000,000. Reading must have been somewhat surprised when he received a letter from Crosby dated 17 October wherein Crosby stated

[51] United States Senate, 74th Congress, 2nd session, Special Committee on Investigation of the Munitions Industry, *Munitions Industry*, report no. 944, 7 vols (Washington, DC, 1936), vi, pp. 164–6.

[52] Ibid., vi, p. 164.

[53] Crosby to the President, 24 Oct. 1917, file GB 132.1, box 117, US Treasury.

[54] F. 118/114, Lord Reading Papers, India Office Library, London.

[55] Reading to Chancellor, 8 Oct. 1917, pp. 105–6, PRO, T 172/437.

that Reading might have had $200,000,000 in his mind, but that Crosby had had only $150,000,000 in *his*, and the latter figure would stand – although the British could apply for more later if necessary. Reading agreed and, after representations from Hoover, the Food Administrator, further agreed that half of the wheat surplus destined for the Allies would go through American flour mills, which were running at only half capacity,[56] thereby helping Hoover with a political problem of his own.

When looking at wheat for Britain the focus must be international, not domestic. This is largely because it proved to be impossible to extend domestic wheat tillage very much, since the political forces ranged against this were too great. In 1917, for example, while attempts were being made to increase the supplies of wheat for Britain and the Allies from North America, attempts were also made once again to increase domestic supplies. As John Turner has written, the Board of Agriculture under the Defence of the Realm Act made orders

> requiring farmers to cultivate derelict land and in some instances to plough up pasture for grain crops. Compulsory tillage orders were applied by local inspectors acting under the authority of the board and on the advice of County War Agricultural Executive Committees made up of farmers and landowners. They were often resisted, both by landlords and their tenants, and thus set neighbour against neighbour as well as against the government. This made for entertaining politics, as the still-powerful agricultural lobby within the Conservative Party battled with the government and its own conscience.[57]

Such entertaining politics were not restricted to the countryside. As Turner continues:

> A greater piquancy was lent to the situation by divisions among ministers. As former chairman of [a] departmental committee, Milner naturally took an interest in agriculture, and on a number of occasions was appointed by the War Cabinet to be an 'overlord' for agricultural matters. Against him Walter Long and Lord Derby, the largest landowners in the Cabinet, took up positions in the tillage campaign . . . Since Derby as Secretary of State for War was responsible for the conscription of ploughmen into the army, and Long as chairman of the Petroleum Committee had to find petrol for tractors, there was plenty of room for obstruction and disagreement.[58]

The fact, therefore, that much political blood was spilt over the passage of the Corn Production Act, which became law in August 1917, will come as no surprise. Its purpose, in the end, was coercion: although

[56] Reading to Chancellor, 12 Oct. 1917, pp. 91–3, PRO, T 172/437. Crosby to Reading, 17 Oct. 1917, Reading to Crosby, 23 Oct. 1917; Hoover to Crosby, 11 Oct. 1917; and Reading to Crosby, 25 Oct. 1917, all file 30, box 221, US Treasury.

[57] John Turner, *British Politics and the Great War* (London and New Haven, 1992), p. 174.

[58] Ibid.

it provided for guaranteed prices for wheat (and for oats) for six years, it also stipulated a minimum wage for farm labourers, supported by an Agricultural Wages Board, provided means to prevent landlords from raising rents in response to the changes provided by the Act and gave 'special authority for the Board of Agriculture to enforce cultivation'.[59] It was an Act difficult to get passed and difficult to enforce. In the end it made little difference as far as wheat was concerned.

Enforcement was difficult, not only because decisions taken for administrative convenience could not always be worked satisfactorily on the ground, not only because its cost aroused outraged resistance from other sections of the community, and not only because its attack on property rights stimulated and focused resistence in the Lords. Beyond this, land and nature resisted. The sloping fields and differing soil conditions in the UK meant that tractors imported from the States could not be used efficiently. Furthermore, the combination of overcropping of grain and the lack of fertilisers meant declining yields; and repeated crops of grain in the same fields exhausted the soil. When farmers did plough under grassland – and they did so under protest, since meat shortages meant that the raising of livestock continued to increase in profitability – they ploughed the poorer rather than the richer fields, those for which no amount of artificial aid would have increased yields by very much.[60]

In the end, the increased yield of wheat was encouraging but insufficient. With regard to the 1917 harvest, there were only 4000 more acres under wheat than in 1916, with yields very little higher due to poor weather and the shortage of fertiliser. For 1918, the intention was to increase the amount of acreage under wheat by 150 per cent, from 2,000,000 to 5,000,000 acres which, Lloyd George claimed, would make the UK self-sufficient in wheat. Final figures showed that wheat acreage had increased by only 750,000 acres, much of which turned out to be unsuitable for wheat and infested with pests. Nevertheless, the average increase for the UK was 65 per cent – but as with all percentage increases the size of the base is all-important. As Barnett notes, 'although a great improvement over the normal ten weeks supply, home-grown grain still only satisfied sixteen weeks of the year's needs'.[61] Therefore, the emphasis had still to be on imported wheat, on paying for it and shipping it safely.

Paying for it continued as an intermittent problem. Negotiations took place from February to October 1918 over the manner of financing of wheat bought in the US for the use of the Allies. Britain treated the whole of the world supply of wheat purchased for the Allies as one unit, while the Americans wished American wheat to be treated separately, because of their desire to restrict spending of the dollars loans to the Allies to purchases in the US (i.e., tied foreign aid). Discussions went

[59] Barnett, *Food Policy*, p. 195.
[60] Ibid, pp. 195–206.
[61] Ibid., pp. 202–5; quotation on p. 205.

on in Washington at the same time as in Europe. A special committee was set up by the Inter-Allied Council for War Purchases and Finance (which had itself been set up at the insistence of the Americans in the autumn of 1917 in order to co-ordinate Allied purchases), of which J.M. Keynes was a member, to reconsider methods of purchasing and financing cereals. Agreement to a complex formula was finally reached in the last week of October 1918.[62] This was not the only example during the war of a bureaucratic structure reaching perfection just as the war ended.

In the end, the experience of the British Government in providing wheat for itself and its allies was a qualified success. Domestically, the rise in production by 1918 was high in percentage terms but low in absolute terms, while the cost had been political rancour of an intense sort, both at Westminster and Whitehall and in the localities. Internationally, the provision of wheat was achieved: nobody starved, the prices paid were not outrageous and the organisations eventually put in place to buy and, especially, to transport the grain were models of their kind. Hoover at one point indeed suggested that the Wheat Export Company extend its ambit beyond grain to other foodstuffs, he found it so impressive. The Wheat Executive worked so well that in the spring of 1918 a whole series of inter-allied 'programme committees' was set up on the same model for textiles, meat, petroleum, metals, in fact for all of the chief categories of imports.

In spite of their perfection, though, at the end of the war 'the imposing structure of economic collaboration' soon melted away.[63] The Europeans wished it to remain, but the Americans emphatically saw controls of this sort as specific to wartime and refused to agree. Yet as two of the official historians of the next war wrote:

'The memory of . . . war-time achievements survived, and so did the painfully acquired mastery of principles and methods. Some of the men survived. In the autumn of 1939, Frenchmen and Englishmen who had shared the experience of a great constructive partnership set to work to renew and extend that partnership . . . When France fell, the same experienced heads . . . found that they had still the same constructive work to do in laying the foundations of economic partnership between the United Kingdom and the United States. The story of their work . . . [gives] an impressive illustration of the continuity of historical experience in this century'.[64]

---

[62] A. Rathbone, 'Memorandum of Conversation with Mr Blackett, February 23', 23 Feb. 1918, file GB 132/17–10, box 119, US Treasury Papers. G.O. May, 'Memorandum re: Cereals', 7 March 1918; Crosby to Hoover, 22 June 1918; McAdoo to Reading, 12 Aug. 1918; Lever to McAdoo, 10 Sept. 1918; and Rathbone to Crosby, 24 Oct. 1918, all file 30, box 221, US Treasury.

[63] W.K. Hancock and M.M. Gowing, *British War Economy* (London, 1949), p. 40.

[64] ibid.

6

The Impact of the First World War on the British Labour Movement

Chris Wrigley

As the twentieth century comes to a close, the importance of the First World War to its history appears massive. For some seventy years its effects were very clear in Russia and much of central and eastern Europe. In Britain the war was decisive in changing the pattern of British politics and, at least for a while, enhancing the economic and political position of the Labour movement.

If the political outcome in Britain was less spectacular than in Russia and Germany, it nevertheless set British politics on a course which by no means had been inevitable before the war. Indeed the politics of the Left might even have followed the US pattern had it not been for the war. There might have been a relatively small socialist movement largely separate from mainstream organised labour; with British organised labour, like Samuel Gompers and the American Federation of Labour, reaching a working accommodation with capitalism and associating with the Liberal Party in the way that much of US labour associated with the Democrats.

This was a distinct possibility before 1914. The British past – political, economic and social – was very different from that in which the US labour movement emerged. Nevertheless, the British labour movement's evolution in a partial liberal parliamentary democracy was closer to the US experience than that of Russia, Germany, Austria or Hungary. Yet in Britain in the two decades before 1914 there were developments which clearly were leading towards the emergence of a substantial European style independent socialist working class party. The First World War was decisive in boosting these possibilities into probabilities.

Anyone claiming 'A Labour government within a decade' would have met with a response of incredulity in early 1914. Yet a minority government was in office, albeit briefly, from January 1924. The First World War and its aftermath transformed the position of the British Labour Party. In parliamentary terms it cast off its pre-war position of being not much more than an auxiliary to the Liberal Party. Most of its parliamentary seats depended on an electoral pact with the Liberals which had operated in the 1906 and the two 1910 general elections. Had there been no war, in a 1915 general election Labour would have fought only a handful more seats than the 65 of January 1910; and its realistic scope for gains would have been in coalfields or inner-city areas.[1]

By the end of the First World War the Labour Party had emerged as a major political force. It was seen by political opponents and political commentators alike as being likely to form a government within a few years. In the 1918 general election Labour endorsed 363 candidates and in addition there were ten allied Co-operative Party candidates and thirty-one unendorsed Labour candidates. Labour's number of MPs went up from the forty-two of December 1910 to fifty-seven (with in addition one Co-operative Party and three unendorsed Labour); a total notably greater than the thirty-seven of the Asquithian wing of the Liberal Party who were also in Opposition.[2] Labour's 1918 total of MPs was then seen as artificially low due to the unfavourable timing of the election, with Lloyd George exploiting the 'Khaki' spirit of victory. Arthur Henderson, Labour's experienced organiser, was to claim credibly in 1920 that in 1918 Labour had 'polled its minimum vote'.[3] In 1918 Labour polled 22.2 per cent of the vote and in the next election, in 1922, it polled 29.5 per cent of the vote and secured 142 MPs.

Labour's enhanced political power owed most to its increased industrial strength arising from the war. Indeed, before the war the most striking feature of the British labour movement had been the considerable strength of the trade unions and, relative to many continental European countries, the slowness of independent labour and socialist politics to develop. British trade unionism stretched back into the eighteenth century and, in 1895, numbered just under 1,500,000 members, a density of 10.6 per cent, at a time when there were only a third of a million German trade unionists, a density of 2.5 per cent. By 1913 British trade union membership had risen to 4,107,000, a density of 24.8 per cent, while the German total had grown to 3,023,000, a density of 16.4 per cent.[4] In contrast, in 1893, the year the Independent Labour Party was formed in Britain (and seven before the Labour Representation Committee was formed) the German socialist party, the SPD, stood for the Reichstag in all but a handful of constituencies and gained 23.3 per cent of the votes on the first ballot and elected 44 deputies. In the last election before the war, in 1912, it polled 34.8 per dent of the votes and elected 110 deputies, becoming the largest party in the Reichstag. In Britain in the December 1910 general

[1] D. Tanner, *Political Change and the Labour Party, 1900–1918* (Cambridge, 1990), pp. 317–37; R. McKibbin, *The Evolution of the Labour Party, 1910–1924* (Oxford, 1974), pp. 72–87.

[2] G.D.H. Cole, *A History of the Labour Party from 1914* (London, 1948) pp. 83–87.

[3] C.J. Wrigley, *Arthur Henderson* (Cardiff, 1990), p. 127.

[4] G.S. Bain and R. Price, *Profiles of Union Growth* (Oxford, 1980), pp. 39, 133. Union density is defined here as the proportion of those in unions of all those who were legally permitted to be in unions, whether currently employed or unemployed. The German figures exclude salaried employee associations. If these were included the German figure for 1913 would be 3,929,000, with a density of 21.3 per cent.

Table 1

Increase in Trade Union Density (percentage) between 1911 and 1921

Sector	1911	1921
Agriculture, horticulture and forestry	0.7	23.5
Bricks and building materials	14.7	47.0
Chemicals	9.6	23.6
Electricity	2.2	33.4
Entertainment	12.2	50.2
Gas	20.2	56.4
Insurance, banking and finance	6.7	22.4
Paper and board	5.8	50.2
Pottery	14.7	50.1
Timber and furniture	13.2	28.2

Note. In these sectors the numbers of trade unionists rose from 106,900 to 580,600 between 1911 and 1921.
Source: G. Bain and R. Price, *Profiles of Union Growth* (Oxford, 1980), pp. 43–75.

election Labour only contested fifty-six seats, polled 371,772 votes (7.1 per cent of the national total) and elected forty-two MPs.[5] While the scale of German trade union organisation was catching up with independent political organisation by the turn of the century, in Britain the Labour Party became a clearly separate challenger for political power only with the First World War.

The number of British trade unionists grew by 57 per cent between 1914 and 1918, reaching a density of 38.1 per cent. By the end of the post war boom in 1920 the number of trade unionists had doubled since 1914, with union density reaching 48.2 per cent, a level only surpassed in 1974–81. Areas which had been strongly unionised before 1914 became stronger still. This was so in such sectors as coal mining, metals and engineering, printing, railways and textiles. In the case of metals and engineering the workforce rose by a third between 1911 and 1921, while trade union density rose from 29.2 to 55.5 per cent.[6]

Yet equally important for the greater strength of the British labour movement was the rapid trade union expansion in other sectors. This is illustrated by ten notable examples in Table 1. The war saw a substantial

[5] W.L. Guttsman, *The German Social Democratic Party, 1875–1933* (London, 1981), pp. 80–81. In the January 1910 election Labour had fielded 78 candidates, polled 505,690 votes (7.6 per cent) and elected forty MPs. McKibbin, *The Evolution of the Labour Party* pp. 12–13, 16.

[6] Bain and Price, *Profiles of Union Growth*, p. 39; J. Waddington, 'Unemployment and Restructuring: Trade Union Membership in Britain, 1980–1987', *British Journal of Industrial Relations*, 30 (1992), pp. 287–305.

increase in trade union membership among manual workers, rising by 57.6 per cent between 1914 and 1918 and nearly doubling (up 98.9 per cent) by 1920. The most dramatic rise was the tenfold increase in membership of the National Union of Agricultural Labourers and Rural Workers. During the war the membership of the Workers Union quadrupled and the three other major general unions trebled their membership. One notable feature of this expansion was the increase in female membership. The Workers Union and the National Union of Gasworkers and General Labourers had fewer than 10,000 women members in 1913. By 1918 this number had grown to some 140,000 between them. Women trade unionists went a long way towards the trebling in number between 1914 and 1918. Membership rose from 436,000 to 1,182,000, a rise in density from 8.6 to 22.8 per cent. Like male, female trade unionism continued to expand until 1920, reaching 1,316,000 and a density of 25.2 per cent.[7] Another notable feature was the growth of white collar trade unionism. H.G. Wells' Mr Lewisham and Mr Kipps were moving to Labour, at least for a while. The density of union membership among white collar workers rose from 11.6 to 24.2 per cent between 1911 and 1921. During the war the numbers in unions rose from 534,500 to 815,600, and in 1920 reached 1,129,200. The National Union of Clerks, led by Herbert Elvin, was sufficiently radicalised in the post-war euphoria to restructure its organisation on a decentralised, industrial guild basis.[8] The war provided the unions with superb conditions for growth. The labour market was highly favourable, with unemployment marginal from 1915, and wartime inflation was sufficiently high to ensure workers were anxious about their real wages (even if long hours and bonuses helped with actual earnings).[9]

Perhaps the most notable feature about most trade unionists in the First World War was generally the degree of patriotic restraint shown in conditions exceptionally favourable for them. They did not cash in on their opportunities in the manner of the many war profiteers.[10] The effect on the labour market of the wholesale withdrawal of fit male labour was immense. During the course of the war some 5,670,000 men were enlisted

[7] Bain and Price, *Profiles of Union Growth*, pp. 39, 41; H.A. Clegg, *A History of British Trade Unionism since 1889*, ii, *1911–1933* (Oxford, 1985), pp. 196–97.

[8] Bain and Price, *Profiles of Union Growth*, p. 41; B. Nield, 'Herbert Henry Elvin', in J. Saville and J. Bellamy (eds), *Dictionary of Labour Biography*, vi (London, 1982), pp. 106–7.

[9] G.S. Bain and F. Elsheikh, *Union Growth and the Business Cycle* (Oxford, 1976). See also A. Booth, 'A Reconsideration of Trade Union Growth in the United Kingdom', *British Journal of Industrial Relations*, 21 (1983), pp. 379–91; and A. Carruth and D. Disney, 'Where Have Two Million Trade Union Members Gone?', *Economica*, 55 (1988), pp. 1–19.

[10] The very strong post-war public pressure for action against wartime profiteers led to the Profiteering Act of 18 August 1919 and serious consideration of a capital levy. R.C. Whiting, 'The Labour Party, Capitalism and the National Debt', in P.J. Waller (ed.), *Politics and Change in Modern Britain* (Hemel Hempstead, 1987), pp. 140–60; C.J. Wrigley, *Lloyd George and the Challenge of Labour* (Hemel Hempstead, 1990), pp. 236–40.

in the Armed Forces out of a total male labour force which numbered some 15,000,000 at the outbreak of the war. The labour market was further affected by the increase in employment in war priority areas. Between 1914 and 1918 the numbers in civil employment fell from 19,440,000 to 17,060,000 (down by 12 per cent) while the numbers employed in the metal trades rose from 1,804,000 to 2,418,000 (by 34 per cent). Part of this increase in numbers was due to more women working in this sector, as in many other sectors (see Table 2). It was also due to more men being employed in metals and engineering. Between 1914 and 1918 in private metal firms the number of male workers rose from 1,634,000 to 1,876,000 while in private chemical companies there was a small rise from 159,000 to 161,000. In government establishments (arsenals, national factories and dockyards) the increase was very substantial: from 76,000 to 277,000.[11]

There were many strikes, but the majority of these were aimed at holding real standards of living in the face of rapidly rising prices. If wholesale prices, the cost of living index and wage rates are weighted each as 100 in July 1914, by July 1918 they had risen respectively to 233, 205 and 175–80 (wage rates only equalling or just passing the cost of living index in July 1919). In contrast, during the Second World War, when the items in the cost of living index were subsidised by the government and there was extensive rationing, the July 1944 figures (September 1939 weighted 100) were 170, 130 and 143.[12] Thus in the First World War governments made few attempts to maintain real wages. Indeed in the early part of the war the Committee on Production, which acted as an arbitration body when strikes were made illegal under the Munitions of War Act 1915, was under instructions from the government to respect the need for economy and to see that any wage advances granted 'should be strictly confined to the adjustment of local conditions'.[13] Many in governing circles were happy for working people to contribute to the war effort involuntarily through higher prices. Such an attitude underlay the views in a letter by one leading Liberal MP at the end of 1915:

> It is very difficult indeed to deal with those working folk who wont save. The only valid method, finally, seems to be the income tax and the taxes on tea, tobacco etc. In the end their expenditure gets into the pockets of the traders who do save and are taxed on excess profits. But there remains the evil waste on food and drink, and that can only very gradually be brought under control.[14]

[11] A.W. Kirkaldy (ed.), *British Labour: Replacement and Conciliation, 1914–21* (London, 1921), pp. 1–3.

[12] W.K. Hancock and M. Gowing, *British War Economy* (London, 1949), p. 152.

[13] *History of The Ministry of Munitions*, iv, pt 4 (HMG, printed but not published), p. 128.

[14] Robertson to H.A.L. Fisher, 31 December 1915, H.A.L. Fisher Papers, 2, Bodleian Library, Oxford. The author, the Rt Hon. J.M. Robertson, had been Parliamentary Secretary to the Board of Trade until earlier in the year.

Table 2

Women and War Work

Occupation	No. of females employed (000s)		% of females employed		No. of females replacing males (000s)
	July 1914	Nov. 1918	July 1914	Nov. 1918	
1 Government dockyards, arsenals, national factories etc.	2.2	247	3	47	232
2 Private and Municipal Industries					
Metal	170	597	9	24	363
Chemical	40	103	20	39	52
Textile	863	818	58	67	107
Clothing	612	556	68	76	54
Food, drink and tobacco	196	231	35	48	62
Paper and printing	148	141	36	47	33
Wood	44	83	15	32	46
Building	7	31	1	7	28
Mines and quarries	7	13	1	2	7
Other (including municipal utilities)	90	156	16	34	80
Total	**2177**	**2729**	**26**	**35**	**832**
3 Agriculture	80	95	9	14	34
4 Transport					
Railways	12	66	2	11	55
Municipal trams	1.2	19	2	34	18
Other trains and buses	0.4	9.3	1	30	9
Other transport	4.6	21	1	10	18
Total	**18**	**115**	**2**	**12**	**100**
5 Finance and Commerce					
Banking and finance	9.5	75	5	43	66
Commerce	496	880	29	54	411
Total	**506**	**955**	**27**	**53**	**477**
6 Civil Service					
Post Office	61	121	24	53	65
Other Civil Service	5	107	8	59	90
Total	**66**	**228**	**21**	**56**	**155**
7 Hotels, pubs, cinemas etc.	181	222	48	66	61
8 Teachers (local authority)	142	154	73	82	18
9 Other professions (persons employed by accountants, solicitors etc)	18	40	12	37	27
10 Municipal services (excluding teachers, trams, utilities)	54	75	14	26	33
11 Hospitals	33	80	n.a.	n.a.	n.a.
Total 1–11	**3,277**	**4,940**	**24**	**37**	**1,969**

Note: In each sub category the figures were rounded to the nearest thousand, as a result the category totals are not always equal to the sum of the parts.
Source: A.W. Kirkaldy (ed.), *British Labour: Replacement and Conciliation 1914–21: Being the Result of Conferences and Investigations by Committees of Section F of the British Association* (London, 1921).

Table 3

Women's Employment in Selected Industries, April 1915

Trade Groups	Approx. numbers, 1911 Census (000s)	April 1915 compared with July 1914		
		Change in numbers employed	on short time	on overtime
Boots and shoes	49	+2.8	0.8	20.6
Clothing	994	+3.9	4.0	21.0
Electrical engineering	12	+19.7	0.9	26.5
Engineering	9	+45.0	4.4	62.9
Food	103	−4.7	1.4	14.5
Hosiery	52	+10.9	2.3	14.4
Leather and leather goods	13	+36.6	4.3	55.1
Woollen and worsted	158	+4.2	2.4	16.9

Source: Lloyd George Papers, D/11/4/1.

While patriotic restraint was a major feature of most trade unionists' behaviour during the war, it was reinforced by high cash earnings. Real wages were eroded, but there were ample opportunities to earn extra money. A.L. Bowley has commented:

> In many cases it became easy to make high earnings on piece work both because the work was well systematized and repetitive on a large scale and because the same rate being ensured whatever the output, there was no fear of any cutting of prices. At the same time night work and overtime at enhanced rates were common. The earnings of piece workers consequently increased greatly, independently of any increase in rates, time workers received more in return for more work, and a very large number of persons passed from unskilled to skilled rates of pay. These processes were particularly marked in 1917 and 1918.[15]

The expansion of overtime working, for instance, is well illustrated by figures early on in the war for overtime and short time working drawn from a survey of the expansion of women's employment in industry (some of which was munitions, some – such as elastic webbing and brush-making – was production replacing German imports).[16] See Table 3.

Patriotic restraint did not involve an abnegation of all bargaining power. Far from it. The unions, the employers and the government were well

[15] A.L. Bowley, *Prices and Wages in the United Kingdom, 1914–1920* (London, 1921), p. 125.

[16] C.F. Rey, Ministry of Munitions, to Lloyd George, 15 July 1915, Lloyd George Papers, HLRO D/11/4/1.

aware of the strength of labour's position in such wartime conditions. Arthur Henderson, while a member of Lloyd George's War Cabinet, observed during one set of negotiations with trade union leaders, 'I think I can safely claim that never during the whole history of trade unionism has organised labour been consulted as it has been during the period of the war'.[17]

The government needed the co-operation of the trade union leaders in key sectors of the economy if they were to gain increased output in spite of the massive loss of labour to the Armed Forces. This was especially the case in munitions. At a conference of members of the Ministry of Munitions and leaders of the Amalgamated Society of Engineers in September 1915 Henderson commented:

> if you had compulsion for industry tomorrow I am not satisfied that you could get very many more skilled men placed at your disposal. When I came to that conclusion two or three weeks ago I put it before my own [National] Advisory Committee ... whether we should not attempt to dilute skilled labour by putting a skilled engineer in charge of 10 or 12 semi-skilled or unskilled men and women and then spread the skilled labour, and probably have a matter of 500 or 1000 supervisors to 10,000 or 20,000 workers ... I am convinced that if you had industrial compulsion tomorrow you have not the workmen to draw upon ... if you do that you will be up against the whole of the trade union movement in this country ... We cannot afford the next two months fighting them.[18]

Henderson was basically right. The expansion of engineering required trade union co-operation in reorganising skilled labour within the industry rather than industrial conscription. By the time of the Battle of the Somme in the summer of 1916 huge amounts of munitions were being produced. A Ministry of Munitions memorandum of that time noted:

> The relaxation of these restrictive rules and customs has been accompanied by the use of trade union discipline to increase production in the national interest. The combined effect of these two forces has been colossal. About three million workers have been drained from industry by military requirements yet the productivity of the country has been maintained at the highest pitch.[19]

The desirability of trade union co-operation was recognised by many employers as well as by Whitehall. George Booth, a businessman who worked for the War Office and then the Ministry of Munitions, told a meeting held with engineering employers from Manchester in April 1915

[17] At a conference with the Amalgamated Society of Engineers (ASE) on trade cards, 2 May 1917, PRO, MUN 5/62/322/19.

[18] Minutes of conference with ASE, 13 September 1915, PRO, MUN 5/57/320/3.

[19] Memorandum, Intelligence and Records Department, Ministry of Munitions, 4 August 1916, PRO, MUN 5-91-344/9.

that it was highly desirable to set up joint committees with the local trade union organisations. He commented,

> it is very essential that the labour side should be satisfied. Mr Henderson and his special committee [the National Advisory Committee] have a room in our office at Cecil Chambers . . . Mr Henderson meets us there, and when we have labour disputes – for instance, in the last two days there has been a dispute over the releasing of military men, and certain conditions at Hereford gave rise to a strike – Mr Henderson has helped to settle matters quickly. The labour people are, indeed, helping us very much, and we want them to feel that they are considered and consulted and appreciated in anything that is done in this patriotic local effort. Each area must work with labour, which is a very sensitive thing.

When one of the employers respondd by saying, 'We have already existing a splendid machinery for settling disputes', Booth commented, 'We ask you to keep that machinery particularly alive at this time, because we think on the whole that the Labour Party has behaved pretty well'.[20] As the war progressed the government pressed a widening range of employers to recognise the trade unions in their industries and encouraged the setting up of joint committees. The Whitley Councils were one later aspect of this.

The involvement of many trade union leaders in assisting industrial reorganisation for the war effort both boosted the unions concerned and gave them problems. The major role of the unions in the war effort, with very full recognition by the employers and government and a substantive say in industrial matters, greatly enhanced their prestige with the workforce. The war legitimised them. They were part of a wartime corporate economy and, indeed, wartime industrial democracy. There was also a widening of their sphere, a going beyond being primarily bodies for skilled male workers. Trade unionism embraced a wider range of unskilled workers, both male and female.

Yet the degree of involvement of the national trade union leadership in expanding munitions production (in its widest sense) did exacerbate tensions within many unions.[21] Lloyd George, when meeting the Shipbuilding Employers Federation in August 1915, commented to a Scottish employer,

> The trade union leaders are fairly reasonable; the difficulty comes from the local leaders and not from the men at the top. I found them very willing to

---

[20] Conference with Manchester Engineering Employers, 29 April 1915, PRO, MUN 5/7/171/1.

[21] This is well surveyed in a large literature. See, in particular, J. Hinton, *The First Shop Stewards Movement* (London, 1972); and W. Kendall, *The Revolutionary Movement in Britain, 1900–21* (London, 1969).

assist . . . but they have not the control over their men in the districts that they would like. You have some very turbulent fellows down in your country.[22]

The ASE leadership found itself in conflict with its members in some engineering areas over the relaxation of working practices, the intro- duction of dilutees and the increased regulation of workplaces under the Munitions Act. To this was added concern that trade union members were making sacrifices which boosted employers' profits. Yet, Arthur Henderson and the ASE leadership were in tune with most trade unionists' support for the war. On many occasions, when the war needs were emphasised, skilled trade unions reluctantly acceded to the workplace changes. For instance, when Lloyd George saw a deputation from the ASE on 31 December 1915 he was told: 'You will realise the importance of my words when I say that 80 per cent of the [ASE] Delegates came to London thirsting for the blood of their Executive Council, and the most important resolution [for the EC] was carried by 87 votes to 14.'[23]

The involvement of the leaderships of the ASE and some other skilled unions in implementing government policies did create a conflict of interest for them. They had taken on the commitment of assisting the war effort. Indeed on one occasion William Mosses, Secretary of the United Pattern Makers Association, wrote to Lloyd George on behalf of the National Advisory Committee on War Output stating 'that generally trade union officials were doing, at present and were prepared to do in the future, everything in their power to facilitate the acceleration of government work'.[24] Yet this purpose could and did cut across one of their prime functions as trade union leaders of representing their members' workplace grievances. The leaders of the skilled unions, especially the ASE, angered those at the Ministry of Munitions when they did press their members' concerns over dilution and the relaxation of working practices. Herbert Llewellyn Smith in a brief prepared for Asquith for the end of 1915 caustically observed:

> The serious part of the situation is that we have reached a position in which the nation is being held up by a single union. If we allow the obstruction of the Amalgamated Society of Engineers to prevail there is little or no chance of being able to fill the National and other munition factories.
> The negotiations with this union appear to be interminable, and no sooner

[22] Conference with the Shipbuilding Employers Federation, 12 August 1915, PRO, MUN 5-48-300/9. For all this, leading figures in the Ministry of Munitions frequently raged at the ASE executive for doing too little. For example on this, H. Llewellyn Smith's notes for H.H. Asquith, 31 December 1915, MUN 5/70/324/2/1; or Christopher Addison's diary, 15 and 21 February 1916, Addison Papers, box 97, Bodleian Library, Oxford.

[23] Meting with deputation from the ASE, 31 December 1915, PRO, MUN 5/70/324/3.

[24] At the time of Lloyd George's allegations on drink and loss of working time. W. Mosses to Lloyd George, 19 June 1915, Lloyd George Papers HLRO, D/11/1/4.

is one agreement arrived at then it is broken, and new black-mailing conditions are proposed.

The demand at the last moment for drastic amendments to the Munitions Bill as a condition of fulfilling the agreement as to dilution already entered into is the last stage of a series of obstructive tactics, and any yielding will only be the signal for the putting forward of some fresh conditions.[25]

Equally the skilled union leaders angered part of their membership by not keeping aloof from government entanglements in the way that Robert Smillie and the Miners Federation of Great Britain (MFGB) did and by helping to bring in rather than resisting the workplace changes. Where there was resistance to such workplace changes, it was usually led by shop stewards. Several of the leading figures of the wartime shop stewards' movement were later to be founder members of the Communist Party of Great Britain. This radicalisation of many engineering and metal workers was not a purely British phenomenon. It was a feature in all the European belligerent countries during the First World War.

In Britain the government was wary of the shop stewards' movement and was concerned that it should not link up with pacifist campaigners. The government was also anxious to remedy the social and industrial conditions behind the near national engineering strikes of May 1917.[26] The government's fears of revolutionary unrest in 1917 and early 1918 appear, with hindsight, to have been unduly great – just as they were in the period after the end of the war. Petrograd in March 1917 was taken as a warning. Generally British strikes did not have the increasing political content of many in Berlin in 1917–18, where demands included changes to the Prussian electoral system, the freeing of prominent left-wing socialists from gaol and a peace without annexations.

Nevertheless in Britain, especially in the later part of the war, there was a fairly thin line between strikes for industrial and strikes for political objectives. In Britain strikes were not over democracy, as Britain had broadly democratic institutions (though not then universal male let alone female suffrage), nor – John Maclean apart – over prominent left-wing political prisoners. However, there was unrest over the incidence of conscription, with a major strike at Sheffield in November 1916. There was also increasing concern expressed over war aims, especially after the Bolshevik Revolution in Russia when Trotsky published secret treaties showing annexationist aims on the Allied side. Perhaps of wider significance was the fact that, in an economy increasingly controlled by the

[25] Notes for Asquith by H. Llewellyn Smith, 31 December 1915, PRO, MUN 5/70/324/2/1. Christopher Addison, the Parliamentary Secretary, was similarly severe in comments in his diary, Diary, 15 and 21 February 1916, Addison Papers, box 97, Bodleian Library, Oxford.

[26] C.J. Wrigley, *David Lloyd George and the British Labour Movement* (Brighton, 1976), pp. 180–204.

government, a high proportion of strikes were aimed at the government
and its policies. In 'them' and 'us' terms, for many working people in
the wartime economy the 'us' was organised labour and the 'them' was
the predominant Conservative and Liberal participants in the coalition
governments. Again, this was a feature of other belligerent countries, not
least Russia between the two revolutions of 1917.

Moreover the very controls in the wartime economy boosted collectivist
attitudes among the British population. What would have been deemed
untried, or even Utopian, before 1914 was put into practice during the
war. The First World War, like the Second World War, produced a very
substantial shift in common assumptions about society and how it should
be organised. Though Lloyd George on such occasions was prone to be
glib, there was something in his comment on the Munitions of War Act
to a conference with trade unionists in November 1915:

> One chief object of the Act was to give state control over unlimited competition,
> a principle that many labour men had been advocating for a long time – and
> during the progress of the war more things had been done to further the
> principles of the labour movement than the propaganda of a generation had
> been able to secure.[27]

The changes of the war affected wider groups than skilled male trade
unionists. While unions like the ASE negotiated direct with senior Cabinet
ministers from early on in the war, later unskilled unions also did so. The
general shortage of labour, as in past cyclical booms in the economy,
enhanced their bargaining position.[28] The moment of truth came over
the government's trade card scheme of November 1916, which gave
preferential treatment to skilled workers in exemption from conscription.
It had been first conceded to the ASE and then, given the outrage of other
skilled unions, extended to them. It was never operated, in recognition
that it was unworkable as unskilled workers were also essential for war
output.[29]

Unskilled and semi-skilled labour benefited as the old accepted wage
differentials collapsed in the general upheaval of war. The wartime
price inflation encouraged the Committee on Production to make wage
awards which would protect the less-well-paid. In munitions the process
of dilution for a time created all manner of anomalies. Addison, speaking
of unrest among skilled workers in Sheffield, commented:

[27] Speech of 30 November 1915, *Manchester Guardian*, 1 December 1915.

[28] This came as a surprise to the government in April 1915. When an employer
commented 'there is a considerable lack of ordinary labourers. You cannot get ordinary
labourers today' Mr Booth responded, 'I think this is the first time that anybody has told
us that'. Minutes of Armaments Output Committee's meeting with Manchester Engineering
Employers, 29 April 1915, PRO, MUN 5/7/171/1.

[29] Deputation of engineering unions other than the ASE, 22 November 1916, PRO,
MUN 5/57/320/18.

I am told that a skilled supervisor gets £3 a week but a pawnbroker's assistant who has come in quite recently earns 11d. a dozen [fuses], and the unskilled wages vary from 17 shillings to 20 shillings a day, or two or three times the wages of the skilled man who is supervising them.[30]

This was an extreme, temporary situation. Overall, though, as Bernard Waites has commented, 'the wartime economy compressed the economic and social distance between the poorest and the artisan state'. Indeed he argued that the combination of economic changes with shifts of popular attitudes were of sufficient importance 'for historians to talk of a re-making of the English working class'.[31]

The Labour Party's particular strength lay in the scale of its trade union membership. The war enhanced this strength. Before the war the dominant ethos of the party had been that of the skilled male trade unionist. The war did not change that. Moreover the skilled trade unionists during and after the war were brutally blunt as to their desire to exclude women as far as possible from skilled work. This hardly helped the Labour Party after the war to reach out to working-class women electors. Indeed, according to Michael Savage, in Preston, a textile town, the keenest Labour supporters were male trade unionists who felt threatened by female labour.[32] As many working women would have shared many assumptions about work and wages with the men, this may well not have been too great an obstacle. Indeed the propensity of many working women to vote Conservative reinforces this point.

The war years did see, however as in much of Europe, political support for Labour growing beyond the confines of large, trade unionised workplaces. Nationally Labour tried to mobilise its strength to exert pressure on the government to remedy social problems arising from the war. This was done through the War Emergency Workers' National Committee (WEWNC), which was made up of representatives from the Labour Party, TUC, General Federation of Trade Unions (GFTU), the Co-operative Movement and the Socialist societies. Arthur Henderson chaired it before he entered Asquith's Coalition government in May 1915.[33]

The WEWNC did much to establish the Labour movement as a champion of working people generally. It took up many wartime issues,

[30] Conference with the ASE, 24 February 1916, PRO, MUN 5/71/324/44.

[31] B. Waites, *A Class Society at War: England, 1914–18* (Leamington Spa, 1987), pp. 16–17. The fairer shares achieved by the poorer sections of society have been discussed by J.M. Winter, *The Great War and the British People* (Cambridge, 1986).

[32] M. Savage, *The Dynamics of Working Class Politics: The Labour Movement in Preston, 1880–1940* (Cambridge, 1987), pp. 163–71.

[33] On the WEWNC see R. Harrison, 'The War Emergency Workers' National Committee, 1914–20', in A. Briggs and J. Saville (eds), *Essays in Labour History, 1886–1923* (London, 1971), pp. 211–59; and J.M. Winter, *Socialism and the Challenge of War* (London, 1974), pp. 184–233.

including high food prices, lack of coal and the very poor provision of separation allowances for the dependants of soldiers and sailors. Arthur Henderson, when speaking at a public meeting held on the issue of controlling wheat and coal prices, made it clear that the WEWNC was campaigning on behalf of more than organised labour.

> It was not for the highly skilled and organised workers the conference was interested, they could look after themselves and were doing so. They were claiming and, he was glad to say, in many cases obtaining substantial increases in wages. They pleaded for the great body of the unskilled, unorganised and detached bodies of workers ... The men had left their homes to fight for their country, and upon their kith and kin left behind fell the hardships and sufferings from high prices which might have been avoided or minimised had the government taken action.[34]

During the war the WEWNC and the Labour Movement generally made food prices as well as war allowances and pensions very much their own issues. In February 1915 Henderson spoke in Parliament of 'the most serious issue with which the civil population had been confronted since the opening of hostilities ... the terrible prices now ruling for food and coals and other commodities'. In calling for a special debate on the subject he spoke of 'almost famine prices'. When that debate took place just over a week later, J.R. Clynes vigorously criticised the government for leaving supplies at 'the mercies of those who are exacting the highest prices according to the laws and practices of their trade and business'.[35]

Similarly the Parliamentary Committee of the TUC took up food prices on behalf of the whole community. When the Parliamentary Committee of the TUC saw the Prime Minister, Asquith, in July 1916, food prices and then the position of old age pensioners were early items on its agenda. Fred Bramley commented that discontent was 'not due to the suffering which the increased cost of living entails' so much as to awareness of massive profits being made by shipping companies and others. Bramley urged:

> We prefer the method of keeping down food prices ... for if an increase of wages were to be sought in the way of adjustment, only those who are well organised and strong will get the advantage; but if the action can be taken to keep down the cost of living the community generally will benefit, and particularly the very poorest who as a rule represent the unorganised mass of people who cannot collectively express their discontent or secure any readjustment of their position.[36]

[34] Wrigley, *Arthur Henderson*, pp. 78–79.
[35] 69. *H.C. Deb.* 10–12 and 776–84, 2 and 11 February 1915.
[36] Deputation of the Parliamentary Committee of the TUC, 19 July 1916, Asquith Papers, 91, fos 81–104, Bodleian Library, Oxford.

It was significant that when Lloyd George saw the National Executive Committee of the Labour Party and Labour MPs on 7 December 1916 to seek their support for his government one person present felt that 'All he definitely promised was a ministry of Labour and a Food Controller'.[37] J.R. Clynes was appointed Parliamentary Secretary to the Ministry of Food in July 1917 and he became the Food Controller the following July.

While the WEWNC's activities in organising meetings, deputations and the like nationally and across the country are relatively well known, it needs emphasising that the Labour movement locally was actively campaigning on social issues thrown up by the war.[38] For instance members of trades councils, socialist societies and co-operative organisations came together in many urban centres to form Food Vigilance Committees. Local activists also took up such issues as overcrowding in munitions producing areas. Uproar over rent rises on the Clyde in 1915 led to the government freezing rents.

Housing was but one area where from fairly early on in the war thinking went well beyond immediate war concerns. The issue was briefly debated at the January 1917 and January 1918 Labour Party Conferences. At the former the conference agreed to call on the government to ensure that local authorities prepare 'housing schemes on garden suburb lines, without block or tenement dwellings'. At the latter, the conference agreed to demand 'a national housing and town building scheme' involving 'the establishment of new towns, and the reconstruction of the smaller existing towns, on garden city principles'. It added that the 'land for this purpose to be compulsorily acquired and development financed by the state, and the whole enterprise to be administered by a municipal authority or non-profiteering democratic body in the interest of the community'.[39] Whatever else, the war encouraged the Labour movement to think about social issues both during it and for the future post-war reconstruction.

While Labour MPs and leading trade unionists participated in the government or became members of Whitehall committees, at the local level trade unionists and some socialist activists also became involved in running local affairs through committees dealing with such matters as recruiting, hearing the pleas of conscientious objectors, relieving distress and issues concerning food. Outside of cities their presence was novel. When they took their places by right in many country towns, it was often much to

[37] Sidney Webb's account, recorded in Beatrice Webb's diary, 8 December 1916, M. Cole (ed.) *Beatrice Webb's Diaries, 1912–1924* (London, 1952), p. 72. Lloyd George's own account to a group of Unionist leaders of what he had promised Labour was notable for omitting all mention of food. Lord Beaverbrook, *Politicians and the War, 1914–16*, ii (London, 1932), pp. 320–22.

[38] On this see, for example, J. Bush, *Behind the Lines: East London Labour, 1914–1919* (London, 1984); and J. Holford, *Reshaping Labour: Organisation, Work and Politics – Edinburgh in the Great War and After* (London, 1988).

[39] On 25 January 1917, Labour Party, *Report of the Annual Conference 1917*, p. 146. On 24 January 1918, Labour Party, *Report of the Annual Conference, 1918*, p. 126.

the chagrin of the local squirearchy, clergy and middle class who had hitherto seen such committee work as their preserves. Once involved in such work, trade unionists were often radicalised, as they were frustrated either by restrictions on the committee's powers or by unrepresentative majorities.[40]

The war also radicalised the co-operative movement. Arthur Henderson reported almost euphorically to January 1918 Labour Party Conference,

> largely as the result of the attitude of ... governments towards the Co-operative Movement, particularly in regard to the taxation of co-operative dividends and the neglect of the assistance proffered by the movement in dealing with the national Food Supply, together with unfair treatment of the staffs of Distributive Societies under the Military Service Acts, a very representative emergency conference ... was held on October 16 and 17 [1917]. In addition to passing a series of ... resolutions ... the conference also decided with practical unanimity in favour of the Co-operative Movement taking up direct political activity in the electoral field. Reference need only be made to the overwhelming manner in which such proposals have been repeatedly defeated by Co-operative Congresses in the past to realise the remarkable change that has taken place in all sections of the Co-operative Movement.

He added that in some districts negotiations had already been taking place between local co-operative societies and local Labour organisations. This was so in Scotland and Plymouth, with strong support for such moves also being present in parts of West Yorkshire, Manchester, Tyneside and Wales. Before the war co-operators collectively had avoided political action but individually had probably been predominantly Liberal or Lib-Lab in their politics, with some notable exceptions which had been Labour.[41]

The pressures of war boosted the co-operative movements in most belligerent countries. In France the numbers of constituent societies of the National Federation of Co-operatives increased by a quarter and its overall turnover increased in value from 9,000,000 to 42,000,000 francs. In Britain individual membership of co-operative societies rose from some 3,000,000 to well over 4,000,000.[42] Like the trade union movement, the British co-operative movement warmly supported the war effort. Yet by 1917 speakers at co-operative meetings were declaring 'that they were about to receive their Taff Vale'. The co-ops, unlike many private traders, did not hold back goods or food to gain higher prices. They were

---

[40] A. Clinton, *The Trade Union Rank and File* (Manchester, 1977), pp. 54–55.

[41] *Report of the Annual Conference, 1918*, p. 22. Henderson reported on moves to find 'about a dozen constituencies where Co-operative candidates might be adopted with the full support of our own local organisations' to the June 1918 Labour Party Conference. Labour Party, *Report of the Annual Conference, June 1918*, p. 5.

[42] J. Horne, *Labour at War: France and Britain, 1914–1918* (Oxford, 1991), pp. 95–96, 223–24.

generous with contributions to war relief committees, yet private traders were often successful in keeping co-op representatives off these and other committees. When eventually the government introduced rationing for sugar, it ignored requests that the Co-operative Union have representation on the body which controlled it, even though the co-ops were the largest wholesalers and retailers of sugar in Britain. Lloyd George's repeated refusal to see a co-operative movement delegation, in spite of press reports of him seeing all manner of other groups, convinced many co-operators that the government was hand-in-glove with the private traders and was actually eager to disadvantage co-ops.[43]

Government reluctance to take measures to ensure fair food shares for all angered many working people beyond organised labour. Food shortages were far worse in continental European countries. Nevertheless in Britain, as elsewhere, food queues were great radicalisers. People who spent hours queuing, often before or after lengthy factory work, were prone to be critical of free market forces and lack of government regulation. Sugar was one particularly sore point. Lloyd George's friend, the newspaper proprietor Sir George Riddell, warned him in June 1917

> that sugar queues were causing grave discontent and that sugar distribution called for immediate reform. The working classes are angry that their wives and families should be compelled to undergo this trouble and indignity, while the wants of the rich are supplied much as they were before the war.[44]

In Battersea in May 1917 a magistrate, when fining a tradesman for refusing to sell customers sugar unless they bought other goods, observed that 'to impose conditions on the sale of sugar is to grind the face of the poor'.[45] Wartime conditions brought about a vigorous revival of notions of 'the moral economy', of social fairness rather than unrestricted profit making.

In Britain, as in parts of continental Europe, political support for Labour spread out from factories and workplaces to the wider community.[46] More men and women came into contact with trade unionism at a time when it seemed notably effective but also more found themselves in tune with co-operators and trades councils over food, dependants' allowances,

[43] T. Carberry, *Consumers and Politics* (London, 1968); S. Pollard, 'The Foundation of the Co-operative Party', in Briggs and Saville (eds), *Essay in Labour History*, pp. 185–210; A.J. Adams, 'The Formation of the Co-operative Party Reconsidered', *International Review of Social History*, 32 (1987), pp. 46–68; and McKibbin, *The Evolution of the Labour Party* pp. 43–47, 178–82.

[44] Diary entry, 2 June 1917, Lord Riddell, *War Diary, 1914–1918* (London, 1933), p. 253.

[45] C.J. Wrigley, *Changes in the Battersea Labour Movement, 1914–1919* (Loughborough, 1977), pp. 2–3. More generally see C.J. Wrigley (ed.), *Challenges of Labour* (London, 1993), pp. 7–12; and, for Britain, Waites, *A Class Society at War*, pp. 225–31.

[46] For example, D. Koenker, *Moscow Workers and the 1917 Revolution* (Princeton, 1981).

housing and other issues. The inequalities of sacrifice on the Home Front inexorably moved these working-class bodies towards collectivist solutions. A large proportion of Lib-Lab or Liberal sympathies, which had still been present in the trade unions, trades councils, the co-operative movement and even the Labour Party in 1914, had evaporated by 1919.

This is not to say that there was a sizeable move towards revolutionary socialism or to trade union Direct Action. The unions had gained in strength and after the war were willing to use it to achieve improved wages and conditions and, in the case of the miners, to press for nationalisation. Yet this should not obscure the fact that the solid centre of the British trade union movement remained happier in seeking solutions through co-operation with employers on joint committees rather than confrontation. Whitley Committees and 'the spirit of Whitleyism', the National Industrial Conference, the National Alliance of Employers and Employed all had strong support from prominent trade unionists and Labour politicians.[47] Nevertheless the general bias of the British Labour Movement did move towards the Left during the war.

In assessing the Labour Movement during the First World War the trade unions deserve the substantial consideration given in this essay. The war reinforced their powerful position within the Labour Party. The withdrawal of Ramsay MacDonald, Philip Snowden and other non trade unionist Independent Labour Party MPs in 1914 was a foretaste of 1931 and the subsequent enhanced role of the unions in the Labour Party. The unions resisted calls from Labour's Right to create a purely trade union party. The greatly increased membership and the much lower expenditure on unemployment or strikes boosted the unions' finances. These more than doubled during the war, rising from £6,471,000 in 1913 to £14,948,000 in 1918. This indirectly helped their political activities in so far as it was used to strengthen their organisations. There was also a steady increase in their political funds, rising from £7,000 in 1913 to £43,000 in 1917, £133,000 in 1918 and £185,000 in 1920.[48]

While these aggregate sums for trade union financial strength are significant, the amounts spent by the individual unions, and whether this was done in particular areas, was important. In the case of the United Society of Boilermakers, before the war it had aspired to run one parliamentary candidate and its political fund had peaked at £863 in 1906. In 1918 it ran five parliamentary candidates, one successful, and had a balance of £8100 in its political fund.[49] In the case of the Durham

[47] See, *inter alia*, Wrigley, *Lloyd George and the Challenge of Labour*; idem, 'Trade Unionists, Employers and the Cause of Industrial Unity and Peace, 1916–21', in C.J. Wrigley and J. Shepherd (eds), *On the Move* (London, 1991), pp. 155–84.

[48] For the hundred principal trade unions see B.R. Mitchell, *British Historical Statistics* (Cambridge, 1988), p. 139.

[49] C.J. Wrigley, 'Labour and the Tade Unions', in K.D. Brown (ed.), *The First Labour Party, 1906–1914* (London, 1985), pp. 129–57.

Miners' Association, organisational assistance to Labour candidates in its area was very substantial indeed. In Barnard Castle, Blaydon, Durham, Houghton-le-Spring, Sedgefield and Spennymoor it provided assistance in the form of seventy-six sub-agents, 107 polling agents and 162 clerks. Overall, in the 1918 general election trade unions directly sponsored 163, nearly half of Labour's 363 candidates.[50]

Arthur Henderson's return to Labour Party organisation after resigning from the War Cabinet in August 1917 provided him with the time and added motivation to reorganise the party. As for this, he observed to the January 1918 Party Conference, that while 'a new organisation based solely upon individual membership . . . might be worth aiming at' the reality was the Party depended on the trade unions. Hence he proposed to maintain the existing 'political federation consisting of trade unions, socialist bodies and co-operative societies . . . but to graft on to it . . . a form of constituency organisation linked up with the local Labour Parties or trades councils'.[51]

Henderson emerged from Lloyd George's government determined to make a democratic challenge for power in Britain. Beatrice Webb noted in her diary at the time of the January 1918 Labour Party Conference: 'He is ambitious: he sees a chance of a Labour Party government, or a predominantly Labour government, with himself as Premier.' The previous December Henderson himself was telling C.P. Scott that he 'thought the policy would be to run a Labour candidate wherever there was a tolerable chance of carrying him'. Scott in his diary further noted,

> He thought they might run as many as 500 candidates now that members were paid and election costs so greatly reduced as they were under the Franchise Bill. They were better equipped for doing this than either of the other two great parties, because they had an existing trades union organization in every town. As to the country districts [they had] the assistance of the co-operators, if they should decide to work with them, as, in many of the country districts . . . 8 out of 10 households were co-operators.[52]

Participation in the Asquith and then the Lloyd George Coalition Governments had greatly enhanced the prestige of Henderson and other Labour leaders. Indeed this had grown as time had gone on. Henderson, who had been something of a political dogsbody under Asquith, had

---

[50] Tanner, *Political Change and the Labour Party*, p. 465. G.D.H. Cole, *A History of the Labour Party from 1914* p. 87.

[51] Labour Party, *Report of the Annual Conference, January 1918*, pp. 98–102. On party reorganisation see also Winter, *Socialism*, ch. 8 and McKibbin, *The Evolution of the Labour Party*, pp. 98–102.

[52] Diary entry, 21 January 1918, M. Cole (ed.), *Beatrice Webb Diaries*, p. 107. Diary entry, 11 December 1917, T. Wilson (ed.), *The Political Diaries of C.P. Scott, 1911–1928* (London, 1970), p. 317.

become weightier in his own and others' estimations as a member of the War Cabinet and as the leading representative of an important element in Lloyd George's Parliamentary support. J.R. Clynes also grew in political stature as Food Controller. There was a similar development of confidence and a taste for power at the local level.

Much the same is true of the TUC and the larger trade unions. No more cap-in-hand visits to junior ministers. The Parliamentary Committee of the TUC expected – and did – see senior ministers or the Premier. At times of conflict so too did the big unions. When Lloyd George wished to declare his democratic war aims in early January 1918 he did so at a trade union gathering, not in Parliament or to a gathering of businessmen. During the war the TUC eclipsed the General Federation of Trade Unions, which was to continue to service the small unions but no longer was a rival authority to the TUC.

The Labour Party's post-war strength also owed much to the Liberal Party's problems. The latter's divisions proliferated. Some backed Asquith or Lloyd George, others joined Labour or the Conservatives. Asquithian Liberal policy statements increasingly seemed old fashioned or 'vague and colourless'. In many areas Liberal organisation disintegrated. According to Duncan Tanner, 'In West Lancashire, the West Midlands, London and the dockland seats of the south coast, the Liberal Party had almost ceased to exist by 1918'.[53] The continuation of Lloyd George's coalition with the Conservatives until 1922 did further harm to the Liberals, with labour, Irish and other policies appearing notably illiberal to many former Liberal voters.

The war did not split the British Labour movement as it did many of the continental European movements. After the outbreak of war Henderson was careful not to drive MacDonald and his followers out of the party. When he himself resigned from Lloyd George's government in 1917 it was not through disillusionment with Lloyd George's policy of defeating Germany and her Allies. Hence Henderson was out of office and could raise issues of concern, yet remain in tune with the preponderantly pro-war working class opinion. He used this opportunity to reunite most of the Labour movement around what was required for a democratic peace settlement and for substantial social reconstruction. Those who split away to the right – the 'super-patriots – did not sustain much electoral support after the 1918 general election. Those who were to adhere to Lenin's Third International were more significant but not great in number.

The British Labour Movement distinguished itself by its solidity and its growing confidence during 1914–20. The Labour Party offered a new formulation of policy in its *Labour and the New Social Order*. It also went a long way to capturing the high moral ground, previously often held by the Liberal Party. Beatrice Webb, who was not backward

---

[53] Tanner, *Political Change and the Labour Party*, pp. 378–81.

in making sneering and scathing comments about Labour's major trade union figures, was moved to write in her diary in December 1918: 'The one outstanding virtue of the Labour Party, a virtue which is its very own, not imposed upon it by its intellectuals, is its high sense of international morality. Alone among British politicians the leaders of the Labour party do honestly believe in the brotherhood of man.'[54] As well as occupying a growing space on the Left of British politics, Henderson, MacDonald and other Labour leaders did so internationally. Afer 1918 they were to play a central role in the activities of the remnants of the Second International, much as the mighty SPD had done in the pre-war years.

[54] Diary entry, 12 December 1918, M. Cole (ed.), *Beatrice Webb's Diaries, 1912–1924*, p. 139.

7

The Foreign Office Political Intelligence Department and Germany in 1918

Michael Dockrill

The Political Intelligence Department (PID) was created in the Foreign Office on 11 March 1918 following a circular minute to the Office by Lord Hardinge, the Permanent Under-Secretary.[1] Amongst its functions were 'collecting, sifting and co-ordinating all political "intelligence" received from our own, Admiralty and War Office sources . . .' Hardinge established this new department partly to counter what he regarded as the efforts of the Prime Minister, David Lloyd George, to reduce the powers of the Foreign Office by setting up a rival and personal secretariat – 'the Garden Suburb' – in the garden of 10 Downing Street, comprised of Lloyd George's cronies who were all, in Hardinge's opinion, amateur meddlers in foreign affairs. By contrast, Hardinge's new department would consist of professional experts whose authoritative analyses of foreign affairs would, he hoped, greatly enhance the role and standing of the Foreign Office. While 'this innovative new Department, and its expert personnel . . . emerged as the cornerstone of British preparations for the peace conference' in 1919, its main task during 1918 was to collect information about the political, economic and military conditions in Allied, enemy and neutral countries and to prepare reports on developments in these countries for the Foreign Office, the War Cabinet and other government departments. This essay will be concerned with PID's information gathering and reporting on Germany during the final months of hostilities in Europe from March to 11 November 1918.

Hardinge was determined that the PID should become a major Foreign Office Department, with the fullest access to the information which was sent to the political departments in the Office by British embassies, legations and consulates overseas and by the various intelligence agencies,

---

[1] For further details, particularly PID's role in Britain's planning for the 1919 Paris Peace Conference, see Erik Goldstein's excellent monograph, *Winning the Peace: British Diplomatic Strategy, Peace Planning, and the Paris Peace Conference, 1916–1920*, (Oxford, 1991). Information in this essay on the origins of PID and about the careers of its functionaries is taken from pp. 57–89 of Dr Goldstein's book. Dr Goldstein kindly read a draft of this article and I am grateful to him for pointing out some errors therein. See also Alan Sharp, 'Some Relevant Historians: The Political Intelligence Department of the Foreign Office, 1918–1920', *Australian Journal of Politics and History*, 34 (1989), pp. 359–68.

War Office and other, whose activities had greatly expanded during the war. To that end his minute continued:

> I am anxious that the new Department should be kept very fully informed, and Departments should err, if anything, on the generous side in marking papers for the Political Intelligence Department or otherwise furnishing it with information.

The personnel of the new Department was recruited almost wholesale from the Intelligence Bureau of the Department of Information (DIIB). This Bureau had been created in April 1917 to provide the Department of Information with reports on foreign countries in order to assist Britain's overseas propaganda campaign. The bulk of the staff of the DIIB had been recruited from universities, the 'quality' press and government departments, and were regarded as a kind of bureaucratic intelligentsia possessing an unrivalled knowledge of the countries they were studying. Hardinge wanted to enrol these specialists in his new Department. After a protracted wrangle with the new Minister of Information, Lord Beaverbrook, Hardinge prevailed – ten members of the former DIIB transferred to the Foreign Office on 27 March 1918.[2] The feud with Beaverbrook continued for the rest of the war. When the Minister of Information sent a T.L. Gilmour to Holland to investigate the British propaganda effort there, Sir Eyre Crowe, the superintending Under-secretary at the Ministry of Blockade, complained to Sir William Tyrrell, the Director of PID, that, 'it looks as if Gilmour's primary object is to denounce the imbecility of the Foreign Office to Lord Beaverbrook and his second object is to furnish him with a case for demanding a voice in the directing of foreign policy. If all Beaverbrook's agents are going to be like this, God help us.'[3]

PID's new officials included such future foreign service and academic luminaries as the Leeper brothers (Allen and Rex), Lewis Namier, A.E. Zimmern (who came from the Ministry of Reconstruction), Professor J.Y. Simpson and Arnold Toynbee. J.W. Headlam-Morley,[4] a former Board of Education official and assistant director and head of the German Section at the DIIB, who had written three books on recent German history and politics, was made assistant director of the new Department and head of its German section. Five more experts were recruited later.

As an example of the kind of employee PID preferred, Lord Henry Bentinck, an influential Conservative MP, recommended a Mr F.R. Harris for a post in the Foreign Office in April, praising him as 'a very cultivated man of exceptional knowledge and ability', with 'plenty of tact and savoir

[2] Goldstein, *Winning the Peace*, pp. 16–61.

[3] Crowe to Tyrrell, 29 March 1918, PRO, FO 371/4363.

[4] His surname was Headlam until July 1918, when he inherited the Morley estate and added Morley to his name. Goldstein, *Winning the Peace*, p. 68.

faire.' Headlam-Morley interviewed Harris on 27 May and proposed to Tyrrell that Harris be taken on provisionally – 'we do not have personal knowledge of his work like most we have taken on' – and put in charge of Swiss affairs. He could also help 'edit an edition of the Russian treaties' since 'he has done historical work and is particularly interested in diplomatic history'.[5]

Another recruit in March 1918 was A.E. Zimmern, who was employed at the specific request of Headlam-Morley, who wanted someone capable of analysing 'the economic aspect of things and the influence which this must have on political decisions'. He pointed out that, while of German origin, Zimmern was 'English by birth' and 'entirely sound on the war'.[6] Zimmern had been educated at Winchester College and had then become a Scholar and Fellow of New College, Oxford, where he had worked on the 'economic interpretation of history'. During the war he had taken up temporary employment at the Ministry of Reconstruction but, because he did not think that his talents were being utilised properly there, he had decided to go to France to lecture to the troops. He had been rescued from this prospect by Headlam-Morley. He was highly thought of in the Political Intelligence Department.[7]

Sir William Tyrrell's appointment as Director was intended by Hardinge to placate the long-established Foreign Office hands who were likely to resent the sudden appearance of this new and rather curious department: Tyrrell was a highly respected and long-serving Foreign Office official, albeit rather unconventional in his working methods. Both Hardinge and Tyrrell realised that, if the PID was to become accepted in King Charles Street, it would need to co-operate closely with the other Foreign Office Departments and with Britain's Missions overseas. With this in mind, Lord Eustace Percy, a diplomat who was attached to PID to deal with League of Nations affairs, wrote to Tyrrell on 20 April that, in case Foreign Office Departments and Missions abroad felt that PID memoranda were written without reference to them and were based on less accurate information than they had at their disposal, a circular letter should be issued explaining the purpose of the PID and inviting criticisms about anything written by the Department. Tyrrell agreed and a circular letter was signed by Hardinge on 5 May, pointing out that

> a new political intelligence department . . . has now been brought into the office with the purpose of making it a permanent integral part of our organisation. The primary duty of the new Department is to collect information and to take, to some extent, off the shoulders of the administrative departments

[5] Lord Henry Cavendish Bentinck, London to Tyrrell, 19 April 1918; Headlam to Tyrrell 27 May 1918, PRO, FO 371/4363.

[6] Zimmern was born in Surbiton. His family had emigrated from Germany after the 1848 revolution.

[7] Minute, Headlam to Tyrrell, 11 April 1918, PRO, FO 371/4358.

the task of keeping up to date, in a readily available form, the knowledge of foreign countries which exist here.

He continued that one of the tasks of the new department would be the production of memoranda for the government on the situation in particular countries or on current problems of foreign policy, and that these memoranda would be based on reports from missions, on material the Ministry of Information had agreed to supply (despite Beaverbrook's hostility, the head of the Ministry's Intelligence Department agreed to co-operate fully with the new department), and on information in the press and from other sources.[8]

After 13 July PID received a weekly summary of propaganda intelligence from the Ministry of Information's Intelligence Department.[9] Colonel G.S.H. Pearson of the Directorate of Military Intelligence offered to send PID 'the slips relating to intercepted letters . . .', including those of foreign correspondents in the United Kingdom. Percy asked Pearson to send 'slips' either of political importance or giving personal information about press correspondents to P.A. Koppel of PID. Pearson also sent over a 'Daily Summary of Information' on economic and commercial matters and in July replaced the 'slips' by MI9's fortnightly reports on press correspondents, while MI9 provided fortnightly reports on 'the affairs of Poles, Czechs and other odd people'.[10]

The War Trade Intelligence Department sent PID any useful material its postal censors and the Directorate of Special Intelligence had secured from intercepted mail. PID also received voluminous reports on conditions in enemy countries from the US State Department and assessments from the French General Staff intelligence, for instance on the supply of food in Germany.[11] There were more unorthodox methods of securing information: in June 1918 PID was sent a short-hand notebook which had been 'removed' from the office of the German Military Attaché in Sweden.[12]

To reinforce Tyrrell's determination that PID should be fully integrated into the Foreign Office, he circulated a further minute to the Foreign Office on 13 May 1918 requesting that telegrams and despatches should

[8] Eustace Percy to Tyrrell, 20 April 1918; circular letter from Hardinge to Heads of Missions, 5 May 1918, PRO, FO 371/4363; Sir Roderick Jones, Ministry of Information to Tyrrell, 1 May 1918, FO 371/4363.

[9] 'Weekly summary of Propaganda Intelligence', from Ministry of Information Intelligence Department, week beginning 13 July 1918, PRO, FO 371/4364.

[10] Colonel G.S.H. Pearson, Chief Postal Censor, MI9, to Lord Eustace Percy, 23 April 1918; Percy to Pearson, 24 April 1918; Pearson to Percy 24 April 1918; Percy to Pearson, 26 April 1918, PRO, FO 371/4362. For details of press censorship and its problems, see Christopher Andrew, *Secret Service: The Making of the British Intelligence Community*, (London, 1985), pp. 176–77.

[11] See PRO, FO 371/3222 for details.

[12] Shorthand notebook circulated to PID on 24 June 1918, PRO, FO 371/4364.

be sent in their jackets directly to PID from the War Department. This would give PID the opportunity to make observations on the jackets, as was customary when files were minuted to established departments, before the files were sent to the heads of the Foreign Office. PID personnel were enjoined that such files

> must be treated urgently and given precedence over other work ... Observations should be as brief and clear as possible aiming at pointing out whether the information in a telegram or despatch is in accordance with other sources of information, discussing reliability and elucidating obscure points.[13]

Tyrrell's efforts at least met with the approval of one British diplomat. Sir Horace Rumbold, the British Minister to Switzerland, wrote to congratulate him on his venture: 'your new Department sounds very interesting and you will get the cream of intelligence from every source.'[14]

PID also undertook work for other government departments, such as the Colonial Office and the War Cabinet Secretariat, in the latter case after an appeal by Sir George Aston to Tyrrell in June for 'one of the able writers of the PID' to write a paper on Germany's policy of extending her sea power in order to defeat Britain, if not during this war, then in the next.[15] PID also produced a weekly telegram on enemy countries for the Dominions governments.[16]

German affairs were the concern of Headlam-Morley, Edwin Bevan and George Saunders, all of whom had performed the same task at the Ministry of Information. Beven had been educated at New College, Oxford. He had worked in India, Greece and Egypt before the war and had written a number of scholarly books. During the war he had published works on Mesopotamia and on German war aims during the war. George Saunders, who had been educated at Balliol College, Oxford, had served in Germany for twenty-three years as a newspaper correspondent and was considered as one of the leading experts on German politics.[17]

Much of the information these officials received about Germany came from Britain's missions in neutral European capitals and often came from not always very reliable second- and even third-hand sources. Correspondence intercepted by the postal censors for the War Trade Intelligence

[13] Tyrrell, minute 13 May 1918, PRO, FO 371/4363.

[14] Rumbold, British Legation, Berne, to Tyrrell, 3 March 1918, PRO, FO 371/4363.

[15] Sir George Aston, War Cabinet Offices, to Tyrrell, 11 June 1918. Harris was given this task: Tyrrell to Aston, 11 June 1918, PRO, FO 371/4364. The outcome was a 'Memorandum on the Position and Prospects of German Sea Power and Shipping', which forecast that Germany aimed to secure naval supremacy in the future to lay a firm foundation for 'Germany's ambitions of world-wide domination ...', PID Memorandum, Germany/013, 24 July 1918, FO 371/3226.

[16] Goldstein, *Winning the Peace*, pp. 62–63.

[17] Ibid., pp. 70, 73–74. Like Headlam-Morley, Saunders had married a German, the daughter of a Berlin banker.

Department and passed on to PID during 1918 contained descriptions of acute shortages of food and clothing in Germany, of the German people's increasing hatred for their government and of increasing war-weariness among all sections of the German population. Cumulatively these reports might have created the impression that Germany was on the verge of collapse, had not the War Office and Foreign Office also been receiving rather more reliable intelligence reports of the movement of large numbers of German troops from the Eastern Germany to the Western Front during the early months of 1918.[18] Rumbold had access to the reports of an agent – code-named 'Jean' – inside Germany who supplied information of military interest, such as the movements of German troops.[19] Undoubtedly there was some hardship and grumbling in civilian Germany, but it had not the slightest effect on the preparations for the German Army's major offensive in the west in March 1918.

In February, before the PID was established, the Foreign Office, no doubt exasperated by the conflicting and inaccurate reports coming out of Germany, asked its Ministers in neutral Europe to be more precise in their assessment of the reliability of the various sources of information about conditions in enemy countries. Rumbold replied on 28 February that, since most of the information reaching his Legation came through the Military Attaché's Office there, he had persuaded the officer in charge of the Attaché's Eastern Department to provide him with a list containing the general particulars of the various agents employed in Eastern Europe, Russia and Turkey, and to place them on a scale ranging from 'very reliable', 'reliable' to 'moderately reliable' etc. Rumbold was arranging with the officer in charge of the Attaché's Western Department to furnish him with a similar list about agents in Germany and Austria when the Military Attaché informed him that the Secret Intelligence Service (MI1c) was opposed to this procedure, as they were 'apprehensive of my employing any information that might give the slightest clue to the identity of the agents'. Eventually the Foreign Office persuaded the War Office's Directorate of Military Intelligence (DMI) to agree to Rumbold being informed as to the degree of reliability of the various informants, but not with any particulars about them. This at least gave the future PID some indication of the relative usefulness of the information it was receiving.[20]

On 31 March 1918 the Political Intelligence Department produced

---

[18] Earlier examples of misinformation included a report by Sir Ralph Paget, the British Minister in Copenhagen, in January, that 'information from reliable sources is . . . to the effect that Germany cannot hold out beyond April', and in the same month a telegram from Rumbold that he had heard 'on good authority from [a] traveller just returned from Berlin that it is generally thought that it will be impossible to feed [the] civilian population between February and May'. Paget, Copenhagen, telegram 19, 3 Jan. 1918, Rumbold, Berne, telegram 7, 3 Jan. 1918, FO 371/3222.

[19] Rumbold, Berne, despatch 396, 8 Feb. 1918, PRO, FO 371/3222.

[20] Rumbold, Berne, despatch 168, 28 Feb. 1918, despatch 168, PRO, FO 371/3223.

its first memorandum on Germany. This was written by Bevan and was entitled 'Memorandum on Recent Events concerning German Social Democracy and Labour'. It was circulated to the Foreign Secretary, A.J. Balfour, the War Cabinet, the War Office, the Admiralty, and inside the Foreign Office, to Sir Eyre Crowe and to the War Department. This was the usual circulation pattern for these documents, although other government departments and the Dominions were added when the information was relevant to them. An appendix to this memorandum concluded that 'the balance of evidence tends to show what the great majority of the German people desire is the earliest possible end to the war. But there is naturally great divergence of opinion as to the best method of achieving it', with the bulk of the population sharing the view of 'the Generals that the German sword should be given another trial on the Western front'.[21]

On 29 April Headlam-Morley produced a memorandum in which he tried to analyse the aims behind Germany's spring offensive in the West. Clearly the main object of this assault was the destruction of the British Army, 'before America could intervene effectively', thus achieving the ultimate German aim of rendering France 'helpless'. The current German strategy, he wrote, sought to divide the British and French armies, drive the British back to the Flanders coast and smash them there, using the German fleet to prevent the Royal Navy from covering a British amphibious retreat across the English Channel. To succeed in this design, the German fleet would need a harbour accessible to the Straits of Dover. Headlam-Morley conjectured that, since the only such harbour was at the mouth of the Meuse and the Scheldt, the Germans might invade Holland in order to occupy the banks of these two rivers. Tyrrell commented that 'the point raised by Mr Headlam is so obvious that it is not worth while calling attention to it or it may not prove to be chimerical in which case I feel bound to put it forward'. Hardinge noted that 'such contingencies as are here foreshadowed have, I understand, been foreseen'.[22]

Switzerland was an important source of Foreign Office and PID information about conditions in Germany.[23] Rumbold had written to his mother-in-law, six months after his appointment to Berne in 1916, that Switzerland was 'a clearing house for intelligence', and that, as a result, he was 'able to keep the F.O. well informed and well supplied with news about all our enemies'.[24] A hot-bed of rumour and speculation,

---

[21] PID, memorandum, no. 001, 'Memorandum on Recent Events concerning German Social Democracy and Labour', 31 March 1918, PRO, FO 371/3226.

[22] PID, memorandum by Headlam, 'Germany and Holland', 29 April 1918, minutes by Tyrrell, 29 April and Hardinge, PRO, FO 371/3457.

[23] Earlier in the war British secret intelligence operations in Switzerland had not been very successful: the Swiss police kept a close watch on spies and revolutionaries. For details see Andrew, *Secret Service*, pp. 148–53.

[24] 12 Feb. 1917. Quoted in Martin Gilbert, *Sir Horace Rumbold: Portrait of a Diplomat, 1869–1941*, (London, 1973), p. 137.

Switzerland swarmed with German refugees and visitors, many claiming to be of an anti-war, anti-militarist, liberal or socialist persuasion, seemingly anxious to provide the Allies with up-to-date assessments of German political and military thinking. There were also a host of agents from the belligerent countries, who were willing recipients of such information, irrespective of its credibility. Hardinge described the country as 'a sort of happy hunting ground for all the political malcontents and intriguers in Europe'.[25] The resulting avalanche of material was carefully sifted by the PID in an effort to discern the reality behind the half-truths and falsities which were part and parcel of the game of intelligence and counter-intelligence.

One of the German informants was a Professor Edgar Jaffe, an economist, whose information was accepted by Rumbold as more reliable than most he received. A PID report in April described him as a member of a well-known German Jewish family prominent in the German scientific and business community. According to MI1c he was the editor of a German Foreign Office publication and had close ties with Dr Karl Helfferich, a former director of the Deutsche Bank, economic adviser to the German government and holder of a number of posts in the war-time German administration. Jaffe was supposed to be of a liberal inclination, although his criticisms of the Allied proposal for a post-war League of Nations, which he described 'as a pretty dream, unsuitable to this workday world', and remarks that 'treaties would always be "scraps of paper"', cast some doubt on this assumption. He visited Switzerland several times during the war. During the summer of 1916 George Saunders, then on a 'mission' to Switzerland, heard him talking in a hotel and was struck by Jaffe's 'volubility'. According to Saunders, 'Jaffe could be heard talking loudly in the smoking room about personal and political matters'. However the PID shared Rumbold's assessment of Jaffe's reliability, praising 'a very remarkable appreciation of the financial and political situation in Germany', which Jaffe had provided to a British agent in September 1917, and which was eventually forwarded to PID by MI1c.

However, despite PID's praise for the quality of information which Jaffe supplied, both the department and military intelligence suspected that the professor had been 'planted' in Switzerland by the German authorities and that his activities could be interpreted in a more sinister light than a mere willingness to enlighten the Allies about developments in Germany. When, in April 1918, PID received reports of conversations between Jaffe and a Professor Herron, a Liberal Swiss academic, which had been obtained by the American Minister in Geneva, PID commented:

it is difficult to understand the mentality of a man, having much information and on the whole showing such good judgment, who would talk as freely as he did. He is not apparently a refugee in Switzerland and therefore can only come

25 Hardinge to Rumbold, 26 April 1917, quoted ibid., p. 144.

with the consent of the Germany Government. We naturally ask what is the interest or object in giving these confidences. Is it in order to bring about some kind of rapprochement or is it personal vanity and sheer garrulousness? . . . The German Government may allow and even encourage these conversations to take place because they may be used to create the impression that once peace is made it would be possible to depend upon a liberal movement in Germany which would be supported by higher financial interests; the parallel is: if the war is stopped, then England will find Germany quite a reasonable nation.

In another report PID noted that 'he [Jaffe] seems at liberty to recommend his utterances to non-German listeners by frequent denunciations of German policy and German personages'. PID suspected that Jaffe's activities were part of a peace campaign by the German Foreign Office, which, 'unable to oppose any open resistance to the Hindenburg–Ludendorff policy of a militarist "German peace", is redoubling its efforts through agents and neutrals in Switzerland to bring about "conversations" with the enemy'. PID commented that, 'even if Bismarck himself arose from the dead to denounce German pre-war policy, he would make no practical impression, unless and until the German armies were beaten in the field'.

During his conversation with Herron, Jaffe feared that, if peace did not come in 1918, there would be another two years of war which would mean the ruin of Europe. He said that Ludendorff believed that peace would come eventually as a result of smashing German victories combined with a defeatist campaign in Allied countries. He quoted a saying of Ludendorff's that 'one does not fight battles to defeat the opposing army but to stimulate the desire for peace behind the opposing army'. Jaffe added that, if Germany defeated the Allies, the German military and conservatives would 'dictate their terms of peace careless of consequences and without any regard to political considerations . . . If their success is not as complete as they anticipate moderate counsels will have more chance of being heard'.

Jaffe outlined the military's vast schemes of conquest in the east and the west which would make Germany the master of all Europe which 'will amply provide [her] with raw materials and will be completely independent of the continents of North and South America, with which she will have no further concern'. Clearly, if Jaffe was reporting accurately the opinions of Ludendorff and the military, he must have been in touch with high circles in the German military establishment. Balfour was equally perplexed, minuting that 'Professor Jaffe's position seems curious – and ambiguous'.[26]

[26] Rumbold, telegrams 466 and 469, 1 April 1918; telegram 473, 2 April 1918; telegram 499, 6 April 1918. Report by PID on Professor Edgar Jaffe, 7 April 1918; minute by Balfour, undated, April 1918; PID, memorandum, no. 002, 'The Lichnowsky Memorandum', 18 April 1918, PID, memorandum, 'Czernin and Germany', Germany/003, 25 April 1918, FO 371/3222.

Another informant in Switzerland was Dr Wilhelm Mühlon, a former managing director of Krupps, who told a British agent in February 1918 that he had once been employed by the German Foreign Office but had left Germany in 1914 to go into exile in Switzerland because he was disgusted with the part his country had played in causing the war.[27] According to the Secret Intelligence Service,

> it would appear from his own account therefore that he abandoned a position which was both remunerative, bringing him into contact with the highest personages in Germany, including the Kaiser, and condemned himself to permanent exile from Germany, in obedience to the dictates of his conscience. It must be admitted that Mühlon does not convey the impression of a man with a conscience with this degree of tenderness. He is essentially a man of affairs, clever, practical, cynical, without illusions; in fact he creates the impression of being anything but an idealist. Yet if his own account be true he is an idealist with a quite exceptional capacity for sacrifice.

Nevertheless MI1c accepted that the information he provided about Germany was useful and, because of his connections, authoritative. In May, Mühlon told the British Military Attaché in Berne that the Allies should distinguish between the heavy industrialists in Germany, who were all pan-Germans, and the ordinary businessmen, who wanted commercial prosperity after the war. Allied threats of a post-war blockade would destroy the latter's hopes and strengthen the hands of the annexationists and the heavy industrialists, who were determined that Germany should retain economic and political control over Belgium, annex Longwy and Briey, and remain in control of Russia in order to exploit its food and raw materials.[28]

However there were other activists in Switzerland in whose sincerity British Military Intelligence had less confidence. A Dutch pacifist resident in Switzerland, De Jon Beek en Donk, Secretary of the Dutch based 'Central Organisation for a Durable Peace',[29] and a member of the 'Netherlands Anti-War League', who, according to MI1c, kept their representative in Switzerland informed about his intrigues, joined forces with Professor Stephen Bauer of Basle University, the Director of the 'International Labour Office' in Switzerland, to try to promote a meeting in that country between German Centre Party deputies like Konstantin Fehrenbach and Conrad Haussman, reputedly anxious to end the war, and supposedly influential British politicians like Lord Henry Cavendish Bentinck and Lord Fitzmaurice of Leigh, a former Liberal Parliamentary

---

[27] See Fritz, Fischer, *War of Illusions: German Policies from 1911 to 1914* (London, 1975), p. 463.

[28] Rumbold, despatch 122, 15 Feb. 1918, PRO, FO 371/3226; MI1C to R.H. Campbell, Foreign Office, 21 Feb. 1918.

[29] The Central Organisation's publications had been banned in Britain by the Censor. Goldstein, *Winning the Peace*, p. 34.

Undersecretary at the British Foreign Office and Chancellor of the Duchy of Lancaster.[30]

Donk stated that the purpose of such a meeting was to discuss moderate peace terms, which were to include the German evacuation of Belgium and northern France. The British agent who was in touch with Donk told the Military Attaché's Department in Geneva that he thought that the proposal was a German trap: any such Anglo-German contacts would soon be leaked to the world's press as a means of raising German morale by pretending that Britain wanted peace. British Military Intelligence and PID needed no such advice: both had dismissed previous German efforts to arrange Anglo-German meetings in Switzerland on the same grounds. Tyrrell commented that 'this Dutch pacifist [Donk] is a mischievous busybody' while Balfour thought that 'his proceedings are as tiresome as his name'.[31]

In August Hardinge minuted that Saide Reuste, a wealthy German, in exile in Zurich because he did not 'see eye to eye with the present regime in Germany' and who, Rumbold thought, 'may be described as a pacifist', 'is a Zanzibari half caste who lived at one time in London and has strong German proclivities. He is regarded as thoroughly disreputable.' Balfour remarked that 'I don't know why a Zanzibari half-caste should have his judgement perverted by "patriotic pride" in Germany.'[32]

The reports of a British military agent in Berne, Captain W.L. Blenner-hassett, to MI1c, and forwarded to PID, were very revealing about the activities of German agents in Switzerland and confirmed PID's suspicions of the reliability of some of the information it received from that country. Blennerhassett identified the 'most formidable' German agent active in Berne as a man called 'Bismarck', who used 'typically German' methods to achieve his ends – 'a mixture of cunning and childish simplicity'. All the concierges in the major hotels in the city were in Germany pay, and they intercepted the mail of the most important 'opposition' Germans and Entente agents and passed them to 'Bismarck'.

Blennerhassett reported that another 'formidable' German agent in Berne was a man named '"Loewengard" who poses as a naturalised Englishman who has switched to me and disclosed a number of points the Germans want information about', including the damage inflicted on London by German aircraft, whether there was a shortage of horses in England and the state of British manpower. 'Loewengard' controlled a group consisting of 'a whole clan of shady agents' who insisted, 'with parrot-like precision', that the war would last for years and would ruin all the belligerents and that therefore 'the British were ill-advised to reject the

---

[30] Rumbold, telegram 1280, 1 Aug. 1918, minutes by Hardinge and Balfour (undated, Aug. 1918), PRO, FO 371/3435.

[31] Rumbold, telegram 996, 22 June 1918, minutes by Tyrrell and A.J. Balfour, PRO, FO 371/3436.

[32] Rumbold, telegram 996, 18 June 1918, minutes by Hardinge and Balfour (undated 1918), PRO, FO 371/3436.

Kaiser's peace offer (sic)'. Blennerhassett complained that 'the Germans have tried every kind of trick here already . . . one agent of theirs who poses as a naturalised British subject however . . . forgot himself for a moment and asked whether I thought 'WE' would get Amiens . . .'

However Blennerhassett had uncovered a genuine German opposition group in Switzerland but they refused to contact the British except under secure conditions which would safeguard them from being compromised, and presumably from the attentions of the ever-vigilant Swiss police. One of their number was General Count Max von Montgelas, who had served in 1914 on the German General Staff and had been a trusted adviser to the then Chief of the German General Staff, General von Moltke.[33] From information Blennerhassett had secured about the Montgelas group's knowledge of current German military thinking, 'there is no serious intention to abandon their [the German military's] policy of reaction unless military failure or the indecisive prolongation of the war threatens a fresh deterioration in the moral of German and Austrian public opinion', an accurate reflection of German policy down to 15 July 1918, when the German assault on Reims was repulsed by the Allies and the German Army was forced to retreat behind the Marne.[34] For instance, a conference of civilian and military leaders, all still confident of victory, at Spa on 2 and 3 July, presided over by the German Emperor, insisted on an expansionist peace which would ensure German domination of the Continent. Moreover Fritz Fischer asserts that 'the aims of leaders reflected exactly the ambitious and political philosophy of the overwhelming majority of the German people'.[35]

As discussed above, most of the reports reaching London about the state of German morale in the early months of 1918 mentioned food shortages and some disillusionment with the endless sacrifices German civilians were being forced to make for the sake of the war. None of this, however, had much effect on the determination of the German people to continue the war, especially while Germany was winning victories in the West; nor was it likely to dent Ludendorff's confidence in ultimate victory. The information was patchy and usually came from, or was about, well-to-do Germans whose circumstances had deteriorated during the war. For instance, the Norwegian Ambassador to Paris, Baron Wedel-Jarlsberg, while visiting Spain in mid May, told the British Ambassador, Sir Arthur Hardinge, that his impression on talking to enemy ambassadors in Madrid, was that

Germany and Austria were utterly sick of and despondent about the war, in spite of the partial success of their offensive, and though they had not yet

[33] See Fischer, *War of Illusions*, p. 464.

[34] MI1c, War Office to PID, 27 May 1918, enclosing reports by Blennerhassett, PRO, FO 371/4364.

[35] Fritz Fischer, *Germany's Aims in the First World War*, (London, 1961), pp. 621–24.

made up their minds to propose an acceptable peace, but that if the Allies stuck to it for some time longer, we should force them to do so.

As an example of the supposed low state of German morale, Wedel-Jarlsberg cited the recent experiences of the Dutch Military Attaché in Paris,

> who had lately been to Christiania through Germany, [where he] had found a somewhat insubordinate spirit among the lower orders. The first-class carriage in which he had travelled had been invaded by a mob of ragged holders of third-class tickets, and when he had complained to the guard, the latter had said he could not help it: an attempt to evict them and make them travel in their own carriages, as he would have done on old days, would cause a nasty riot.

How useful did PID find these reports on developments inside Germany for their analyses of German policy towards the war? In general PID, as has been shown, were sceptical of the veracity of much of the information supplied by often self-serving and unreliable sources, some of whom had been planted in the neutral countries by agencies of the German government. In any case PID did not rely solely on this kind of intelligence: it had numerous other sources of information about Germany on which it drew. Since its foundation PID had built up a filing-system which contained press cuttings and information from elsewhere about conditions inside the various countries with which it was concerned and 'material of substantial importance to contemporary history', such as the negotiations for the Brest-Litovsk Treaty, all of which were stored in the library for easy access. By May the Foreign Office Library was also beginning to acquire a large number of books, especially about commerce, industry and banking in Germany.[36] Certainly its assessments showed a clear understanding of the development of German policy during the final months of the war, although, in common with practically all observers of the German political scene, it was taken by surprise by the speed of Germany's collapse in October 1918.

During the spring, however, it was hardly likely to be taken in by reports of domestic hardship in Germany or of the supposed yearning of many Germans for peace. With General Erich Ludendorff and the military firmly in control of Germany, and the apparent success of the German army's March and April offensives in the west, any peace the German Government was likely to offer would be one based on annexation and conquest, as the Treaties of Brest-Litovsk and Bucharest clearly demonstrated. A PID memorandum of 8 May on 'Statements of

[36] Headlam, minutes, 17 April 1918, Alwyn Parker, minute, 22 March and 20 April 1918 and Tyrrell, minute, PRO, FO 371/4360; Headlam, minute, 23 May 1918, PRO, FO 371/4366.

German Political Aims since the Western Offensive Began', which was widely circulated throughout Whitehall, made this clear, noting that 'the frankness with which these ambitions [of annexation and aggrandizement] are avowed, has increased since the beginning of the Western offensive' and

> the idea has become widely accepted that policy will be determined by the fortune of German arms on the Western front . . . [Up to mid-April] German politicians and journals of all shades, except the Minority Socialist, had cast prudence and even hypocrisy to the winds and were rallying to the cry of annexation in the West. It was freely assumed that Britain and France would be so soundly beaten that they would be unable to offer any effective opposition to this policy and that America had come in too late to effect the issue . . . It is useful to remember all these recent boasts and schemes if, in consequence of increasing difficulties and embarrassments both in the West and in the East, the Germans should presently initiate a new 'peace initiative'.[37]

However PID did not think that such an initiative was imminent even in mid June, when the German offensive in the west began to falter and the confidence of the German public in its military leaders was beginning to decline, despite rigorous press censorship which sought to conceal the true military state of affairs from the German people. A PID memorandum on 15 June entitled 'A "Peace Offensive" in the German Press' pointed out that

> the German masses seem to be divided between stolid and helpless resignation and the belief that the continuation of German sanguinary offensives furnishes the only hope of attaining the peace which is so desperately desired before Germany is totally exhausted and ruined.[38]

Nor did PID believe in the existence of a potentially influential peace party in Germany. A PID memorandum on 'Recent German Pronouncements on Economic Policy' on 14 June 1918 did however identify some German business and governmental circles whose misgivings about the effects of the war on Germany's economic future were increasing, thus providing the Entente with the opportunity of using the economic weapon as a means of further undermining the morale of this group: 'economic pressure is by far the best leverage at our disposal for influencing German opinion'.

PID was convinced that, while the German public were not interested in an idealistic peace,

[37] PID, memorandum 'Statements on German Political Aims since the Western Offensive Began', 8 May 1918, PRO, FO 371/3222.

[38] PID, 'Memorandum on a "Peace Offensive" in the German Press', Germany, 007, 15 June 1918, PRO, FO 371/3457.

it was vitally and anxiously interested in questions of economic policy, for upon their settlement depends the prospect of the restoration of domestic comfort and prosperity ... If it were made perfectly clear that the Allies intended to pursue the economic weapon to its fullest extent in order to achieve their declared purposes, including full reparation, it would have a far more disintegrating effect upon German opinion than any statement of purposes hitherto issued from the Allied side.[39]

Although the military tide turned in favour of the Allies from mid July 1918, PID remained dubious about the accuracy of the increasing number of reports describing the rapid deterioration of the German economy to the point where the country appeared to be on the verge of collapse. After mid July the legations at Stockholm and Geneva sent PID records of interviews with German deserters in Sweden and Switzerland, and with foreign travellers, describing, in graphic detail, the increasing collapse of discipline in the German army,[40] the desperate shortages of food and the growing demoralisation of the German middle and lower classes. Headlam-Morley, for one, remained 'very sceptical as to the truth of' these reports.[41]

In July and early August peace hints from German sources, including one PID believed emanated from Prince Max von Baden via Prince Charles of Sweden, began to circulate in the neutral capitals. Most suggested that a conference of the belligerents should meet to discuss a compromise peace whereby Germany made concessions in Belgium and northern France in return for a free hand in the east. Such proposals were dismissed by Hardinge and Balfour as 'another German trap', and this was confirmed by British Minister Erskine in the Rome Embassy who warned London that some of these hints were orchestrated by an Austrian, Robero de Fiore, 'one of Germany's ablest spies', who headed an enemy espionage system at Berne and 'who would be a most dangerous person to deal with in negotiations'.[42]

On 17 July 1918 Zimmern and Lord Eustace Percy produced a long joint memorandum on 'Economic Policy towards Enemy Countries,' the gist of which was the suggestion that the Allies should now concentrate on:

the conditions which we desire established between the present Allies ... to build up a body of political and economic doctrine which will reach German

[39] PID, 'Memorandum on Recent German Pronouncements on Economic Policy', 14 June 1918, PRO, FO 371/3222.

[40] See Esmé Howard, Stockholm, telegram 253, 13 July 1918, reporting rumours of ill-discipline in the German army. Cecil minuted 'if true this is the most important symptom we have heard of yet'. Cecil Minute (undated), PRO, FO 371/3222.

[41] Headlam-Morley, minute, 20 Aug. 1918 on A. Percy Bennett, British Consul, Zurich, despatch 104, 7 Aug. 1918, PRO, FO 371/3222.

[42] Esmé Howard, Stockholm to Hardinge, 10 July 1918, minutes by Hardinge and A.J. Balfour; Erskine, Rome, telegram 591, 11 Aug. 1918, PRO, FO 371/3442.

ears and commend themselves to German minds without those adventitious aids to publicity the use of which we are now driven by the vagueness of our ideas and the conflicting currents of our political life. The best propaganda that we can conduct in Germany is to make the present alliance the embodiment of the kind of international action which will become the centre of the world's desires.

This was much praised by the higher reaches of the Foreign Office – Crowe described it as 'a document of great merit', Hardinge 'as based on the German mentality' and Lord Robert Cecil as 'brilliant'. This enthusiasm might have been the result of Foreign Office frustration, hinted at in the paragraph quoted, with the increasingly hysterical and ill-formed demands for a punitive peace which, in the Foreign Office's opinion, would merely convince the German people that their only alternative was to fight to the bitter end.[43]

Cecil thought that the Zimmern–Percy memorandum was too long to be absorbed by the War Cabinet, and sent it instead to the Chancellor of the Exchequer's War Cabinet Economic Defence and Development Committee, which, with Austen Chamberlain, a Minister in the War Cabinet, in the chair, considered it on Tuesday 13 August. Cecil told the Committee that the question raised in the memorandum 'was how best we could accentuate German fears in regard to economic conditions after the war. What was needed, the FO thought, was to ignore Germany and build up [a] unified system of control over commodities which Germany most needed.' This proposal was approved and Percy and Zimmern were assigned to work out a detailed scheme.[44]

With Germany's military prospects becoming ever more bleak in August, reports poured into the Foreign Office from the neutral capitals about the mounting clamour within Germany for peace. The PID was now inclined to accept the accuracy of accounts of increasing war weariness in Germany and of the acute shortages of raw materials. However the department did not anticipate that this would lead to a renewed 'peace offensive' until early November, when the Reichstag was due to reassemble.[45] On 8 August 1918 Sir Ralph Paget, the British Minister in Copenhagen, forwarded to the Foreign Office two memoranda drawn up by the British Naval and the Military Attachés in Stockholm about an interview with a Professor Nicholai, 'a well known German pacifist' who had escaped to Denmark from Germany in an aeroplane to avoid prosecution for publishing an anti-militarist book *The Psychology of Wars*.

[43] For example, see Zimmern, minute, 19 Aug. 1918, PRO, FO 371/3474.

[44] PID, memorandum by Zimmern and Percy, 'Economic Policy towards Enemy Countries', 17 July 1918; Crowe, minute, 17 July 1918; Hardinge and Cecil, minutes; Cecil to Austen Chamberlain, 9 Aug. 1918; 6th meeting of War Cabinet Economic Defence and Development Committee, Tuesday 13 Aug. 1918, PRO, FO 371/3475.

[45] PID, 'Memorandum on the Coming German Peace Offensive', Germany, 0015, 28 Aug. 1918, PRO, FO 371/4358.

Nicholai told the Attachés that a great peace movement, which was anti-militarist and anti-Hohenzollern, was attracting enormous support in Germany but it was leaderless, disorganised and voiceless. As a result only the German Army, may of whose officers and men, Nicholai claimed, were anxious for an end to the war, was in a position to overthrow the military party. He urged the Entente to appeal to this gathering sentiment by offering a peace of reconciliation.

Lancelot Oliphant, an official in the War Department, was 'rather sceptical' of Nicholai's account. George Saunders minuted that, 'while we have plenty of evidence of discontent in the Army and Army officers as high as General (Xylander, Montgelas) who realize the perfidity and brutality of German methods', there appeared to be no links between any of these discontented elements, 'nor any widespread disintegration of discipline as would bring about a real revolutionary movement in the Army ... ' 'It seems as if only the debacle of a big military disaster could open the path for revolution.' Nor would it be an easy task to persuade the Allies to agree on a provisional statement of peace aims sufficient to make an impression on the Germans while the German government 'would pick holes in it. As a general principle it might be good to keep on telling the Germans that their only chance of getting equal treatment in the matter of raw materials is to end the war on Allied terms. But I doubt if this policy would provide immediate and tangible results.' Tyrrell thought that:

> Mr Saunders's comments strike me as very sound and much to the point. A big military disaster alone will start a revolution in Germany: most of the remedies suggested for this purpose are not only ineffective but are likely to play into the hands of the German Government.

On 5 September a PID 'Memorandum on German War Aims ... drawn up by a well-informed and reliable authority on German affairs, who has had exceptional and recent opportunities of testing public opinion both private and official on Germany on the subject of peace terms', set out the latest PID thinking on the prospects for peace. PID now believed that a new 'peace offensive' would be launched at the end of October and:

> in as much as the methods of the enemy never vary, the new peace offensive is certain to receive the best possible democratic window dressing so as to make appeal to pacifist opinion throughout the world, but to England in particular, where the partisans of 'peace by negotiation' are to be strengthened from without ... [T]he whole object of a so-called peace offensive, even in the eyes of the relatively moderate men ... [is] *to obtain by negotiation the greater part of what the extremists previously sought to acquire by force of arms alone* ... As things stand today, moderate and sane men have no adequate share in the responsibility of government [in Germany] which is in the hands of ... the powerful party at Imperial Headquarters.[46]

[46] PID, 'Memorandum on German War Aims', 5 Sept. 1918, PRO, FO 371/3222.

While, during September, reports continued to flow in of increasing demoralisation in Germany, especially in the army,[47] Rumbold described a recent conversation with 'a writer of liberal opinion', who had just returned to Switzerland from Germany and who could find no evidence of despair or indiscipline in the country; on the contrary the writer insisted that bulk of the population expected Germany to go on the defensive and continue with the war, even if Austria collapsed.[48] Another report from Berne stated that a German officer on the German General Staff, on a visit to Switzerland, had informed the German legation there that the German government and General Staff no longer believed in the possibility of victory. They now hoped to persuade the Entente that Germany would soon be transformed into a democracy. Oliphant commented that 'neither the German Staff Officer nor the German Legation credits the Entente with having heard the story of "When the Devil was ill etc!"'[49]

Mühlon also suggested that the time was ripe for the Entente to put forward 'reasonable' peace proposals, but Gerald Spicer, another War Department official, thought that such an appeal to the German people would have very little chance of success while the military were keeping the war away from Germany's frontiers and that 'the main thing is the defeat of the military party in the field'. Headlam-Morley did not think that Mühlon and other German exiles had 'any information to speak of from the German people or any faction of it'.[50] On 18 September Rumbold telegraphed the Foreign Office to report rumours of an impending political crisis in Germany but in his opinion the 'Germans would do their utmost to get the rest of the world to believe that they had entered on the path of democracy while in reality maintaining their present system. We should have to look out for this pitfall'.[51]

With the appointment of Prince Max of Baden as Chancellor, PID provided the Foreign Office with a lengthy description of his antecedents and his political opinions. 'From such information as is available ... it would appear that Prince Max is a man of some character and of considerable ability. He is described as being animated by a spirit very different from that of Prussianism.'[52] However there were those in the PID who refused to accept that the constitutional changes over which Prince Max presided were genuine. A PID memorandum of 21 October

[47] See Maxse, Rotterdam to Campbell, telegram, 14 Sept. 1918; Robertson, The Hague, telegram 3225, 16 Sept. 1918, PRO, FO 371/3222.

[48] Rumbold, telegram 1622, 20 Sept. 1918, PRO, FO 371/3222.

[49] Rumbold, telegram 1576, 13 Sept. 1918, Oliphant Minute, 22 Sept. 1918, PRO, FO 471/3437.

[50] Rumbold, despatch 666 10 Sept. 1918, Spicer, minute, 19 Sept. 1918; Headlam-Morley, minute, 19 Sept. 1918, PRO, FO 471/3225.

[51] Rumbold, telegram 1604, 18 Sept. 1918, FO 371/3223. Also Rumbold telegram 1670, 23 Sept. 1918.

[52] PID, 'Memorandum on Prince Maximilian of Baden', 3 Oct. 1918, PRO, FO 371/3224.

1918 pointed out that the German Chancellor was not a Reichstag deputy, and under the constitutional reforms he would remain an appointee of the German Emperor, who alone represented the sovereignty of the federal German government. The writer therefore doubted that there existed 'a true constitutional spirit' in Germany.[53] On the other hand, another PID memorandum praised the constitutional reforms as 'undoubtedly the commencement of far reaching changes in Germany . . . the recognition of some form of parliamentary democracy . . . It is obvious . . . that this event cannot be without its effect upon the diplomacy of the war.'

This memorandum, probably written by Headlam-Morley, warned of the consequences which might result from these political changes. Since 1914, Allied statesmen had argued that they were at war with the German government and not with the German people. Recently Britain and the United States had promised that their policy towards peace with Germany would change if a democratic government came to power in Germany. 'So if a Liberal Government were established we might be confronted with a curious and embarrassing problem.' Such a government would ask the Allies to enter into negotiations for a peace based on Wilsonian principles. 'How could an offer of this kind be met?' If the Allies refused to make concessions to the new German regime at the ensuing peace conference, the Germans 'will say that all our talk about German democratisation was mere war propaganda and hypocrisy: as soon as we got what we asked for we have merely taken this line to weaken Germany's powers and resistance and it was obvious that our real aims were aggrandizement'. As a result the spirit of resistance in Germany would be strengthened:

> we may easily get into a very awkward and delicate position . . . It may be suggested that it would be wise to get back to the old and sound principle that the internal forms of government in any one nation are not the concern of other nations. Even as regards Germany, it is not so much the forms of the constitution as the spirit of the nation with which we are at issue. In particular we must avoid being entangled in any discussions to particular changes in the constitution which would meet our demands.[54]

Headlam-Morley, in another minute, pointed out that, if Germany had become a genuine democratic state,

> the full responsibility for accepting terms of peace, which would undoubtedly be very humiliating to Germany, would attach to the Liberals and Socialists. This would therefore enable the Conservatives and Military elements to wash their hands of the whole thing. This is a contingency which it seems desirable to avoid. It seems in fact that it ought to be our object to bring it about that

[53] PID, memorandum 'Provisional Note on the German Reply to President Wilson as Regards Constitutional Changes in Germany', 21 Oct. 1918, PRO, FO 371/3224.

[54] PID, 'Memorandum on the Situation in Germany and Peace Overtures', 3 Oct. 1918, PRO, FO 371/3224.

those who have been responsible for both the outbreak and the conduct of the war should share the odium and unpopularity which will attach to accepting the conditions of peace imposed by [sic] Germany; we should not enable them to evade this responsibility. From this point of view, great importance attaches to the personal signature, not only of the Emperor but also of Ludendorff.

Percy secured Balfour's approval to show this paper to Colonel House, Woodrow Wilson's emissary to negotiate the armistice terms, when he arrived in London.[55] It was sound advice but not taken by the Allied leaders, who were anxious to bring an end to the war as soon as possible, without raising issues that might either complicate the armistice discussions or encourage the Germans to continue fighting.

Count Montgelas, as reported by Agent 'G. 100' in Montreux, stated that 'a Revolution . . . [in Germany] has already begun, and it was this Revolution which made the sudden request for an Armistice necessary . . . There is a reason for it. Something special had happened since September 26, . . . something bigger than Europe has experienced since Napoleon.' He assured his interlocutor that Max's request for an armistice was genuine and was the forerunner of complete surrender. Headlam-Morley declared that 'these words deserve more attention than many of the reports we receive from Switzerland, for General Montgelas is a man of high position and in a position to be well-informed'. Headlam-Morley surmised that the 'something special' to which Montgelas had alluded was the possibility that Bavaria (Montgelas was a Bavarian) had threatened to separate herself from Prussia if the war was not brought to a speedy end. He was puzzled about 'the sudden surrender of Germany' – this was what he believed the request for an armistice amounted to – since it appeared to be much more rapid and complete than Germany's military situation could explain. Germany could have continued to fight a defensive war, even without Bulgaria and Austria. He doubted that fear of Bolshevism and social revolution provided an adequate reason. He could only return to the possibility that the 'missing link' was a Bavarian ultimatum to secede from the Empire and withdraw her troops from the western Front.[56]

Meanwhile, as chaos threatened to engulf Germany,[57] the Dutch Minister of Foreign Affairs warned British Minister Townley that the imposition of a harsh peace on Germany might result in a Bolshevist take-over there with the danger that Bolshevism would spread across western Europe. Townley retorted that 'in my opinion, even at [the] risk of Universal Bolshevism, [the] German people must now be taught that German militarism is beaten and that the civilised world will have no more of it'.[58] However Headlam-Morley did not think that the danger

55 Headlam-Morley and George Spicer to Tyrrell, 22 Oct. 1918, minute by Percy.

56 Montreux, 8 Oct. 1918, Headlam-Morley, minute, 16 Oct. 1918, PRO, FO 371/4368.

57 For instance, see Townley, The Hague, telegram 3942, 8 Nov. 1918, PRO, FO 371/3224. On 9 Nov. the socialist Ebert replaced Max von Baden as Chancellor.

58 Townley, The Hague, telegram 3717, 24 Oct. 1918, PRO, FO 371/4368.

of Bolshevism could be dismissed so lightly: while he agreed that the German government might be encouraging Entente fears of Bolshevism for their own ends, he argued that the warnings of liberals like Montgelas could not be ignored. The consequences would be serious if Bolshevism were to spread across western Europe. Headlam-Morley urged that to counter this danger 'the discussion of peace terms be hastened as much [as] possible and the condition of strain which now exists be got over'. Peace terms should not be alleviated but 'every possible means should be taken to put them in such a form as to make it easier for the present Government of Germany to accept them', for instance, by assuring the Germans that there would be 'no further partitioning of German territory' after the peace conditions had been communicated to Germany. He feared that a Bolshevik uprising in Germany would make the prospects for a future liberal Germany problematic and would probably end in a military dictatorship. He hoped that the Allied armies could press forward as quickly as possible and occupy Germany in order to maintain order there – indeed he hoped that the German government might be induced to appeal for Allied military assistance against Bolshevism.[59]

Earlier Headlam-Morley had demanded that 'there can be no cessation of hostilities till there has been a military defeat and surrender: this will complete the conversion of Germany'. He had consistently demanded that 'the responsibility for her defeat must be fastened on the military and the former rulers of Germany; it would be disastrous to allow them to say that it was all the fault of the Liberals – that is what President Wilson's policy will lead to'. Now that Germany seemed to be moving in a democratic direction he was anxious that peace negotiations should be started as soon as possible. A constitutional German regime was for him the best hope for the future of Germany and Europe and everything possible should be done to make the peace terms as palatable as possible, without of course compromising Britain's peace aims. He rationalised the change from his earlier demand for a complete Allied military victory by suggesting that the armistice request was tantamount to a complete military surrender.[60]

On 1 November a PID review of 'Internal Conditions in Germany' cast doubt on German press assertions that Germany was now a democracy, since it had received evidence that the military authorities were still intervening in political affairs, despite Ludendorffs' resignation. However the memorandum concluded that this was now of little significance since:

> it is like discussing domestic squabbles indoors in the midst of and earthquake to review these internal German affairs while the fate of Empires, nations and ancient Crowns is being decided in the vast theatre of War and of Revolution.

---

[59] Headlam-Morley, minute, 28 Oct. 1918, PRO, FO 371/4638.

[60] Headlam-Morley, minute, 25 Oct. 1918 on Rumbold telegram 725, 11 Oct. 1918, PRO, FO 371/3225.

But it is precisely these matters that are preparing the German contribution to the vast general upheaval in Central Europe. The mass of the people, including a great portion of the professional and middle classes, is now under the full influence of sudden disillusionment, the realisation of its own terrible sacrifices and the contagion of revolution in the great neighbouring states. The question of guilt for these immeasurable calamities has now been raised and the answer is being given that the responsibility for what has happened lies with the Prussian Junker and the great industrialist governing class, the military caste and, last but not least, with the Emperor and the dynasty.[61]

When revolutionary outbreaks began in Germany at the beginning of November, PID concluded that:

the patience of the people, whose sons and brothers have been slain by the million in the calamitous Imperial gamble for world-power, who themselves are underfed, unwarmed, miserably clad, has come to an end.[62]

However there was little sympathy for Germany's predicament inside the Foreign Office – for instance, Hardinge minuted after the Armistice: 'As Mr Asquith said: the Germans have brought it on themselves'.[63] Clearly Woodrow Wilson's appeal for an idealist peace was unlikely to be supported by the more hard-line elements within the British establishment.

How far did PID justify Hardinge's initial hope that it would become a valuable part of the Foreign Office policy process? As far as the German section was concerned, PID certainly justified its existence during 1918, producing wide-ranging reports on Germany which often displayed a shrewd insight into German thinking about war and peace. It also wrote memoranda containing useful syntheses of German press commentary, Allied and enemy statements about war aims etc. Its officials sifted through the avalanche of information which descended on it and was usually successful in separating the accurate from the inaccurate. A report by a sub-committee investigating the staffing of the Foreign Office drew attention to the 'information of all kinds from competing sources', which poured into the Office and recommended that,

some effort should be made to obviate the duplication which undoubtedly exists, to define precisely the work of each intelligence branch, and to limit

---

[61] PID, 'Memorandum on Internal Conditions in Germany', Germany 019, 1 Nov. 1918, PRO, FO 371/3224.

[62] PID, 'Memorandum on Internal Conditions in Germany', 021/Germany, 8 Nov. 1918, PRO, FO 371/3224.

[63] Hardinge Minute, undated, probably end Nov. 1918, PRO, FO 371/3222.

the production of information to what can really be read and digested by those whose business it is to decide on, and formulate, policy.[64]

Press sources were unreliable: Rumbold pointed out in June that 'as a rule German speeches and newspaper articles are of small importance. If they mean anything at all, it is something quite different from what they say.'[65] Nevertheless, PID gauged the situation in Germany in 1918 with uncanny accuracy and its record of forecasting future developments was also good. Headlam-Morley stands out as a significant figure. He was once described by E.H. Carr as 'considerate, enlightened, rational, and commonsensical, averse from every fanaticism, from any emotional indulgence'.[66] These qualities are reflected in his reports.

He and his section recognised that the military were firmly in control of Germany until the autumn of 1918 and they rightly refused to attach any significance to reports that the German masses were yearning for peace. They equally dismissed so-called German peace proposals either as propaganda stunts or attributed them to wishful thinking on the part of German emigrés in neutral countries. However they did accept that Montgelas and Mühlon were providing the most reliable information about developments in Germany during 1918.

Inevitably they were as bewildered as most observers about the impact of the dramatic changes which took place in Germany's military fortunes and in her internal political situation during the autumn of 1918. This explained the differences in interpretation and the conflicting advice in the reports which PID issued during this period and these in turn resulted from the conflicting information they were receiving about Germany. Some officials suspected that talk of constitutional changes in Germany in September simply reflected the military defeats the Allies were inflicting on the German Army; such cosmetic changes, and the peace proposals that were made, were merely attempts to gain time while the German army regrouped behind its frontiers.

During October and early November PID became converted to the view that the changes taking place in Germany were genuine. Headlam-Morley, for one, was concerned that the military elite would try to saddle the new constitutional regime with the responsibility for both the Armistice and the subsequent Peace Treaty. He wanted the allies to ensure that the blame for the war was laid squarely on the shoulders of those responsible – the German Emperor, Ludendorff and the other military leaders.

Finally Headlam-Morley became obsessed with the fear of Bolshevism sweeping across Germany and the rest of Europe in the wake of Germany's

[64] Report of the Sub-Committee on the Foreign Office and Ministry of Blockade of the Committee on Staffs, 29 July 1918, Sir Bernard Mallet, W. Russell and S. de Jastrezebski, PRO, FO 371/787.

[65] Rumbold, telegram 982, 19 June 1918, PRO, FO 371/3222.

[66] Quoted in Goldstein, *Winning the Peace*, p. 68.

collapse. He wanted to make it easier for the new constitutional German government to make peace quickly, although his suggestions as to how this might be put across to Berlin were not very convincing. His desperation increased as the spectre of revolution appeared to loom larger in mid October when he urged that Allied troops should rush into the country to restore order there. Crowe gave this suggestion short shrift – it would, he wrote 'unite all the vital forces in Germany against us'.[67]

At the end of the war Headlam-Morley and other members of the PID began to concentrate on peace issues and PID itself was reorganised on 15 November 1918. Many of its officials went to Paris in January 1919 to work at the peace conference. By the middle of 1919 PID, which Hardinge had originally feared would become a pariah, had become firmly established as a regular Foreign Office department and was now valued by most senior officials. In 1920 it became a victim of Treasury demands for retrenchment and was abolished, although some of its members joined the Foreign Service. Its worth had however been proven and in 1939, on the outbreak of the Second World War, it was re-established.[68]

[67] Crowe, minute, 16 Oct. 1918, on Headlam-Morley to Tyrrell, 12 Oct. 1918, PRO, FO 371/3444.

[68] For details see Goldstein, *Winning the Peace*, pp. 79–89.

8

Major-General J.F.C. Fuller and the Decline of Generalship: The Lessons of 1914–18

Brian Holden Reid

In December 1932 there appeared in the *Sunday Express*, a feature entitled 'Dodderers in Brass Hats'. This story did not concern initiation rights or bullying in the lower ranks; quite the contrary, it lambasted senility in the upper reaches of the Army. Many British Generals, so the article claimed, were simply not up to the physical demands of command. In the days before the Director of Public Relations (Army) and 'clearance' (by the Ministry of Defence of all service publications), there was unanimous agreement as to the author – a Brigadier, who had the reputation of being a trouble-maker: a man who ridiculed his seniors, heaped scorn on the achievements of distinguished commanders in the Great War (and he took no pains to conceal his contempt either in conversation or in print); and who had the temerity not only to write articles, but books – indeed nineteen to date. Before his death in 1966 he was to write a total of forty-six books; the year 1932 alone was to see the appearance of no less than three of them, an extraordinary rate of production for a busy soldier who usually wrote in the evenings or at weekends. This Brigadier was shortly to be promoted to Major-General and was the British Army's leading military thinker, a pioneer of armoured warfare – J.F.C. Fuller.

Fuller was undoubtedly self-opinionated and conceited; by his own description, an 'unconventional soldier'. He was fearless, articulate and a ceaselessly diligent worker – virtually a one-man 'think tank'. His career had certainly been unusual. He was an intellectual when that breed of officer was conspicuous by its absence in the British Army. He preferred reading books to playing games. But throughout his career Fuller had made himself something of a nuisance. It was indicative of the extent to which Fuller had bucked the system that when in November 1931 he was offered command of the Second Class District of Bombay – perhaps a typist and half a dozen punkahwallahs, as General Fuller acidly observed – he declined it on the grounds that he had no confidence in the Government of India, and that his previous military experience was wasted. Privately he considered the offer an insult which was doubtless why it was made. General Ironside, a previous Commandant of the Staff College, a future wartime CIGS and his long-serving mentor, summed up the position accurately. He thought Fuller imprudent, even cheeky, 'a difficult man to place and not everybody's man. But he is straight and fearless and ingenious. How many of our leaders are that? Very, very few.' He continued: 'I am not saying that he has not been stupid, but he was not handled properly just because his critical spirit was considered disloyalty.' In December 1933 he was placed on the retired list.

In this chapter the focus will be on one aspect of this 'critical spirit', that is to say, the 'lessons' that Fuller drew for the command of armies from the First World War. The historical perspectives that he brought to bear both on this and other wars, were profoundly influenced by his own experience of the Great War, (as GSO 1 of the Tank Corps), during which he personally witnessed the command style of many senior British generals. His judgements on them became progressively harsher the further away in time he progressed from the Great War itself. Clearly, his views reflected his own frustration at the way the Army appeared to be stagnating, especially after 1933. This feeling now appears rather exaggerated. Nevertheless, his preoccupation with the nature of command is of enduring interest. A military writer of Fuller's experience, shrewdness and skill always provides food for thought – even when he is wrong. The article which had provoked so much fury in the War Office was in fact not written by Fuller. 'I thought the *Sunday Express* article rather ungentlemanly,' he wrote to his friend and fellow military pundit, Captain B.H. Liddell Hart, 'and did not want to be connected with it.' Nevertheless, though the style of the article offended Fuller, it was a sensationalised treatment of ideas which Fuller himself has put forward in print – in books and articles which by prevailing military standards of the day were brazen and impertinent in tone. In a nutshell, Fuller argued that British generals of 1914–18 were too old and that in the event, for a variety of reasons that will be discussed in more detail shortly, they did not command.[1]

By the late 1920s Fuller had put the finishing touches to two substantial studies of command that were clearly influenced by the new perspectives afforded by 1914–18: *The Generalship of Ulysses S. Grant* (1929); and *Grant and Lee: A Study in Personality and Generalship* (1933) – two of the finest books ever written on Grant which have stood the test of time remarkably well. But this essay will concentrate on another book which appeared in 1933 that reveals his views about command and, though very short, distils much good sense albeit in a provocative and mischievous way. This book is entitled *Generalship: Its Diseases and their Cure*. Fuller argues in this book that generalship as an art had declined since the end of the American Civil War (1861–65). By rounding upon British generalship in the First World War as an object lesson in how not to command, moreover, he indicted by implication an entire generation of British general officers as at best well-meaning failures or at worst incompetent bunglers. This

[1] Fuller to Liddell Hart, 15 Dec 1932, Liddell Hart Papers, 1/302/235.

was perhaps not the most tactful way to ensure further advancement in the Army; it is little short of a miracle that Fuller was promoted Major-General in 1930.[2]

Generalship had started life as a long article originally submitted to the *Journal* of the Royal Artillery, but the editor rejected it prudently on the grounds that the then CIGS, Field Marshal Sir George Milne ('Uncle George'), might object. The flavour of its brazen tone may be savoured in the preface. Here Fuller recounted a story in which a brave and meritorious officer, Colonel Clement, was wounded in the head and carried off the field of Waterloo. Napoleon was so impressed by his bravery that he instructed that he be forthwith promoted to the rank of Brigadier-General. On arrival in the field hospital he was so badly wounded that the Surgeon-General, Larrey, removed the top of his head and took out the brain. Suddenly an aide-de-camp from the Emperor arrived and announced his promotion. Revived by the splendid news, Clement rubbed his eyes, jumped up, picked up the top of his head, placed it back on his skull and ran out of the room, 'Mon Général, your brains!' shouted Larrey. To which the gallant Clement, running faster, replied, 'Now that I am a General I shall no longer require them.' It is perhaps not surprising that a number of conservative reviewers, who did not share Fuller's impish sense of humour, failed to see the joke. Indeed a somewhat pompous review in the *Times Literary Supplement* claimed that *Generalship* was 'a hasty and unconvincing piece of writing' essentially designed 'to throw discredit on British generals and British General Staff'.[3]

What, then, were these 'diseases' of generalship that Fuller felt so strongly about? An analysis of these cannot be divorced from a discussion of Fuller's view of the post-1918 role of the British Army and the doctrine that was evolved to fulfil this role. Here Fuller found nothing but muddle and confusion. He was convinced that in peacetime thinking British soldiers had to make 'bricks without straw and with precious little clay'. What was the British Army designed to do and how precisely was it commanded? There were few answers to these questions. The main reference point for any discussion of command in the inter-war years had to be the campaigns in France and Belgium 1914–18, which represented the culmination of a style of generalship that had developed in the British Army during the nineteenth century as a response to its role as an imperial police force. Its command style had also been influenced by trends in the industrialisation of war, the scale of which rendered personal command so much more difficult. This could be

[2] Brian Holden Reid, 'British Military Intellectuals and the American Civil War: F.B. Maurice, J.F.C. Fuller and B.H. Liddell Hart', Chris Wrigley (ed.), *Warfare, Diplomacy and Politics: Essays in Honour of A.J.P. Taylor* (London, 1986), pp. 45–47.

[3] Fuller to Liddell Hart, 9 Jan 1932, Liddell Hart Papers 1/302/215; *Generalship: Its Diseases and their Cure* (London, 1933), pp. 7–8; Reid, *Fuller*, p. 123.

characterised as essentially 'hands-off'. Fuller likened British generals to 'managing directors sitting in dug-outs, in châteaux and in offices'. They did not command directly and consequently, 'battles degenerated into subaltern-led conflicts, just as manufacturing had degenerated into foreman-controlled work. The glitter and glamour had gone, the man was left without a master – the general in flesh and blood . . . who could swear and curse, praise and acclaim, and above all who risked his life with his men, and not merely issued orders mechanically from some well-hidden headquarters miles and miles to the rear.'[4]

The real target of this biting criticism is a system which, whatever its advantages from an administrative point of view, contributed to a vagueness in the conduct of war at what we would now term the operational level. (Fuller used the anachronistic term 'grand tactics' to describe this area of military activity.) As Fuller commented on the Third Battle of Ypres (Passchendaele) in July–August 1917, though

> no one in their senses would have expected the general-in-chief [Haig], or his subordinate army commanders, to lead their men over those desolate shell-blasted swamps, very little was done outside formulating a plan to fight an offensive battle in a most difficult defensive area, with the result that soon after the battle was launched on July 31, 1917, all contact between the half-drowned front and the wholly dry rear was lost.

Apart from the enunciation of certain overall principles, very little attention was devoted to the means of achieving a breakthrough in Flanders. Control over the operational level – the management of armies in campaigns in a given theatre of operations in pursuit of their political object by means of the manoeuvre of armies and the fighting of battles – that category of conflict lying between grand strategy and fighting tactics – was feeble, and Fuller homed in on this deficiency with brutal clarity. In Fuller's opinion, the fundamental pivot which co-ordinated the operational level with the object of the war was the commander. Yet he had abdicated this most crucial role.[5]

It was Fuller's cardinal thesis to argue that the experience of the last war was of supreme importance in preparing for the next. The First World War is significant in the study of command because it is the only war in British history in which the British Army assumed the main burden of fighting in a large-scale continental war. Despite the crucial part played by the British Army in the Battle of Normandy in 1944, it very quickly assumed a subordinate role, and also, the function of the manoeuvre wing was allotted to the American armies. In the months August–October 1918, the British Army engaged the great bulk of the best German divisions on

[4] J.F.C. Fuller, *Generalship*, pp. 12. 14–5.
[5] Ibid., p. 16.

its front and defeated them in the field.[6] The campaigns of the Great War are, therefore, of tremendous intrinsic importance from the vantage-point of the study of command, not merely because Fuller focused his attention upon them, but because of the dominating role played by British forces in bringing that war to an eventual victorious conclusion.

The Great War, then, offered a great reservoir of experience. Indeed, in Fuller's opinion, it showed how at the operational level war should not be fought. His criticisms carry weight because of his assertion that the British Army would repeat many of the mistakes of the Great War if it continued to neglect the operational level and doctrinal discussion, which was particularly serious because the next war would be a war of manoeuvre. Manoeuvre warfare makes greater demands on the intellect and imagination than attritional warfare. Fuller contended that the British Army would risk disaster if it neglected the problem of movement and relied on trial and error in wartime – as it had during the First World War, and was indeed to do again in the Western Desert during the Second World War. He argued throughout the 1920s that there was a very real possibility that, if the Army rested on its laurels, it might be crushingly defeated in the first phase of the next war It hardly needs pointing out how near the military operations that the British Army engaged in during the years 1940–42 came to fulfilling this prediction.[7]

In considering the problems that the British Army would face in the next war, Fuller focused primarily on the moral dimension of generalship. He argued that generals should personify the spirit of their armies; they should identify with their men, and their men should identify with them. The style of command that prevailed in the British Army during the First World War did not fulfil this demanding requirement. The root cause was that 'the same factors which in industry have led to a separation, and consequently, to a loss of sympathy, between employer and employed, have also quite unseen, been at work in all modern armies from the year 1870 onwards'. The increased industrialisation of war, with a resultant vast increase in scale, had to be controlled by military commanders and it could not be avoided. Commanders could only counter-balance this increasing emphasis on material factors by accentuating, by whatever means, the moral factors underlying personal command. 'The true general', Fuller wrote, 'is not a mere prompter in the wings of the stage of war, but a participant in a mighty drama . . . his men cannot possibly feel for him as they would were he sharing danger with them.' If such moral imperatives were ignored, 'the most rapid way to shell shock an army is to shell-proof

---

[6] This is the view advanced by John Terraine in a number of books, most notably in *To Win a War* (London, 1978), p. 14; Tim Travers, *How the War was Won* (London, 1992), p. 179, sees the failure of the German Spring Offensive as more decisive; it was certainly important, but the German Army still had to be defeated.

[7] Reid, *Fuller*, pp. 218–20.

its generals; for once the heart of an army is severed from its head the result is paralysis'.[8]

A central theme of Fuller's discussion was that command in war could not be separated from leadership; generalship was a compound of the two. Thus 'heroism is the soul of leadership . . . for until a man learns how to command himself, it is unlikely that his command over others will prove a profitable business'. Clausewitz wrote that 'War is the realm of danger; therefore courage is the soldier's first requirement'. Fuller stressed that this line of argument was even more relevant to the general, for only by asserting the moral qualities of leadership, that is, by asserting his character and martial spirit, could a commander forge an enduring link with those who served under him. If a general lived 'outside the realm of danger', Fuller believed, 'then, though he may show high moral courage in making decisions, by his never being called upon to breathe the atmosphere of danger his men are breathing . . . he will seldom experience the moral influences his men are experiencing . . . But it is the influence of his courage upon the hearts of his men in which the main deficit will exist.'

So what qualities did Fuller believe would act as a stimulus to counteract the symptoms of the 'diseases' that afflicted generalship? Fuller quoted Marshal Saxe, whose writings he greatly admired, when arguing that a commander needed three attributes above all others, first, courage; secondly, brains; and thirdly, good health. In combination these qualities should produce a commander who was both steadfast in adversity, balanced in judgement, and original in conception. 'Originality, not conventionality, is one of the main pillars of generalship', he wrote. That is to say, a general should be capable of producing and implementing an imaginative yet practicable plan. 'To do something that the enemy does not expect, is not prepared for, something which will surprise him and disarm him morally.' To achieve this would be to capture the soul of manoeuvre warfare, the main ingredients of which are initiative, drive and imagination. The distillation and maturing of these attributes is not easy, or even possible, when the military system is geared to producing bureaucrats, or those who instinctively turn to conventional and plodding solutions to operational problems – an extension of 'routine' paperwork to the battlefield. 'Leadership', Lord Moran once explained, '. . . is the capacity to frame plans which will succeed and the faculty of persuading others to carry them out in the face of death.' 'The art of command', he continued '. . . is the art of dealing with human nature. The soldier is governed through his heart and not through his head.' Those generals most able to arouse their subordinates and soldiers are those who are still

<hr />

[8] Fuller, *Generalship*, pp. 13, 25, 20.

inspired by the fires of youth rather than by the comforts of middle age, or worse.[9]

Marshal Saxe's views on command, Fuller pointed out, had been developed in the pre-industrial age, but this rendered them all the more valuable because they served as a source of perspective on the command systems that had developed since 1870. Saxe's theory, he concluded, 'is absolutely sound for all types of war, whether shock or missile weapons predominate, or whether missile weapons are of short or long range, are slow to fire or rapid to load'. But, of course, the prevailing conditions of war affect greatly its application. Fuller pointed to the American Civil War, a conflict of 'vastly increased weapon-power [which] in no way gave a lie to the old theory of generalship, undoubtedly it modified it, but it in no way effaced it – the personal factor remained supreme'. Generals Grant and Lee, though so very different in character and background, were alike in one important respect, 'both these soldiers relied upon the personal factor', and both were scornful of danger. At Shiloh (1862), as in so many other battles, 'With Grant, there was no turning away from danger, he always faced it.' Fuller compared this adversely with the conditions prevailing on the Western Front during the battles of the First World War. Here, he observed with some exaggeration, the generals 'had no more influence on them than had they been lying in their graves'.

A suspicion occasionally surfaces that Fuller would have liked to see First World War generals behave like Coriolanus after the fall of Corioli, 'covered with blood and sweat and leading no more than a handful of men. But when he ran up to the consul with a jubilant expression, stretched out his hand, and gave him the news that Corioli had been captured, and when Cominius embraced and kissed him, the soldiers took courage.' Fuller was heavily influenced by the heroic classical example and upheld an excessively romantic ideal of leadership which permeated his writing. If this is discounted, he does make a number of important, if debatable, points. The first is that 'war is obviously a young man's occupation'; 'the older a man grows,' he continued, 'the more cautious he becomes, and . . . the more fixed becomes his ideas'. He also underlined the fundamental problem that arises when commanders are appointed during a long period of peace: 'Age may endow a man with experience, but in peacetime there can be no moral experience of war, and little physical experience.' When the next war begins and battle opens:

Nothing is more dangerous . . . than to rely upon peace training . . . Consequently, the more elastic a man's mind is, that is, the more it is able

    [9] Ibid., pp. 21, 27, 29, 32; Carl von Clausewitz, *On War* (ed.) Michael Howard and Peter Paret (Princeton, 1976, 1984), i, pt 3, p. 101; Lord Moran, *The Anatomy of Courage* (London, 1945), pp. 192, 195. This is also John Keegan's view: see *The Mask of Command* (London, 1987) p. 329.

to receive and digest new impressions and experiences, the more commonsense
will be the actions resulting.[10]

Fuller built up a persuasive case that seniority in high command –
that is, the promotion of senior commanders simply because they are
senior – should be discarded in favour of the promotion of dynamic and
youthful talent. In a striking passage, based largely on a critical reading
of Brigadier-General John Charteris's two books, *Field-Marshal Earl Haig*
(1929) and *At GHQ* (1931), Fuller pointed out that an older commander

> instinctively shuns discomfort, he fears sleeping under dripping hedges, dining
> off a biscuit, or partaking of a star-lit breakfast, not because he is a coward,
> but because for many years he has slept between well-aired sheets, dined off
> a well-laid table and breakfasted at 9 o'clock, that he instinctively feels that if
> these things are changed he will not be himself, and he is right for he will be
> an uncomfortable old man.

Such criticism expressed a much broader disillusionment in the inter-
war years with the style of leadership displayed in the First World War.
Commanders in that war were usually rotund, uninspiring sexagenarians;
they were men that did not deny themselves comfort, though they denied
others. They often appeared to resemble the worst caricatures of the self-
centred and pompous military. Haig was obstinate, gruff and inarticulate.
'His only gesture,' wrote Charteris, 'was a strange stiff movement of
the forearm as if discarding a used match and an occasional tug at
his moustache'. Joffre, munching his way through a massive breakfast,
seemed rarely to focus his thoughts on any matter more challenging than
the luncheon menu. These are unseemly caricatures which Fuller tended
to encourage and they need not be taken too seriously, but Fuller made
one important criticism that most assuredly can: namely that if a general
does not display leadership, then he will become isolated from reality,
resulting in 'a kind of military scolasticism [which] enwraps his whole life'.
Haig preferred to surround himself with 'Yes Men' who acquiesced in his
opinions, and most of the staff walked in fear of him. Although there
is nothing particularly wrong in principle with a well-ordered life, Haig
seemed obsessed with daily routine – his 'arrangements' – and was usually
grumpy if they were interrupted in any way. Certainly the atmosphere at
GHQ could be considered 'scholastic'.[11]

In summing up his case against the prevailing 'diseases' of generalship,

[10] Fuller, *Generalship*, pp. 33, 39, 41–42, 38: Reid, *Fuller*, pp. 109–19.

[11] Tim Travers, 'A Particular Style of Command: Haig and GHQ, 1916–18', *Journal
of Strategic Studies*, 10 (1987), pp. 365–66; Gerard J. De Groot, *Douglas Haig, 1861–1928*
(London, 1988), p. 220. Comfort was a major consideration: central heating was 'a must',
and GHQ moved three times before finding a suitably salubrious residence at Montreuil
(see pp. 174–75).

Fuller made a number of important points. The first was that age unconsciously dragged a general to the rear. 'The more cautious a general becomes, the more he likes to think over things, and the more he thinks things over the more likely is he to seek assistance from others.' This resulted in a proliferation, and occasionally a dominance of staffs over their commanders; also in command by committee – always an anathema with Fuller. It also tended to lead to a blurring of the lines of responsibility, an abdication of operational control and, moreover, an unpleasant desire to seek scapegoats for failures at the top in the echelons immediately below. Commanders who were not strong leaders and tended to lack confidence often turned for help to their advisers; they tried to avoid taking difficult decisions. 'In place they seek a decision from their staffs, and frequently the older they are the more they seek it, because they so often feel that the latest arrival from the Staff College must know more than they do – sometimes they are not wrong.'[12]

All these factors contributed to a decline in the art of generalship. The paradox of command was that the more complex warfare became, the less capable were traditionally educated generals in handling its multifarious demands. They declined to counteract the increased bureaucratisation of war, refused (or were unable) to project their personalities, and were content to transform themselves into military bureaucrats, tied to their desks. Indeed in 1914 'so intellectually unprepared were our higher commanders that they were at once sucked into the vortex of impersonal command . . . the one idea being, not to improve the quality of fighting, but to add to the quantity of fighters'. This was an important criticism deserving of careful study and reflection. Scrutiny of the writings of many First World War generals reveals that they placed an excessive faith in merely accumulating fighting power. 'With more guns and ammunition and more troops,' wrote Sir Douglas Haig, 'the Allies were bound in the end to defeat the Germans and break through.' But rather less thought was given as to how this breakthrough was to be achieved. Successful generalship was rather more than the sum, as Fuller put it elsewhere, of the coefficient of human tonnage.[13]

Thus, claimed Fuller, 'All these things, size, age, complexity, theory, staff organization, etc, rose to full growth during the years 1871–1914, and coupled with the unconscious whisperings of the instinct for self-preservation, drove the generals off the battlefield, and obliterating the personal factor in command, dehumanized warfare.' Fuller's thesis is interesting, persuasive and penetrating: few readers of his work can but fail to appreciate the sheer courage – the audacity of the man – in writing about such matters so candidly and commenting so freely upon

---

[12] Fuller, *Generalship*, pp. 57–59.

[13] Ibid., p. 54; *The Private Papers of Douglas Haig, 1914–1919* (ed.), Robert Blake (London, 1952), p. 84; Reid, *Fuller*, p. 114.

the performance of his seniors. It is not very likely that a serving officer would try and emulate him today. But herein also lies the book's main weakness. Fuller was prone to be reckless and overstate his case.

It was unworthy of him to suggest – however tacitly, and some of his comments could be misconstrued as innuendo – that First World War commanders were fearful of the front line; perhaps some were, but no matter how headquarters-bound many were, they chafed impatiently under self-imposed restrictions. This is as true of the less able commanders, such as General Sir Hubert Gough, as the more able. Haig himself had demonstrated his imperturbability at the front during the first Battle of Ypres in October 1914 in the finest traditions of the Duke of Wellington, though subsequently he had failed to project his personality to the armies under his command. General Sir Ian Hamilton had failed to stamp his will on the Gallipoli battles, but he certainly did not lack courage. As Fuller observed of the generation of British generals preceding those who conducted the Great War: 'In the good old days of the mid-nineteenth century, though our fox hunting generals may not have been too intelligent, and were in most cases, totally ignorant of the art of war, no one would dream of suggesting that they were lacking in courage.' Fuller did not expressly set out to denigrate the courage of the First World War generals but he gave the opposite impression. Thus Fuller infuriated and provoked and diverted attention away from important criticisms – one of his fundamental faults. The former CIGS, Field Marshal Lord Cavan, wrote to Fuller in 1933, commending his provocative analysis, 'that is what you want', but he focused on Fuller's attacks on the lack of personal example in operations in which he had participated, and which he thought unfair. In fact, Fuller was quite wrong to impugn the courage of First World War generals. Seventy officers of the rank of Brigadier-General and above were killed or died of wounds in 1914–18.[14]

It is thus not very surprising that Liddell Hart should observe that 'It is really extraordinary what letters I get from more senior people about your very mild little book. I am afraid the real truth is that they now suffer a sort of prickly affection of the skin whenever a book of yours appears in sight'. Nevertheless, Fuller's criticisms of British generalship were sound, Whatever the basic instincts of First World War commanders, they were either reluctant or unable to grasp the need to assert their personalities to appeal to mass armies of conscripts. The only exception was Allenby,

[14] Fuller, *Generalship*, pp. 34, 60; Anthony Farrar-Hockley, *Goughie: The Life of General Sir Hubert Gough* (London, 1975), pp. 196–98, 227; John Terraine, *Douglas Haig* (London, 1963), pp. 113–14; Robert Rhodes James, *Gallipoli* (London, 1965), pp. 89, 113–14, 282; Reid, *Fuller*, p. 228. I owe the figures on general officers' casualties to the researches of Keith Simpson, see 'The Officers', in I.F.W. Beckett and Keith Simpson (eds), *A Nation in Arms* (Manchester, 1985) p. 86 n. 90.

who did not feature in Fuller's little book, who completely rejuvenated the Egyptian Expeditionary Force in 1917. Fuller held Allenby, his old army commander in 1916–17 in high regard. When Wavell was writing Allenby's biography in the 1930s, Fuller paid tribute to Allenby's soldierly qualities as an 'extremely natural and simple man'. 'He could not stand the "yes man";' Fuller continued, 'when he spoke he wanted a direct answer, and when one was not given it upset his balance.' He considered Allenby outstanding, both as a commander and a director of his staff,[15] but on the whole, for the First World War generation of commanders, the kind of techniques employed by Montgomery in the Second World War were dismissed as ungentlemanly and tantamount to demagogy – the sphere of despised politicians. Haig, a remote personality, once thawed sufficiently to approach a private soldier and ask haltingly, 'And where did you start the war, soldier?' To which inquiry he received the rather impertinent reply: 'Nowhere, sir; I didn't start the war, sir.' Such diffidence is somewhat disarming, but it should not disguise the importance of the relationship between public relations (or showmanship) and morale in conscript armies. Indeed the mass army demands of a general mass appeal. As Lord Moran observed: 'Men whose personality gives them dominion over others will not be separated from their followers by time and space.'[16]

The importance of age in this equation is a thorny question. Few would dispute that commanders should be physically fit. Here the experience of 1914 was not very edifying. Lieutenant-General Sir James Grierson had died en route to France in August 1914. Fuller had actually watched him leave from Southampton, writing later that he resembled an advertisement for Oxo beef extract, round with rosy (almost purple) cheeks. Indeed his staff had been advised to buy pen knives in order to bleed Grierson should his blood pressure rise excessively. Lieutenant-General Sir Archibald Murray had a complete nervous and physical collapse on 26 August 1914, the critical day of the battle of Le Câteau. Fuller claimed that no less than 74 per cent of the most successful commanders in history were under forty-five years of age; only 4 per cent were over sixty. An impressive table is included as an appendix to *Generalship*, enumerating their ages. This reveals that in 1914 the average age of British Generals and Lieutenant-Generals was just under sixty years of age.[17]

The figures appear to be on Fuller's side, but his preference for youth is excessive. Age in command is a subject that it is unwise to be dogmatic

---

[15] Fuller to Wavell, 10 December 1936, Allenby Papers 6/7, quoted in Brian Holden Reid, 'Preface' to A.P. Wavell, *Allenby: A Study in Greatness*, i (reprint, Andover, 1992), pp. xv–xvi.

[16] Liddell Hart to Fuller, 21 Feb 1933, Liddell Hart Papers 1/302/238; Charteris, *Earl Haig*, pp. 387–88; Moran, *Anatomy of Courage*, p. 205.

[17] Reid, *Fuller*, p. 125; Tim Travers, *The Killing Ground* (London, 1987), p. 14; Fuller, *Generalship*, pp. 87–8.

about. Field-Marshal Earl Wavell pointed out that 'It is impossible really to give exact values to the fire and boldness of youth as against the judgement and experience of riper years; if the mature mind still has the capacity to conceive and absorb new ideas, to withstand unexpected shocks, and to put into execution bold and unorthodox designs, its superior knowledge and judgement will give an advantage over youth.' Some of the world's greatest generals conducted a number of their most accomplished campaigns after the age of forty-five – including Caesar and Cromwell; and Marlborough, Turenne and Moltke after sixty. So long as mental agility remains a constant, increased age is not necessarily an impediment to a commander. Indeed Major-General George B. McClellan, who was only thirty-four and a half when called to command the armies of the United States in 1861, displayed a prudence more worthy of Kutuzov than Napoleon. During the Second World War many (including Auchinleck), thought that Lieutenant-General Sir Henry Maitland Wilson, at fifty-nine in 1941, was 'past his prime'. Though somewhat ponderous in thought and elephantine in appearance, this proved not to be the case. He hardly cut an athletic figure, but Maitland Wilson's experience was of great value to the Allies, and he rose to the rank of Field-Marshal and Supreme Commander Mediterranean.[18]

Yet Fuller deserves the benefit of the doubt on this score. The average age of corps and divisional commanders in 21st Army Group 1944–45 was forty-eight, and regimental COs thirty-five; in the BEF of 1939–40 it had been 54 and 45 respectively. As Wavell said, 'a good young General will usually beat a good old one', and the stamina of youth usually wins in the end. Yet armies must offer a career structure to those who serve them in peacetime, and it must be recognised that what is possible in war is not always practicable in peace. Even the Israeli Army, which had done more than any other army to institutionalise youth in its upper echelons (by 1967 those who had served as junior officers in the 1956 War had reached senior rank), has failed in attempting to ensure that all Generals retire at 40; and, to a certain extent, Israeli soldiers never 'leave' the Army, so the services of those who retire at such a young age are not lost – a very real danger with this system.[19]

How then could this all-important mental flexibility in commanders be cultivated? Fuller contended that fundamentally generalship was based on knowledge and not instinct, and that this knowledge was most valuable in offering psychological insights. 'Here history can help us, and in place

[18] A.P. Wavell, *Generals and Generalship* (Harmondsworth, 1941), pp. 21–22; Reid, *Fuller*, pp. 125–26; David Fraser, *And We Shall Shock Them: The British Army in the Second World War* (London, 1983), p. 134; Brian Holden Reid, 'General McClellan and the Politicians', *Parameters*, 17 (1987), pp. 103–4.

[19] Reid, *Fuller*, p. 125; Wavell, *Generals and Generalship*, p. 22; Gunther E. Rothenberg, *The Anatomy of the Israeli Army* (London, 1979) p. 119.

of being looked upon as a clay pit to dig brick out of, it should be considered an inexhaustible quarry of psychological ore.' Though in peacetime generals could not be trained to cope with the moral demands of war, their minds could be better trained to adapt themselves. Fuller was of the opinion that the Army should select its best officers in the age bracket between thirty-five and forty-five, and that irrespective of their rank at this age, they should be 'thoroughly trained in their future duties, and should wherever possible, be attached to the formations which in the event of war they will command, so that they may get to know their future subordinates'. Then, in a passage predicting the character of the Higher Command and Staff Course instituted in 1987, Fuller suggested that periodically these officers should be assembled at the Staff College without staffs and set demanding exercises in all their details. He added a condition which would neither be popular not very desirable – that any student not gaining 50 per cent marks should be asked to resign his commission. At any rate, 'I am certain that the intellectual sphere of generalship would be vastly extended and the promotion list somewhat eased'.[20]

'The object of education', Fuller stressed repeatedly, 'is not so much to discover "what to think", as to learn "how to think". What is, or was, the nature of an army's machinery; what can it, or could it, make?' When studying it is not so much the contents of the books that should be memorised; facts are only a means to an end; what 'is so important . . . is insight into the personality of the writers including oneself'. Then in a passage written in sulphur, he asked: 'Why are we soldiers so cretinous in this respect? Why have we such a horror for the truth, for facts, for actualities, for possibilities, for probabilities and even for obvious uncertainties? The answer is because our system of mental discipline is cretinous'. The military intellect would not be enlarged until soldiers were given, and were mentally equipped to exploit, intellectual freedom.[21]

Once the mental outlook of commanders was improved, how would they relate to their staffs and the operational problems they would encounter? Fuller's first recommendation in this area was that an executive deputy should be appointed who could relieve the commander of routine duties, permit him to go forward, and yet have sufficient authority to take decisions in his absence and in his name, as the deputy would be immersed in the operational plan. The extent to which a deputy could substitute for the commander while dispensing moral support or direction to subordinates is difficult to gauge. There are occasions when only the commander can fill this role – not least in times of crisis. Nonetheless, it is the man that is really needed, not the rank, and the burdens of the commander may be reduced by conferring on his chief of staff

[20] Fuller, *Generalship*, pp. 67, 68–69, 70.
[21] Ibid., p. 71.

executive authority, as Montgomery did after 1942 on de Guingand. Secondly, Fuller urged, wherever possible, a reduction in the numbers of staffs: 'Whilst in theory the idea of a staff is to relieve a general of work, in practice the last war certainly proved that the larger the staff was, the more a general becomes absorbed in its work.' Certainly the First World War demonstrated an odd paradox: whereas British armies had never been better administered and supplied, levels of generalship were rather less distinguished.[22]

Finally, Fuller revived a valuable aspect of Napoleonic practice, namely, that liaison officers should be deployed as the commander's eyes and ears reporting directly to him, in order to aid his control over the conduct of operations: 'personal liaison officers are in fact an extension of his brain'. If, as Fuller argued, future wars would be more mobile, increased motorisation would increase the ability of the commander to grip the operational level. Here Fuller believed that the role of GHQ on the Western Front had been lamentably deficient. There was a complete absence of any operational doctrine, and no central, organised direction of such thinking as had emerged. British thinking on command before 1914 had underlined that, 'The chief duty of the higher command is to prepare for battle, not to execute on the battlefield.' Sir Henry Wilson, while a corps commander, claimed that 'Haig and GHQ . . . write nonsense and who are wholly inaccessible and who are therefore useless as guides, philosophers or friends'. Training and detailed operational considerations were left to individual army (and corps) commanders. The retreat in March and April 1918 was a good example of how morale and organisation (which was the foundation stone of morale) were eroded by the precipitate withdrawal of HQs in an uncoordinated flight, symptomatic of lack of operational grip; further piecemeal retreats followed which only induced further disorganisation and despair. Such HQs could not cope with mobile warfare backwards – 'at times the chaos was indescribable', recalled one witness.[23]

The system, as expounded by Fuller, did much to increase the commander's control over operations, though it was undoubtedly aided by improvements in communications which were not available in the First World War, such as the use of radio. None the less, it is striking that nowhere in Fuller's book does he consider the demands made by the waging of coalition warfare. All of Fuller's recommendations contribute to an isolation of the commander, surrounded by adoring aides, concentrating primarily on operational problems – like Montgomery in 1945 – and resenting any efforts to bring his thoughts to focus on the implications of narrowly professional concerns. It is not a system which

---

[22] Ibid., p. 79; Reid *Fuller*, p. 79; Moran, *Anatony of Courage*, p. 192.

[23] Fuller, *Generalship*, p. 81; Travers; 'A Particular Style of Command', pp. 364, 374, quoted in Travers, *Killing Ground*, p. 241.

promotes inter-allied harmony, for it ignores this necessity, and nor does it cope well if views diverge over the way in which a war should be fought.[24]

In his little book, Fuller put his finger on much that was wrong with British generalship in the Great War, even though he was ungenerous in not acknowledging its successes. *Generalship: Its Diseases and their Cure* stands as a devastating criticism of a style of command which sought to apply managerial techniques to the conduct of war. The British General Staff believed that warfare could be controlled if managerial solutions were applied to the administration of armies – and this was achieved with considerable success – and yet central guidance over the central issue of the war, namely how it was to be won, was abdicated. Fuller wished to see more mental and material resources being lavished on harnessing an army's fighting power and less on its administration. It is true that he hoped this problem would be eased by a reduction in the size of armies (which certainly did not occur before 1989), but this miscalculation is not central to an appreciation of his writings on generalship. As in all his books, there are acid swipes at sacred cows, such as the inter-war cult of sports – 'the cricket complex'. 'Games and sports', he observed, 'have an immense value as physical relaxers and restorers; but in themselves they have no more military value than playing fiddles or painting postcards.' This 'complex' resulted in 'The comfortable theory that to amuse ourselves is the most perfect way of learning how to become soldiers.' Yet these asides reflect the author, frustrated, acidic, scornful – his talents wasted. Perhaps the most virulent disease afflicting the British Army during this period was its incapacity to harness adequately Fuller's immense talents.

---

[24] Martin van Creveld, *Command in War* (Cambridge, MA, 1985), p. 186; Reid *Fuller*, p. 125.

Index